PELI

BUDDHIST PHILOSOPHY
IN THEORY AND PRACTICE

HERBERT V. GUENTHER was born in 1917. He holds Ph.D. degrees from the universities of Munich and Vienna. In 1950, he went to India to teach at Lucknow University and, in 1958, became Head of the Department of Comparative Philosophy and Buddhist Studies at the Sanskrit University in Varanasi. Since 1964, he has been Head of the Department of Far Eastern Studies at the University of Saskatchewan in Canada. He has published translations, with commentary, of several books on Tibetan Buddhism, among them *The Life and Teaching of Nāropa*. Professor Guenther is married and the father of two daughters.

OTHER BOOKS

BY HERBERT V. GUENTHER

The Jewel Ornament of Liberation

The Life and Teaching of Nāropa

The Royal Song of Saraha

The Tantric View of Life

Tibetan Buddhism Without Mystification

Treasures of the Tibetan Middle Way

BUDDHIST PHILOSOPHY
IN THEORY AND PRACTICE

HERBERT V. GUENTHER

PENGUIN BOOKS

Penguin Books Ltd, Harmondsworth, Middlesex, England
Penguin Books Inc, 7110 Ambassador Road, Baltimore, Maryland 21207 U.S.A.
Penguin Books Australia Ltd. Ringwood, Victoria, Australia

Published by special arrangement with
Shambala Publications, Inc., Berkeley, California
First published in Pelican Books 1972

Printed in the United States of America by
Kingsport Press, Inc, Kingsport, Tennessee
Set in Linotype Times Roman

To Ilse

To The

CONTENTS

PREFACE

A GREAT DEAL has been written about Buddhism, but no attempt has hitherto been made in English to present an account of the various systems and problems of Buddhist philosophy in a single volume. To fill that gap is one of the reasons why the present work has been written; another is that much of what has been said about Buddhist philosophy rests on insufficient factual basis. Certain important systems are not mentioned at all and others are disproportionately emphasized.

On the basis of two comparatively short works in the Tibetan language, dealing with the whole of Buddhist philosophy, I have endeavoured in this volume to deal with the philosophical problems as they were formulated and developed in the course of time. In doing that, I have also taken into account the major works of which the ones translated here are a summary. Not included are the accounts of the non-Buddhist systems, as they fall outside the scope of this volume.

The choice of two different works was prompted by differences of approach to problems of philosophy. dKon-mchog 'Jigs-med dbang-po (1728–1781), author of the *Grub-pa'i mtha'i rnam-bzhag rin-po-che'i phreng-ba,* "The Jewel Garland of the Dissertation on Philosophical Systems," represents the 'traditionalistic' approach. As a dGe-lugs-pa (follower of the 'new' tradition started by Tsong-kha-pa [1357–1419]), he strictly adheres to the tradition which recognizes only works of Indian origin as authoritative; consequently he emphasizes the customary Indian, that is, epistemological aspect of Buddhist philosophy.

Needless to say, even today his work is widely studied by Tibetan monks, particularly those of Mongolian descent.

Mi-pham 'Jam-dbyangs rnam-rgyal rgya-mtsho (1846–1914), author of the *Yid-bzhin-mdzod-kyi grub-mtha' bsdus-pa*, "The Summary of Philosophical Systems as Detailed in the *Yid-bzhin-mdzod* (The Treasure which is like the Wish-Fulfilling Gem)," belongs to the rNying-ma-pa tradition (initiated in the eighth century by Padmasambhava and dating back to the introduction of Buddhism into Tibet). Although inspired by Indian Buddhist philosophers the rNying-ma-pas were independent thinkers and contributed significantly to the development of Buddhist philosophy. Their approach was 'existential' and the question of Being, rather than of perception, ranked foremost with them. Hence the emphasis they placed on Tantrism. Mi-pham's work, a summary of Klong-chen rab-'byams-pa's (1308–1363) monumental writings, is considered an outstanding contribution by present-day rNying-ma-pas.

Since these authors presented the whole of Buddhist philosophy in concise and intelligible terms, it is hoped that through their presentation here a clearer picture of Buddhist philosophy emerges.

The title of this book identifies the two sides of Buddhist philosophy, the one characterizing the clarification of ideas, the other embodying these ideas in life.

ACKNOWLEDGEMENTS

IT IS impossible to mention adequately all who have influenced my thinking. Discussions and books have all become so much part of my thinking that it is sometimes hard to say which are my own ideas and which have been borrowed. Special thanks are due to dge-bshes Ngag-dbang nyi-ma, formerly of Drepung ('Bras-spung) monastery, Tibet, with whom I studied dKon-mchog 'Jigs-med dbang-po's work, and Tarthang Tulku, formerly of Golog monastery, Tibet, who made the rich rNying-ma-pa tradition available to me.

I am greatly indebted to my colleagues and friends, J. F. Pas and G.A.K. Scott, for valuable suggestions in formulating and presenting the material contained in this volume. To Mrs. J. F. Pas I owe thanks for preparing the typescript. To my wife, as usual, goes the credit of having prepared the index and of having given me the unfailing help needed to prepare this book.

H.V.G.

The Buddha and his two disciples, Śāriputra and Mahāmaudgalyāyana

CHAPTER ONE

THE DEVELOPMENT AND CHARACTER OF BUDDHIST PHILOSOPHY

ALTHOUGH IT IS customary to speak of Eastern philosophy with Buddhism as its most influential exponent, every serious student of Far Eastern thought is struck by the fact that none of the Oriental languages has a word which in any way corresponds to our 'philosophy.' This in itself is not a defect, rather it compels us to reconsider the meaning of the word 'philosophy.' It is evident that any dealings with Eastern thought involve comparative studies, but to take one's own premise for granted, as is most often done, and then to criticize other premises with this bias, is a travesty of comparative research. It will readily be admitted that we may mean many things by 'philosophy,' such as, for instance, the sum of the beliefs which man has held about himself at different times and, above all, about the universe, or the examination of these beliefs. On closer inspection, however, much of what is labelled philosophy turns out to be a mere sham and basically a negation of philosophy. What, then, do we have to understand by 'philosophy'? Certainly, it can never be an achievement; it remains a movement, a continual striving for truth by pre-eminently intellectual means. In this quest for truth philosophy brings about a change in ourselves by opening our eyes to wider horizons. Such a vision is directly related to the desire to cultivate and refine the personality. Moreover, philosophy as an encompassing vision wants to know all that is knowable; unlimited cognition is its basic characteristic. Any limitations imposed on it will inevitably kill it. But the most decisive point is that in this striving for truth, truth itself is the primal source of our thinking. Yet it becomes perverted easily by positing as absolute something which is valid from certain points of view and in certain respects and at a particular level of thinking. It also becomes false by considering the particular knowledge of something within Being as the knowledge of Being as such and as a whole. Philosophy as a quest for truth born out of truth is therefore constantly struggling against its two foes: absolutization and concretization. This is the theme of Buddhist philosophy in particular. It begins with a vision of what there is, and then progressively enlarges this vision. Its rejection of the non-Buddhist systems, all of which in some way succumb to anti-philosophical tendencies, as well as its trenchant critique of its own digressions into this dangerous territory, are due to, and reflect, the endeavour to keep the philosophical spirit alive.

In course of time there developed within Buddhism four major lines of thought, each in its own way endeavouring to fathom the message of the Buddha. The earliest systematic attempt was that of the Vaibhāṣikas, who favoured a 'realistic' approach in dealing with the first great division within Reality as a whole: the distinction between that which is transitory and that which is (or seems to be) eternal. For the Vaibhāṣikas both 'departments' consisted of substances, and for this reason they may roughly be classified as 'substantival dualists.' But inasmuch as there are apparently fundamental differences of kind among the many things and substances constituting the same department, the Vaibhāṣikas held different views about them. The eternal was believed to comprise three or four substances which were not just what might be called substances of a 'natural kind' that were eternal, but which had specific properties, so concerning the realm of the eternal the Vaibhāṣikas were specific-property pluralists.

In the department of the transitory each substance, apart from being of the 'natural kind' that is transitory, had a special attribute which made it of such and such a kind. There were material substances, mind-substances, mind-related substances, and substances which could not be defined as being either of the others, yet had being of their own. Thus, concerning the transitory they were differentiating-attribute pluralists. Believing in different kinds of substance, even within a single department, the Vaibhāṣikas had to accept a great plurality of substances and, on the whole, they accepted a much greater plurality of substances than of kind.

The Vaibhāṣikas' theory of transitory and eternal substances became the target of the Sautrāntikas' critique. Within Reality as a whole, they distinguished between that which exists and that which is real but not existent. The former consisted of the concrete things we encounter in common experience and being a concrete thing entailed its transitoriness, just as everything which is not a concrete thing entails its permanence and not being a concrete thing must be abstract. The Sautrāntikas then initiated the systematic development of the science of logic and developed different epistemological theories. If we accept the account of the dGe-lugs-pas who became the most influential school of thought in Tibet and who were almost exclusively interested in epistemological problems, the Sautrāntikas' line of thought on the whole resembles phenomenalism in the West, not representational realism, as has often been stated. The latter's absurd theory that something unexperienceable can be experienced contradicts the Buddhist claim of all-knowability. A common feature of both Vaibhāṣikas and Sautrāntikas was their belief in physical objects as coinciding with what is assumed to be real and having an ontological status. For the Vaibhāṣikas any physical object was of the nature of being reducible to a substance; for the Sautrāntikas the notion of physical object had been abstracted from the data of sense. This idea of things existing really became the target of all other philosophical trends in Buddhism.

The third great movement was that of the Yogācāra. This doctrine is usually called idealism, which is a misnomer for what is implied by it both in the West and in the East. The Western form should have been termed idea-ism or mentalism which is its essential feature, and the Eastern one experientalism, since experience counts. By idealism, to use this common, though inappropriate, term, we understand the doctrine that nothing exists except minds and their ideas. This is easily misinterpreted and caricatured by the failure to distinguish between sensations and imaginations. Idealism rests its case on two principal contentions: (a) physical objects such as mountains, trees, houses and the like are genuine objects of knowledge; and (b) to know these things is to have an experience of them. It is easy to develop these two theses in terms of sensations, and since sensations are events in a mind, all reality must be sensations and hence mental. While idealists of the Western type insist on this conclusion, the Yogācāra philosophers thought otherwise. They declared that physical objects must be defined in terms of what can be experienced, but that which can be experienced is not just sensations or mental events. The yellows and blues which are the objects of my immediate and direct awareness, are not the awareness itself, but that of which I am aware. There is no point in saying that not only my awareness but also that of which I am aware is mental. Similarly it is meaningless to assert that the colours which I see are physical. After all, to which physical object do the red spots belong which I see when I get hit on the head? To put it concisely, seeing blues and yellows is doubtless a mental event, as any seeing is; but this does not for a moment imply that what is thus seen is mental or physical. The mental and the physical are special constructs within the field of experience, and another such construct is the relation of externality which makes me believe that things exist as such and external to the observer. Once we appreciate that it is the experience that matters, we will never bring up any questions of things existing unexperienced. The Yogācāra philosophers did not deny that there were things external to the observer, but they disclaimed their independent existence and they objected to their being equated with mind. They never accepted the Leibnitzian idea that lumps of coal are colonies of spirits of low sentience.

The bifurcation of Nature into the material and the mental with an unbridgeable gulf between them, which found its extreme expression in Descartes' reasoning and which ever since has overshadowed the thoughts of Western philosophers, makes the understanding of the Yogācāra doctrine rather difficult, inasmuch as certain superficial resemblances make us overlook the tremendous differences between it and the Western mentalistic trends. Some Yogācāra philosophers held sensa—particular existents which resemble physical objects as ordinarily conceived, but which in their dependence on the observer are like mental states—to be either true or delusive, but they would never declare that material characteristics were delusive appearances of certain mental characteristics, as was done by Leibniz, Hegel, Ward, Bradley, Mc'Taggart, and Berkeley who, however, held that sensa do have some material characteristics. Nor would the Yogācāra philosophers claim with Bradley that the Absolute or, as they termed it, the Ideal consisted of 'experience.' A little reflection shows that no experience occurs more than once and that all repeated experiences are in fact analogous. It is this particularity as well as the Ideal, which is not just another particular existent, which they considered as existing really.

This remnant of the earlier beliefs in something really existing became the target of critique by the Mādhyamikas, the fourth great movement within Buddhism. The Mādhyamikas divided into two larger branches, the Svātantrikas who took over certain ideas from the Sautrāntikas and the Yogācāra philosophers, and the Prāsangikas. All of them were unanimous in rejecting the assumption that something exists really. In this respect they followed up the distinction made by the Yogācāra philosophers between that which is held to coincide with what is assumed to be real and that which does not, as for instance that which is termed the notional-conceptual, comprising first and second intentions which have been known in the West since Aristotle. For the Svātantrikas things existed as being-things, as self-evident, and by virtue of that which makes a thing what it is, its essence. But they also realized that the concept of what something is is not as such indicative of the fact that it exists, and even to conceive of it as existing, i.e., of the actual existence of a particular thing, still leaves open the question whether such conceived existence is in fact true.

The Prāsangikas realized that no solution can be reached by pursuing this line of thought any further and they embarked on a philosophical venture which is akin to what the later Wittgenstein has called the 'language-game,' although they would not have equated philosophy with a mere critique of language. However, they recognized that a name is logically independent of the characteristics of the thing named and that the christening ceremony is not the use of the name but the way in which we give it a use.

This short survey of the main trends in the four major lines of thought within Buddhism and their formulation in concise statements might suggest that the task of philosophy is to provide compelling rational insight which everyone must see and can know. This, however, would mean that the nature of truly philosophical thinking has been overlooked. In philosophizing we travel the path to the primal source of our being. As a methodical reflection it can be subsumed under three questions: What do I know? What is authentic or true? How do I know?

The answer to the first question is that everything I know is relational in structure. The objective as well as the subjective are given with the same evidence. Although this becomes evident again and again, there is a strong tendency to slur over this unique intentional phase of our being, and either to reduce the object to a state of the subject, or the subject to that of an object. Buddhism has never lost sight of the intentional and relational structure of our awareness, and thus has avoided both a pan-objectivism and a pan-subjectivism.

The second question cannot be answered by referring to the many existents we encounter, but by apprehending that which only inadequately can be referred to as that which is in itself. This differentiation between that which is in itself and knowable and that which in ordinary parlance is said to exist is technically known as the Two Truths. These have nothing to do with the Western distinction b phenomenal and the noumenal, the one knowa other forever unknowable. To interpret the Two this way is to overlook the all-knowability on which Buddhism insists; and to interpret them as appearance and reality, the one delusive and the other true, is to fail to take into account the Buddhist conception of the unconditional realness of what there is. The Vaibhāṣikas tried to answer this question, in the same way as the philosophers and physicists in the West before the modern age. They thought of the world as composed of things, an idea which they developed into that of material substance, and this, in turn, they thought of as consisting of particles, each very small, and each persisting through all time. It was these 'atoms' that were believed to be ultimately real, while the concrete 'thing' was relatively or conventionally real. The Sautrāntikas and the other philosophical schools understood the Two Truths in the sense of epistemic correlation. It is the aesthetic, intuitive factor that is declared to be ultimately real, while the theoretically designated factor in our experience is only relatively so.

The third question is solved by inquiring into the limits of knowledge. Here it becomes clear that all truth is apprehended in specific modes of thought and in studying these modes we provide a basic tool for philosophical thought. This study makes us aware of what is valid and invalid and thus we are enabled not only to know, but to know how and by what means we know, which is particularly important for the problem pointed out by the second question.

The three points discussed so far are the basis for setting out on a path which is not so much an inert link between a starting point and a goal, but a name given to the process of inducing and experiencing a change in our outlook. Hence 'path' and 'knowledge' and 'awareness' are synonymous in Buddhism. It is here again that the intentionality of all our experiences is most clearly marked. In order to travel a path I must have an idea of where it will lead to, because I cannot go unless I go somewhere. But since the path is my very being I must have an idea of myself as I am going to be. This does not contradict the statement that the objective pole of the 'path,' the content of my 'cognition,' is the fact that there is no self as some unchanging and forever existing individual and 'objective' entity. As a matter of fact, to conceive of myself as either this or that, and thus to prejudge the outcome of my striving, is to block any progress, and such bias instead of clearing my view will only add to my blindness and make me emotionally unstable. But since the way which I travel is said to remove all bias and blindness, its nature must not be predetermined in any way; it must find its determination in the progress along it to a point which is free from all bias.

Such progress comprises different stages. Although the number of the stages is the name for all the three spiritual pursuits, the Śrāvakas', Pratyekabuddhas', and Bodhisattvas', their nature is not of the same order. Each path signifies a specific mode of human response and partakes of an anticipatory response, and each course denotes a variety of fundamental frames of references or leitmotifs which come to characterize man's entire life. The path is therefore essentially a process of learning which begins with the acquisition of knowledge. Knowledge is not merely an accumulation of intellectual data, it is tied up with the social environment. Man learns through being with others, and this social aspect is referred to as 'acquisition of merits.' Both merits and knowledge are futile if they are not used properly, if we fail to gain insight and understanding and through them a more satisfactory mode of being with our fellowmen. But when we succeed in doing so, we have already progressed in the direction of transcending our pettiness, and prepared ourselves for seeing ourselves and others (persons and things) as they are and without the emotional instability that characterizes our self-centred seeing. Afterwards work on ourselves can begin, which is all the harder because it demands that we remain true to ourselves.

Such work, however, is facilitated by 'warmer' feelings which principally tend to reinforce mental life and conduct, although they do not initiate activity. The four degrees of intensity that have been classified clearly illustrate the fact that these warmer feelings lend added strength to action already in progress, and cause it to be continued. Although here the elimination of wishfulness and intellectual fog begins, this does not, as is often assumed, lead to a state of emotional undernourishment and intellectual blankness. Rather it produces a heightened perceptivity and responsiveness which is all the more satisfactory since the disturbing and upsetting elements have been eliminated. Seeing properly, which evolves in the course of this striving, is both a process and a product. As the former, it consists of the phases of eliminating the obstacles which prevent us from seeing things and ourselves as they are and of the free passage after the removal of the obstacles, the security in feeling that the obstructing forces will not make themselves felt again. As the latter, it is the outcome of both the elimination of the obstacles and the feeling of security, although it cannot be designated as being either of the two. What we see and immediately experience is nothing determinate or definite which any adjective referring to a specific quality can designate. It is an utter openness which nevertheless is emotionally moving and aesthetically vivid, even more so than anything else. Seeing properly is but the preliminary step to the essential phase of our being, attending to that which has been seen, making it the leitmotif of our further conduct. This in particular relates to a change in our personality. 'Seeing' is deemed to be sufficient for eliminating all that is due to our upbringing, our environment with all its superstitions and traditions, all of which can easily be overcome by broadening our mental horizon. But 'attending to that which has been seen' is more difficult to practise. It means to live up to that which is absolute in the sense that it holds for all people under all circumstances, that it is not transitory and variable from person to person. In the last analysis it relates to the conquest of the deep-rooted individual self-idea which prevents us from seeing and acting properly and colours our view by some bias or other. Free from all determination, positive or negative, the noetic power is now enabled to understand and appreciate things as they are in themselves, and not merely from a certain point of view and from the demands elicited by a certain fixed position. But at what point the thinker believes he has reached the end of his striving, remains his secret and no universal absolutizations are possible; otherwise Buddhism would not have been able to distinguish between Śrāvakas, Pratyekabuddhas, and Bodhisattvas.

A major division in Buddhism is known as Hīnayāna and Mahāyāna. These two appellations are used to indicate attitudinal rather than philosophical differences. Mahāyāna refers to a socially-orientated attitude, Hīnayāna to an individualistically-orientated one. Since historically the philosophical systems of the Yogācāra adherents and of the Mādhyamikas came after those of the Vaibhāṣikas and Sautrāntikas, and since the development of the former systems coincided with the change in attitudes, it has become customary to list the Yogācāra philosophers and Mādhyamikas as representatives of Mahāyāna and the Vaibhāṣikas and Sautrāntikas as those of Hīnayāna. However, dKon-mchog 'Jigs-med dbang-po makes it clear that a particular social attitude does not necessarily coincide with a certain philosophical belief. A mentalist-'idealist' can be extremely selfish, just as a 'materialist' can be thoroughly altruistic.

While the philosophical systems that evolved in time represented the speculative aspect of Buddhism, they were not an end in themselves, but essentially a means to come to a deeper, more basic form of existence stripped of the fictions of consciousness about it. This 'existential' Buddhism is called Vajrayāna. Vajra is the symbol term for Being-as-such which as the indestructible core underlies all growth and self-realization in the same way that truth itself underlies the quest for truth. It has to be noted that the term 'self' in self-realization does not imply the glorified ego of subjectivistic philosophies with their postulate of a Self. Similarly, 'existential' is not a defining characteristic of some human subject, but refers to Being-as-such. 'Existential' Buddhism is therefore totally different from the various forms of Western existentialism which is purely anthropocentric and ego-centric, unable to realize that Being-as-such and egoness are two different categories. 'Existential' Buddhism, claimed to be the climax of the philosophical quest, is concerned with Being, not with an ego, in however idealized a way it may be presented.

Before the major philosophical systems developed, a great many ideas had been propounded, unsystematically, yet deeply affecting the continual quest. This intellectual activity is reflected in the list of schools, eighteen according to tradition, that we find mentioned in the numerous indigenous works. Sometimes these schools were no more than splinter-groups gathering around a gifted teacher or communities in various parts of India. Although for the most part we have merely the names of these schools, not their ideas, because the tenets attributed to them vary in the various listings, the very existence of these schools indicates the impact of the Buddha's teaching on his contemporaries and on subsequent generations.

In the following passage Mi-pham 'Jam-dbyangs rnam-rgyal rgya-mtsho gives us a glimpse of the beginnings of Buddhist philosophical thought which was both the outcome and the source of a way of life. It is true he gives us this picture of early Buddhism in retrospect and he criticizes its tenets from the viewpoint of a later logician and metaphysician. But his criticism is not meant to destroy, but to open our eyes to wider horizons. Much of what the early Buddhists believed to be the answers to their questions may seem to us to be something of the remote past. Nevertheless these questions and answers made the subsequent development of Buddhist philosophy possible.

Another important point to be noted in his criticism is that he does not attack the early tenets from the outside, but that he reveals their inner weaknesses. When lastly he extols the Mahāyāna he merely re-emphasizes the positive character of Buddhist philosophy as a quest for truth born out of truth.

Guru Padmasambhava (8th cent.) founder of the first Tibetan Buddhist tradition, represented by Mi-Pham (1846–1914) author of *The Summary of Philosophical Systems*

FROM

THE SUMMARY OF PHILOSOPHICAL SYSTEMS

YID-BZHIN-MDZOD-KYI GRUB-MTHA' BSDUS-PA

foll. 9b ff.

THE BUDDHIST philosophical systems that are to be accepted comprise Hīnayāna and Mahāyāna. Hīnayāna, according to the gradation in intellectual capacity, consists of Śrāvakayāna and Pratyekabuddhayāna.

The Śrāvakayāna is discussed here according to schools, character, and philosophical tenets.

SCHOOLS

There were eighteen schools. In the beginning there were the Mahāsānghikas and the Sthaviras.

The Mahāsānghikas split up into the branch-Mahāsānghikas, Ekavyavahārins, Lokottaravādins, Bahuśrutīyas, Nityavādins, Caityakas, Pūrvaśailikas, and Uttaraśailikas.

The Sthaviras split up into Haimavatas, Sarvāstivādins, Hetuvādins, Vātsīputrīyas, Dharmottaras, Bhadrayānikas, Sāṃmitīyas, Bahudeśakas, Dharmadeśakas, and Bhadravarṣikas.

They had different views. All of them have been refuted in the main work [from which the following is an excerpt].

CHARACTER

The Śrāvakas observe impeccable manners and abolish all (positive and negative) imputations concerning the knowable [which is analyzed by them into] the psycho-physical constituents, the elements, and the interactional fields, by studying and pondering over the four truths in every possible way and in a faultless manner. When they are reviled, angered, beaten, or irritated they do not retaliate in any way. They possess the four qualities marking a religious person [1] and with them set out on the Path.

Further, they have few desires and know how to be content; they observe the twelve practices that mark a scrupulous person; [2] they are moderate in eating, try not to sleep during the first and last parts of the night, practise the thirty-seven topics conducive to enlightenment over the five paths by properly meditating on the ugly and other aspects of things as the antidote against the three poisons, on the four truths, and on the chain of interdependent origination.[3] Thereby they reach their goal: deliverance from the three worlds.

Since both their paths and the deliverance [reached by them] are something positive, they must not be discarded, and since also in Mahāyāna these (lower) paths and deliverances are commonly accepted as being necessary for the higher reaches, they are not to be looked down upon. However, the petty selfishness and the philosophical belief that what is only a partial aspect of the ground, the path, and the goal is something existing in an ultimate sense, is what is going to be refuted here in the Mahāyāna.

Philosophical Tenets

The philosophical tenets are listed in two groups: those which are common to them, discussed below, and the individual philosophical systems.*

The Śrāvakas have seven points in common. Since their lower paths must be transcended they must be known here in the Mahāyāna, because it has been said that to transcend is to know and to see with open eyes.

The seven points are: (1) the four truths as objective realities; (2) atoms and moments as ultimate builders of the universe; (3) Arhatship as the final goal; (4) the non-recognition of a primal ground, (5) the non-recognition of the Mahāyāna, (6) the non-recognition of the ten spiritual

* These latter begin with the Vaibhāṣikas. See Chapter Two.

levels; and (7) the claim that the Buddha is merely an individual human being.

1. These are the truths of frustration: its origin, its cessation, and the way to its cessation. The first relates to the psycho-physical constituents representing an affectively-toned and affect-arousing effect. It includes all the sentient beings as they are born in the six kinds of life-forms, as well as their environment, the external world. These four truths are the embodiment and presence or resting-place of frustration because among these beings three kinds of misery are encountered.[4]

Origin means the cause of frustration. It is karmic action and emotive responses. Karmic actions are motivations, perceptions, and that which has been set up by motivations, acts by body and speech. Each of them is good, evil, and neutral. Emotive responses are passion-lust and others.

Cessation means that frustration, together with its cause, has ceased to operate. It is twofold: (i) the psycho-physical constituents still being present, and (ii) their being no more.

The path to the cessation of frustration is the application of [what is termed] the five paths in one's life,[5] so as to realize the cessation of frustration by eliminating its cause through being aware of frustration.

2. Since indivisible atoms as ultimate and primary factors in the physical universe and indivisible moments as the primary instances of the flux of cognition exist in an ultimate sense, it is claimed that they build the physical world [and its cognition].

3. An Arhat who has passed into a state where the psycho-physical constituents are no more does not relapse into the world, because the cause for being born in the three worlds has lost its generating power. There is no Buddhahood, because he is tied to the Śrāvaka pattern. It is claimed that passing into Nirvāṇa is like a flame going out when the oil has been consumed.[6]

4. While the six groups of perceptions are recognized, no common ground for their operation is accepted, because it

does not constitute an objective reference. Moreover, such a ground is said to be inadmissible because if there were a static mind serving as the ground of everything, it would have to be an individual self.

5. While the four sections of the Vinaya and the other scriptures of the Hīnayāna are considered to be the Buddha's words, the Prajñāpāramitā literature is not so considered, because, so they say, this literature has been composed by Māra and outsiders in order to proselytize,[7] and because they seem to contradict the Tripiṭaka and the four axioms.[8]

6. When one sees the truths one cannot stay in Saṃsāra for many aeons more. A highly gifted individual who on the level of an ordinary man is capable of accumulating merits and knowledge during three 'countless aeons'[9] has the power to become a Buddha. He will realize the factors conducive to and forming part of enlightenment during one night session.

7. Some highly gifted persons who for countless aeons have been able to endure hardships in Saṃsāra will become Buddhas when they have studied the Śrāvaka paths and accumulated merits and knowledge during these aeons. Others are not capable of doing so because frustration in the world is overwhelming and because malicious elements prevent them from working for others. Therefore, while 'Buddha' means a sublime individual, it does not mean authenticity (*nirmāṇakāya*), because an (individual) Buddha still has the residua of what is going to mature inasmuch as he bleeds and feels pains in the back.

There also is no continual concentration, because it is said in the scriptures that he came out of a state of deep concentration and went for alms. They also claim that after the Buddha had passed into Nirvāṇa his working for others stopped completely.

The critique of these points is as follows:

1. The four truths do not exist as ultimate realities, because they are found nowhere when one examines the whole of the given, the world and its inhabitants, and the psychophysical constituents and the interactional fields, and because

all that is termed 'rejection,' 'acquisition,' 'riddance,' and 'possession' are indexes, not entities.

2. There are no atoms building the physical world. If they did they would have to meet each other partially or totally. In the former case they would not be indivisible inasmuch as they have parts, and in the latter case a whole closed system would become an atom. Hence they cannot exist as builders of the universe. If they would build the world without meeting each other, atoms of darkness and of light could enter the spaces in between them and still other atoms could enter into the spaces in between the latter, so that into a small grain three thousand atoms and more could enter.

Atoms are also not found when one investigates shadows, distances, and arrows being shot.

Time moments also do not exist as such. The problem is whether the middle moment joins with the previous and subsequent moments or not. In the former case it would have to do so by degrees or at once. If it does by degrees, moments are divisible, and if they do so all at once, even an aeon becomes a single time moment.

If time moments do not join, that which is in between them can be interrupted by other time moments. This latter time moment either comes in between other time moments, or it does not; if it does not, one could not know duration as an addition of time instances, and if it does come in between, the indivisibility of time moments becomes untenable.

3. Arhatship is not final Nirvāṇa because the obscurations of the various patterns of existence have not yet been completely removed; because the radiant light which is the very nature of mind is what constitutes Buddhahood; because the obscurations are incidental; because even if the activity of mentation may be stopped while the obscurations have not yet been removed, the cause for projecting a mind existence is still there; and because the two prerequisites as the cause for final enlightenment must be acquired.[10]

4. A primal ground must be accepted because, if it did not exist, continuity would not be possible; neither could one be born in Saṃsāra nor be liberated from it, because there

would be no substratum for the tendencies moving in either direction; and when there is no mind in which the six perceptive functions operate, a mind could not come into operation again because, when the functions have been stopped, there is nothing from which they might start again. Moreover, if it is a fact that the whole of appearance is of the nature of experience, the ephemeral perceptive functions cannot be the cause of the possible experiences. Hence one must assume a common substratum or a primal ground.

5. The rejection of the Mahāyāna is not admissible. Not only does the Mahāyāna not contradict the Tripiṭaka and the four axioms, it is even superior to the earlier teaching, because in the Hīnayāna the path to Buddhahood is incomplete, while in the Mahāyāna the path culminates in the most sublime goal of enlightenment.

6. There are the ten spiritual levels. Even if one has set out on the Noble Path, the prerequisites must be prepared because there are many hindrances on the path due to the many emotional imbalances, and the prerequisites [for goal attainment] are not complete on the level of ordinary persons because they have not received the initiatory confirmations and empowerments. Hence the levels are not contradictory to the gradation of knowledge on the levels counteracting the ten obscurations which have to be eliminated.

7. If the Buddha is merely a human being and if his working for others ceases with his passing into Nirvāṇa as a result of his having removed the obscurations and ignorance, such an ephemeral and merciless being cannot command any respect. At the time of enlightenment when the radiant light is felt to shine free from all obscurations, the appearance of the Buddha, though He may be seen in different forms and shapes according to the different states of the beings, is not some individualistic phenomenon.

CHAPTER TWO

THE VAIBHĀṢIKAS

THE EARLIEST systematic attempt to work out the implications of the Buddha's teaching was that of the Vaibhāṣikas who are so named after the title of their most authoritative work, the Vibhāṣā, and who grew out of the larger group of the Sarvāstivādins.[1] This accounts for the fact that various tenets are listed as being held by them, although properly speaking, these tenets represent the beliefs of other groups among early Buddhist philosophers.

The Vaibhāṣikas started with an analysis of Being (*yod-pa*). This they understood as meaning 'all that exists.'[2] Existence as such was for them inseparable from the feeling of reality which we know primarily belongs to whatever can have an effect on us. Their analysis led to the first great division within Being as a whole, between that which exists and is transitory and concrete (*dngos-po*) and that which exists but is eternal, i.e. absolute (*rtag-pa*). This division remained valid for all subsequent philosophical schools, although different interpretations and evaluations were placed on it.

The Vaibhāṣikas' approach has often been termed 'realistic.' But here a word of caution becomes necessary because this term, derived from and developed within the Western philosophical framework, hardly does justice to Eastern patterns of thought; at best it merely points to certain, usually inconclusive, similarities. The fact that in indigenous works on philosophy the tenets of the Yogācāras,[3] whom we generally equate with 'idealists,' are dealt with as being on the same level as those of the alleged 'realists' actually should give us pause. The objections raised by the later philosophers of Buddhism against the systems ranging from 'realism' to 'idealism' are directed toward their concretism and reductionism, and since much in our thinking would be open to the same critique, it is extremely hazardous to employ our traditional concepts without distorting the nature of Buddhist philosophy, which as a spiritual movement goes beyond realism and idealism.

Each of the two departments into which the Vaibhāṣikas divided Being consisted of particular existents. For this reason the Vaibhāṣikas may roughly be classified as 'existential dualists.' But inasmuch as there are apparently fundamental differences of kind among the existents constituting the same department the Vaibhāṣikas held different views about them. The absolute was believed to comprise three, and, with certain groups, even four or five particular existents.[4] These can best be understood as inner factors of lived experience, and cannot simply be discussed or ignored as merely subjective, but play an important role in the individual's life-world. One of these existents is termed 'space', which must not be confused with geometric, mathematical space, any point of which is, like any other, at various measurable distances from material bodies. Nor is it the mere absence of resistance. Lastly it also is not sensed space with which it sometimes seems to have been equated even by Vaibhāṣikas. Belonging to the department of the eternal within Being, it is an existential category which has a 'perspectival' character disclosing or, as the texts say, 'not obscuring' the naked facticity of a situation which not only stretches away from the subject towards the object but also refers from the object to the subject. As the oriented space of an individual's life-world it is of course quite distinct from geometric space which is a secondary intellectual construction; and as a meaningful horizon of Being it is closely related to the two remaining existents constituting the department of the absolute. One of these existents is the non-reoccurrence of the processes which involve man in Saṃsāra. Its existential character is clearly indicated by the definition of its being present when the conditions that ordinarily initiate such an involvement with its attending frustration do not obtain in their entirety, and by the qualification that it is not dependent on the use of insight. The other existent is the cessation of the working of the factors causing involvement, due to insight which, however, does not produce the state of non-involvement and freedom but merely discovers it. Actually one and the same 'reality' is here looked at from different angles; the one is viewed *from* the goal, which strange to say is the basis of all activity in freedom and hence truly existential. The other is looked *at* as the goal and its effect on man's life. But since each aspect could be named, it seems that the names were responsible for the fact that this feature of Being was counted as two entities. It also seems that 'insight' as goal-discovery and goal-inspired living and 'space' as the lived world of the individual, rather than his location in a predetermined framework, touch upon the pattern of space and time as aspects of man's being rather than as categories of interpretation.

In the department of the 'transitory' (*mi-rtag-pa*) each particular existent, apart from being of the 'natural kind' that is impermanent, had a specific attribute which made it of such and such a kind. It is here that the Vaibhāṣikas listed everything which we would call the physical-material, the mental-spiritual with its subdivision into mind- (particle or particles) and mind-related substances, and, lastly, concrete entities which could not be defined as being either of the others, yet could be defined as having being of their own. The physical-material, in particular, was constituted of relatively stable patterns, with 'significant forms' such as the material universe both exhibiting a substantive nature and being susceptible of perception. But it also comprised what we would call 'sensa' in the phenomenological meaning of contents of awareness (colours, sounds, fragrances, flavours, and pressures) and in the physiological meaning of the processes of sensing them. Lastly they included in this section an intangible entity which we would rather term a behavioural property or a trait tending to typify reactions favourable or unfavourable, of rejection and acceptance, of likes and dislikes, of withdrawal and approval.[5] From this short survey it is obvious that concerning the 'transitory' the Vaibhāṣikas were differentiating-attribute pluralists. Believing in different kinds of concrete entities and in a plurality of substances, they accepted, on the whole, a much greater plurality of concrete entities than of kind. In the field of the mental-spiritual it becomes even more patent that our Western categories do not fit the Vaibhāṣikas' tenets. They claimed that we have an immediate apprehension of the nature of things as they are in themselves, but as they never lost sight of 'experience,' which may be described as the sum total of appearances and feelings together with ordering thought, they at once were aware of the distinction between (a) data available for ordering and (b) thought as ordering activity. More precisely, they held that we are directly aware of external material objects and that therefore the senses give us trustworthy knowledge. Sensory awarenes, however, is intimately connected with perceptual and conceptual knowledge. Perceiving and conceiving begin when we select and attend to connections which are already 'thought about' in sensory awareness (*dbang-shes*).[6] The distinction between sensory, perceptual and conceptual data was one both of kind and of degree of definiteness. Within this scheme what we translate by 'mind' (*sems*) had merely a 'privileged' position in its co-existence with the various mind-related substances, all of which participated in one way or another in the total conscious experience. Mind seems to have been considered as a homogenous substance exhibiting a specific function in its conjunction with sensations which themselves were cognitive. This suggests the idea that mind represents the possibility of originative response which becomes first selective emphasis and then symbolic construction. The distinction between perception and conception is drawn not between two different entities, body and mind, but between two modes of activity integrated in one actuality. The one is a direct *rapport* with other actualities, the other is a selective and interpretative activity. Mind is thus not just an entity 'decoding' messages received through the bodily organs, but an originative form of activity arising in conjunction with various (physical-mental) activities and through them is in contact with the surrounding universe. This co-operation of mind with the various mental events, accounting for a determinate conscious experience, becomes intelligible when we clearly focus the two modes of cognitive life. The one, which may be termed 'adverbial,' is marked by integral feelings having certain affective tones, motivation and other characteristics of sensitivity and qualifying a state of experience which comes as the result of a response to and *rapport* with the environment. The other, which we shall call 'transitive,' is a differentiation of contents of awareness. The latter seems to call for developed powers of discrimination and therefore opens up new perspectives. This explains why 'appreciative discrimination' belongs to the 'entourage' or group of mental events (*sems-byung*) operating on various levels, practical, aesthetic or theoretic, and is not itself the 'privileged' factor (*sems*), which acts rather as the initiator of cognitive experiences.

The last group of particular existents belonging to the department of the 'transitory' is made up of so-called 'disjunct entities.' They are interpretative schemata by means of which relations between perceptions can be represented. In the creation of this group there has been operative a law of projection of which the Vaibhāṣikas do not seem to have been aware, and which prompted them to consider the relations that obtain between facts when they are rendered as propositions, as something like 'real objects.' Thus, for instance, '*A* attains *B*' tells of a way in which *A* and *B* are combined, but our only means of expressing this way is to name it and, all of a sudden, a new entity 'attaining' seems to have added itself, which is then looked on as a 'thing' or 'particular entity' (*dngos-po*) having power in itself. In looking on these entities as 'particular existents' or 'things' the Vaibhāṣikas were embodying relics of mythical thinking.

The prominence given to the concept of 'particular existents' means that the Vaibhāṣikas' philosophy was formally an *ontology*, a doctrine of what there is.[7] The way, however, they worked it out shows that they were primarily concerned to give a unitary account of experience as a whole.

Metaphysics comes into the picture when those who accept

the foregoing analysis proceed to inquire into the nature of these particular existents. The metaphysical concern is linked with the notion of two truths. Superficially it seems to correspond to the traditional Western conception that the philosophers (metaphysicians) have access to real things which are stable, unchanging and for that reason fully knowable, and as a consequence they recognize the world of appearances for what it is: impermanent, flickering, and unreal like a dream. The key terms here, of course, are 'real' and 'unreal' respectively. Certainly, a dream is quite real in the sense that it is the case that we are dreaming and having certain beliefs; it is also 'unreal' in the sense that the beliefs entertained in dreaming refer to what is not the case. This shows that 'real' is used in an evaluative sense with reference to some interpretation. While it would seem natural to conclude that the 'real' is the genuine, the authentic, as opposed to the spurious, the Vaibhāṣikas did not separate reality from existence, and therefore did not accept some things as unreal or non-existent. Their distinction was that between the ultimately real and the empirically real. The Buddhist philosophers were the last persons in the world to deny the empirical world which for them always remained quite 'real,' but as metaphysicians they saw it in a different light. This had tremendous effect on practice which is summed up in what the called the 'way' (*lam*) and which has remained a means to see things differently. Philosophy, metaphysics, and practice thus formed a unity.

The Vaibhāṣikas' metaphysical interpretation of Being does not, as might be assumed, coincide with their division of Being into that which is absolute on the one hand, and transitory on the other. Ultimately, real was that which, it was assumed, existed *as* substance (*rdzas-yod*), while anything that could be claimed to *exhibit* substantial existence (*rdzas-grub*), though not having existence as substance in itself (which nevertheless might be a constituent of the latter), was considered to be conventionally or empirically real and to have nominal existence (*btags-yod*).

Speaking of substance in the context of Buddhist philosophy needs clarification because this notion, even in Western philosophies, is notoriously ambiguous. It is usually associated with the twin notions of long duration and the possibility of independent existence which, in turn, lack precision. However, according to the commonly accepted view, anything transitory would not be considered as a substance but as an 'event in' or a 'state of' a substance. The Vaibhāṣikas rejected these criteria for 'substance' and were as much in agreement with McTaggart, for whom every particular existent, however transitory, is a substance, as with Spinoza, for whom no existent could count as a substance unless it was eternal. They were, however, not quite consistent in their use of the notion of 'substance' because they understood it both in an absolute sense and in that of consisting of collocation of atoms (which, strictly speaking, fulfilled the Vaibhāṣikas' criterion for the ultimately real). In this respect a certain similarity with the Vaiśeṣikas' idea of substance as being the material cause of derivative substance is evident.[8] Apart from this ambiguity the Vaibhāṣikas' idea of substance does not imply any materiality; their notion rather reflects the 'thingness' of thought so characteristic of the early stages of mental life. Aside from the eternal or absolute and 'ultimately real,' the transitory 'ultimately real' must be understood to include the determinable qualities of temporal and spatial position. This is to say, no particular existent can be characterized by different determinate forms of the quality of temporal position while being the same particular existent. In other words, a particular existent is instantaneous. Similarly, no particular existent characterized by the quality of spatial position can be characterized by two different determinate forms of the quality. Hence all particular existents of the material realm are punctiform, and are instantaneous events and point-instants. The former were the constituents of the 'mental' and the latter those of the 'material.' The mental and the material thus were further characterized by the 'extensional' qualities of duration and spatiality, forming certain ways by virtue of their 'positional' qualities. What we would call a mind would on this analysis be a set of point-instants varying continuously in their quality of temporal position, and its determinate duration would depend upon the determinate relation between the determinate qualities of temporal position characterizing the first and last point-instants of this set. A body, on the other hand, would be a set of point-instants all of which have the same determinate temporal position, but whose spatial position is varying continuously. Thus the constituents of a mind and a body are ultimately real, but the mind and the body are themselves only conventionally or nominally real. The Vaibhāṣikas' conception of Being, both ontological and metaphysical, can be shown as follows:

BEING = THE UNIVERSE OF SUBSTANTIVAL REALITIES

Ontology: transitory (causative) — absolute (non-causative)

(*dngos-po*) (*mi-rtag-pa*) — (*dngos-po*) (*rtag-pa*)

empirically real — ultimately real

Metaphysics:

(*rdzas-grub = btags-yod = kun-rdzob*) (*rdzas-yod = don-dam*)

1. the physical material — 5. the absolutes

2–3. the mental (mind particle and mental events)

4. interpretative schemata

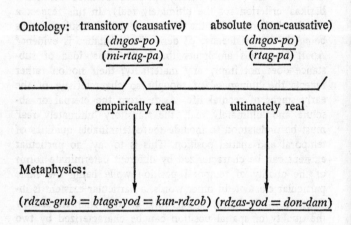

The Buddhist philosophers not only dealt with ontological and metaphysical problems, but also paid close attention to the factors which constitute the foundations of personality. Especially they investigated *feeling, emotions, moods,* and *temperaments,* not only in their overt manifestations but also as to their latent potentialities. It is a well-known fact that some situations tend to call forth reactions which we call pleasant, unpleasant, and indifferent. Others which are more critical arouse emotional responses. An emotion, then, is a stirred-up state of acute disturbance of the individual which is related to certain perceived stimuli. In everyday life we experience a wide variety of feelings and emotions, collectively known as affective states. Each of us, in addition, is characterized by periodic fluctuations in the nature of his or her emotional-feeling tone. We may be gay at one time and depressed at another. These moods may occur daily in periodicity, they also may be of longer cycles. Further, certain patterns of mood may come to dominate the total personality for years and even for a whole lifetime. Even so there may be fluctuations of subordinate feelings, emotions, and moods, all of them tending to disrupt the personality. The recognition of this fact prompted the Buddhist philosophers to discuss still another division in reality: the split into that which brings about emotional instability and that which ensures emotional stability. The latter, in particular, is intimately connected with learning as a process of integration rather than as the acquisition of unrelated bits of information. It is the integrated person that is no longer at the mercy of the affective vagaries, and in the vision of what reality is and means he has been given the opportunity to become and remain integrated by further learning. This vision comes on the so-called 'Path of Seeing,'[9] from which goal-directed learning with its advances and setbacks becomes possible.

The status of an integrated person is closely related to the idea a man has about himself. What, then, are we to understand by 'I'? Indian thought has had the tendency to speculate whether 'I' denotes a peculiar and separate substance, or whether it is merely an index word indicating the one person from whom the noise 'I' issues and therefore is not an extra name for an extra being. While the Hindus hardly ever went beyond the first kind of speculation, the Buddhist fervently upheld the second alternative. Still, 'I,' in my use of it, always and only indicates 'me' and it seems to have a uniquely adhesive quality. Various groups among the Vaibhāṣikas held various views about which constituent of the personality served as the peg on which to hang this 'I.' Apart from this, all philosophers had to face the problem of accounting for what seems to be and to constitute my indivisible and continuing identity. These speculations took the form of centre-theories and non-centre theories. The former ascribe the unity of the mind to the fact that there is a certain particular existent, a centre, which stands in a common asymmetrical relation to all the mental events which could be said to be the states of a certain mind, while non-centre theories deny the existence of such a centre, and ascribe the unity of the mind to the fact that certain mental events are directly interrelated in certain characteristic ways while others are not so interrelated. Centre-theories further divide into those which accept a Pure Ego and those which do not, but which conceive of the centre as an event. The Buddhists, on the whole, have rejected Pure Ego theories and gradually have arrived at favouring a non-centre theory. The Vaibhāṣikas, however, adopted a central-event theory. That is to say, for them the unity of a total state of mind, consisting at any moment of mental events of various kinds and of events of the same kind but with different epistemological objects, depended on a common relation in which all its differentiations stand to a common centre, which is itself an event and not a peculiar extra entity; it is of the same nature as the events which it unifies. There is a single central event (*sems*) which stands in a common relation to a number of other mental events (*sems-byung*), each of which has its own characteristic quality and some of which stand in characteristic relations to objects. As the relation between mind and mental events is so intimate that the one cannot be without the other, the mental events are more precisely termed a function of mind. In listing the mental events related to a central event the Vaibhāṣikas adopted a qualitative method and, in the end, named fifty-one such events, the earlier number having been forty-six.[10] These events included not only emotions and cognitive processes but also behavioristic features. The fact that these latter properties were listed as 'mental events' clearly shows that the Vaibhāṣikas dealt with man in the concrete rather than in the abstract as a mere postulate and that the trend towards emphasizing mind was already present, because on this basis it could be said that the body is mind insofar as a mind animates a body and therefore behaves in a certain way which it would not do if it were not so animated.

The analysis of Being, particularly with regard to its division into the objective and subjective, merely provided the raw material with which the individual had to deal, and in so doing the validity of knowledge arose as an important problem. The Vaibhāṣikas recognized immediate apprehension and inference as the means providing us with valid knowledge. Inference comprised both genuine or mediate and immediate inference. In this respect their conception of inference was wider than ours, which is almost exclusively restricted to genuine or mediate inference. Through the latter we pass to a new fact not already known, but potentially involved in the premise, while through immediate inference we merely pass to a new symbolic formulation which refers to the same existent fact. Judgments of perception which are neither inferences (in our sense of the word) nor immediate apprehension would fall under inference in the Vaibhāṣikas' line of thought.

In the field of immediate apprehension the Vaibhāṣikas distinguished between and recognized three types. The first, immediate sensory apprehension, was considered as not involving the noetic (*shes-pa*).[11] The latter, as has been shown previously, acted essentially as an initiator of cognitive experiences and, if it apprehended anything at all, it merely apprehended the bare haecceity. Yet, we *see* colour-forms, *hear* sounds and so on. This the Vaibhāṣikas explained as being due to the specific function which each sense-organ performs by way of its peculiar structure. The eye, for instance, is a specific sense-organ which has its own peculiar function of 'seeing forms,' and in exercising its function it provides its own validity. 'Seeing' thus becomes an active process of formulation which begins in the eye. It is not a passive storing of chaotic stimuli out of which a mind construes forms to suit its own purpose.

The second type, intellectual apprehension, is an immediate awareness of meaning, not a logical reflection or ratiocination which may develop out of the former.

The third, mystical apprehension, is a manner of knowledge by connaturality; it is beyond concepts and analogies and silent in respect to apprehension through the senses.

This discussion of ontological, metaphysical, psychological, and epistemological problems served as the framework within which the individual had to work out his way of life which was considered to culminate in freedom or salvation. Working out one's way of life was termed the 'Path' (*lam*) which, ensuring the development of the personality, was understood as a continuous broadening of the individual's spiritual horizon. The 'Path' therefore was essentially a cognitive process affecting every aspect of the individual's life. It is here that Buddhism left the realm of philosophy (as we understand this discipline now) and, by assuming the character of ethics, joined with religion. In speaking of Buddhism as a religion we must understand the word 'religion' as implying an ultimate concern for ultimate reality, rather than as a set of doctrinal postulates.

The 'Path' in its last analysis consisted of two major phases, one of learning and one of no-more-learning. The former was subdivided into four stages, each called a 'path' so the following diagram of the 'Path' obtains:

Phases of Learning	Phase of No More Learning
1. preparation	5. no more learning
2. linkage	
3. vision	
4. cultivation of the vision	

The first or preparatory stage is known as 'accummulation of merits and perfection of knowledge.' Its first aspect emphasizes the ethico-social character of learning which never occurs in a vacuum, and, in particular, it refers to those activities which safeguard the existence of man as a human being within the cycle of rebirths.[12] In Buddhist thought human existence is something exceedingly rare and valuable. It is easily lost and difficult to retrieve, and it is possible to find salvation only through a human existence. The second aspect, perfection of knowledge, facilitates the first, inasmuch as knowledge assists in curbing the emotions which underly man's actions and which, jointly with his deeds, make him lose his humanity.

The second stage represents the transition from the preparatory aspect to the central experience of the 'Path' as such, the vision of reality in its true nature. That is to say, whatever we perceive is transitory, death-doomed, and unable to provide emotional satisfaction or to give spiritual sustenance. But inasmuch as everything transitory is merely a temporary differentiation of and in a wider aesthetic field, the transitory itself offers the possibility of escaping its frustrating limitations and of making us more keenly aware of the wider aesthetic field and of prompting us to attend to the latter's presence which alone can provide an essentially spiritual contentment. It is from this third stage that the later 'perfection of transcending awareness' starts, because it is the discriminative-appreciative function (*shes-rab*) that enables man to step 'outside' the death-delivering ravages of all that is transitory.

This vision leads to the fourth phase of the 'Path' as the conscious cultivation of what has been realized in the vision of reality. It is viewed from two angles: the one is experienced as 'obstacle-removing,' the other as the feeling of 'being freed' from what was formerly disturbing and obstructing. Gradually this will lead to a state in which the aspirant has no longer to learn.

With the exception of the third phase, the vision of reality in a new perspective, all phases, including the final one, may or may not arouse affective responses that are related to success or failure in the enterprise, which is itself considered as a fluctuation between 'coarser' and 'subtler' experiences. These relate to the triple division into a world of sensuality, pure form, and formlessness. Each subsequent 'world'-experience is more subtle than the preceding one.

The arousal of affective responses occurs in the wake of the learning process, which is marked by endeavour. This, in turn, is enhanced by the feeling of success and lowered by that of failure, although these feelings may also have the opposite effect. Since the curbing of the emotions that involve man in the coarser and subtler aspects of the world is a continuous task performed on and by the 'Path,' even the last stage of it does not exclude the possibility that these disturbing emotions may reassert themselves. This happens according to the Vaibhāṣikas when the individual, having reached the phase of no-more-learning, becomes negligent in his watchfulness. They therefore held that the saintly sage may fall from his elevated position, although he will not fall so low as to become an unregenerate person again, because by his previous learning he has already moved far beyond this level.

The fact that the Vaibhāsikas distinguished between a 'path' arousing affective responses and one not so doing points to a very important characteristic of the Buddhist way of life which takes into account and emphasizes the transitoriness of all that exists concretely. Inasmuch as the 'Path' is essentially a cognitive process we may know impermanence in two ways: (*a*) by having a keen awareness of it that enables us to make the appropriate compassionate response to a given situation, and (*b*) by having it so grown into our bones that we respond by our immediate being, as having become connatural with impermanence. The former is the way of saintly persons. The latter is the 'noble' path itself. From this idea of connaturality directly follows the Vaibhāṣikas' claim that in spite of the cognitive function of the 'Path,' the so-called 'Truth of the Path' (*lam-bden*) is not identical or co-extensive with the noetic, but is the sum total of what constitutes the individual divorced from the arousal of affective states.

As an index of man's spiritual growth and his experience of it, the path is intentional in structure. That is to say, I cannot go without going somewhere; I cannot think without thinking about something; and I cannot do without doing something. Thus the objective as well as the subjective are given with the same evidence and the objective is present in a peculiar relational mode of becoming. This means that the objective is a challenge to make up one's mind about it and to take a stand (although it may be no standpoint in the ordinary sense of the word), rather than a stubborn clinging to outworn schemes (with which we tend to confuse a standpoint). In grasping or accepting these possibilities man has already made up his mind about what he is seeking, and in following the path he discards whatever may prevent him from attaining his goal. This is indicated by the discussion in the original texts of what has to be and actually is eliminated by the path.

These possibilities form the content of the vision and are summarized as the Four Truths, which for practical reasons are enumerated in the obverse order of effect and cause: The Truth of Frustration, exposing the unsatisfactoriness of all that is, and the Truth of the Coming into Existence of Frustration on the one hand; the Truth of the End of all Frustration and the Truth of the Way towards it, on the other. Each of the four truths is envisaged in four aspects which have been open to different interpretations.[13] Nevertheless each of the four aspects of each truth are logically related to each other.

Although knowledge is essential for the development of the individual, the vision of the Four Truths is not yet knowledge in the proper sense, but an 'acceptance' of what a person ordinarily has avoided facing. This acceptance of things as they are—that is, to see them as truly transitory and for this reason unsatisfactory and causing sorrow—brings about knowledge, which unlike propositional knowledge is an emotionally stabilizing, deeply 'felt knowledge.' The Vaibhāṣikas subdivided the stage of vision into sixteen moments or grades, eight of which were 'acceptance in knowledge' and the remaining eight 'felt knowledge.' But it was only the last grade that was true 'felt knowledge' and as such belonged to the phase of conscious cultivation. Each of the four truths relates to each of the three spheres into which the universe has been divided: the spheres of pure form and formlessness forming a unit here as contrasted with the sphere of sensuality. Each truth thus has two grades of 'acceptance'—the one referring to the sphere of sensuality, the other to the joint spheres of pure form and formlessness—and two corresponding grades of 'felt knowledge.' Each grade was considered to follow the other: the acceptance of the transitoriness of the spheres of sensuality giving rise to knowingly feeling this transitoriness, which in turn gives rise to the acceptance of the transitoriness of the higher spheres of pure form and formlessness and the feeling of it in knowledge. Similarly, what applies to the Truth of Frustration also applies to the remaining three truths.

From the very beginning Buddhism opposed the absolutistic subjectivism of the Hindu philosophers; in other words it rejected any form of a Pure-Ego theory (*ātman*). This rejection was the direct outcome of its functional view of what constituted the individual, and fully harmonized with the observable transitoriness of all that is.

The subjectivism which was to dominate the later Hindu philosophies had in the Upaniṣads before and around Buddha's time assumed the character of an impersonalistic Idealism according to which an eternal solitary and sovereign self, a Pure Ego, is the essential self within each individual. This view was termed a 'coarse' idea of what makes us talk about an individual or a self, and its rejection was accordingly called 'coarse' idea of the nonexistence of a Pure Ego. A modified form of this theory was held by the Vātsīputrīyas and Sāṃmitīyas, who rejected an absolutistic *ātman* but postulated a self-sufficient substance which, being transitory as other substances, did not contradict the Buddhist conception of impermanence,[14] although it violated the functional character of what is called an individual. Their theory, which is halfway between a Pure-Ego theory and a central-event theory, was termed a 'subtle' idea of a self and its rejection was the 'subtle' idea of the nonexistence of a self.

The awareness of the non-existence of a Pure Ego in any form, which originated in the vision phase of the 'Path,' is easily understandable when we bear in mind that the decisive difference between Buddhism and Hinduism consists of the fact that Buddhism took a dynamic-functional world view, while Hinduism remained static-absolutistic. The functional view Buddhism developed concerning the self can be illustrated in the following way. The Kāśyapīyas, who with their insistence on the priority of mind within the constituents of the personality seem to have been the forerunners of the mentalistic schools of advanced Buddhism, considered mind alone as the ground for talking about a self. However, mind and mental events are so intimately related that the one is not without the other. Accordingly, if we let x stand for the 'individual' or 'self,' m for 'mind' and n for 'mental event(s),' the functional character of the 'self' can be expressed as

$$x(m, n)$$

and since n is a function of m, the formula can be rewritten

$$x(m, f(m)).$$

On the basis of the Kāśyapīyas' line of thought, this formula would have to be restated as

$$x(m, n) = x\,(m, 0) + n$$

and developed according to the generally accepted view that five 'mental events' are everpresent with each 'mind.' Thus we have

$$x\,(m, n) = x\,(m, 5) + (n - 5).$$

The Vātsīputrīyas, however, not content with the purely functional character of the 'self,' demanded an additional variable; and, provided that they, too, shared the Buddhist esteem of the mental, they would have set up the impossible formula:

$$x(x') + (m, n)$$

With the realization of the functional character of the 'self' those emotive reaction patterns and possibilities are eliminated which cluster round the belief in a 'self' as an entity in itself. But still those patterns which operate in response to the other contents in experience are present and have to be eliminated by repeated attention to them in the phase of the conscious cultivation of what has been seen of reality in the phase of vision. The latter reaction patterns are divided into nine categories of strong-strong, strong-medium, strong-weak, medium-strong, medium-medium, medium-weak, weak-strong, weak-medium and weak-weak. These nine categories belong each to the nine levels into which the triple division of the universe has been subdivided:

	1. denizens of hell			
A. Kāmadhātu	2. animals			
(sphere of	3. unhappy spirits			
sensuousness	4. men			Level I
and	5. demons			
sensuality)				
		1. Caturmahārājakāyika		
		2. Trāyastriṃśa		
		3. Yāma		
	6. gods	4. Tuṣita		
		5. Nirmāṇarati		
		6. Paranirmitavaśavartin		
		7. Devaloka		
	1st Dhyāna	1. Brahmakāyika		II
		2. Brahmapurohita		
		3. Mahābrahmā		
	2nd Dhyāna	1. Parīttābha		III
		2. Apramāṇābha		
		3. Ābhāsvara		
B. Rūpadhātu	3rd Dhyāna	1. Parīttaśubha		IV
(sphere of		2. Apramāṇaśubha		
pure form)		3. Śubhakṛtsna		
	4th Dhyāna	1. Anabhraka		V
		2. Puṇyaprasava		
		3. Bṛhatphala		
		4. Avraha		
		5. Atapa		
		6. Sudṛśa		
		7. Sudarśana		
		8. Akaniṣtha		
C. Ārūpyadhātu	I. Ākāśānantya			VI
(sphere of	II. Vijñānānantya		Caturārūpya	VII
formlessness)	III. Ākiñcanya		Brahmaloka	VIII
	IV. Naivasaṃjñānāsaṃjñā			IX

Each of the nine categories throughout the nine levels of the universe has to be overcome or eliminated in order to attain the goal. In this process two moments operate, one of eliminating and one of being in the possession of the elimination of the respective category. The Vaibhāṣikas here adhered to a strictly gradual progression towards their ideal. One category after the other was eliminated, first in the sphere of sensuality, then on each level in the sphere of pure form, and lastly, on each level in the sphere of formlessness. They rejected the idea of a simultaneous elimination of one category on all nine levels. This gradual elimination was related to a typology of 'saintly person'; for instance, a person who had succeeded in eliminating the sixth category (medium-weak) had become a 'once-returner,' that is, a person who would only once relapse into the world of sensuality, while a person who had eliminated the ninth category (weak-weak) had become a 'no-returner.' It is when the last category on the last level is eliminated, a process called an 'integrative concentration as solid as a diamond,' that the person may attain the ideal of a 'saintly-sage' (*arhat*).

Essentially the 'Path' is a means to attain a goal. When we talk of goals, aims, ends, or ideals, we are but stating in another way the principle of teleological action, which, in Buddhism, is acquired in the course of living with others and is internally determined by learning. The aim towards which an individual strives is defined both individually or personally, and socially or culturally. Both ways of definition interact because the former does not develop in a vacuum or without reference to social interaction and the latter is made of interacting individuals. Each individual reorganizes his experiences in such a way as to express what he comes to consider his basic want. In this sense each person is unique as he builds up his own style of life. Out of the emphasis that was laid on either the individual or social definition, the major division into Hīnayāna and Mahāyāna in course of time developed, the former giving preference to the individual-personal definition of man's ideal, the latter to the social-cultural one. Both existed side by side and therefore it would be wrong to equate Hīnayāna and Mahāyāna with philosophical tenets, for they represent values, individual and social.

When individual values are emphasized two types of individuals are recognized: the Arhat who has succeeded in curbing his emotional nature and the Pratyekabuddha who, in addition to having curbed his emotions, has developed his intelligence. Where social values are given preference the Bodhisattva becomes the ideal.

The importance which Buddhism attaches to the path and its goal, the individual who through the exercise of his discriminative ability has subjugated and eliminated his passions, must not lead us to assume that Buddhism recognizes the supremacy of moral values at the expense of everything else. It is true that Buddhism stresses morality as a basic factor in the individual's life-world, but morality has only a limited value. As a matter of fact, morality is the outcome and corollary of knowledge which is grounded in freedom. Liberation from the bondage of the passions and of insufficient knowledge is the ultimate value in a man's life. While this ultimate value was more and more clearly elaborated in the course of philosophical enquiry, the early Buddhists, and the Vaibhāṣikas in particular, must be credited with having clearly understood that ethics has nothing to do with metaphysics. They were convinced that in the end man would become extinct—'like a flame going out.' This conviction did not lead them into the fallacy of assuming that what counts in a person's life is the gratification of his desires, in other words, to do only what will give us pleasure. The conviction that every man will finally become extinct does not alter the fact that, as long as I and others are alive, some actions and some states of mind, such as kindness and the appreciation of beauty, are better than others, such as cruelty and the enjoyment of others' suffering. Whether the environment in which we live is better or worse will largely depend on our present actions, and whether we are mortal or not, it is our duty to produce a better state rather than making a bad one even worse. In performing this duty it may be desirable to believe that we shall continue through countless aeons, but this belief in the desirability of immortality or semi-immortality does not give us any reason to assert the actuality of a state of immortality.

In his *Jewel Garland* dKon-mchog 'Jigs-med dbang-po presents the philosophical tenets of the Vaibhāṣikas in their own right and succinctly defines the various categories which, although accepted by all subsequent philosophical systems, were to become the objects of critical investigation. Although there were different philosophical trends, as is easily understandable from the fact that the Vaibhāṣikas were widely spread over the northwestern and central parts of the Indian sub-continent, individual philosophers such as Vasumitra dominated the scene and in one way or another gave coherence to the philosophical endeavour.

Mi-pham 'Jam-dbyangs rnam-rgyal rgya-mtsho, in his *Summary of Philosophical Systems,* singles out certain topics of the Vaibhāṣikas and, by subjecting them to a trenchant criticism, indicates in retrospect how Buddhist philosophy developed. Since he also gives a detailed account of the contents of the categories, his presentation is a valuable complement to dKon-mchog 'Jigs-med dbang-po's.

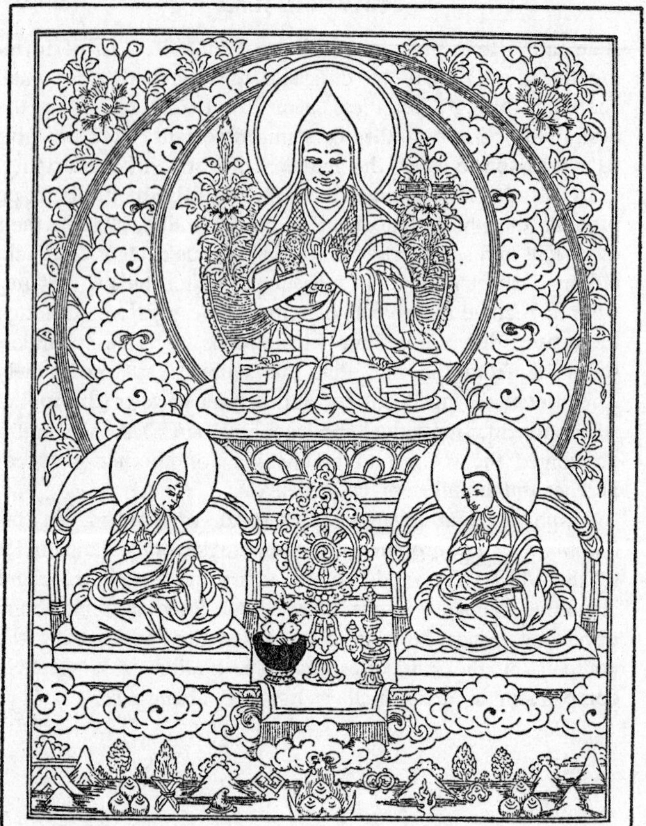

Tsong-kha-pa and his two disciples rGyal-tshab Dharma Rinchen and mKhas-grub-rje. He was the founder of the 'New' tradition in Tibetan Buddhism, represented by dKon-mchog 'Jigs-med dbang-po (1728–1781) author of *The Jewel Garland*

FROM

THE JEWEL GARLAND

GRUB-PA'I MTHA'I RNAM-PAR BZHAG-PA RIN-PO-CHE'I PHRENG-BA

foll. 4b ff.

The Vaibhāṣikas' philosophical faith is dealt with under four heads: intrinsic characteristics, schools, explanation of the name, and the contents.

Characteristics

A Vaibhāṣika is a man following the Hīnayāna line of thought, recognizing external objects to exist in truth, but not acknowledging a non-referential awareness (*rang-rig*).

Schools

There are the schools of Kashmir, Bactria, and India proper.

The Name

The teacher Vasumitra is a representative of the Vaibhāṣikas because he follows the teaching to the Vibhāṣā which is as vast as the ocean, or because he accepts concrete existence throughout the past, present and future.

Contents

There is here the triple division into Ground, the Path, and the Goal.

THE GROUND

This is twofold: object(ive situation) and owner of the object(ive situation).

The Objective Situation. Here everything knowable is classified under five primary factors:

appearance or 'form,'
the dominant or 'the noetic,'
the entourage or 'mental events,'
'disjunct entities,' and
'the absolutes.'

These five primary factors are said to be 'particular existents.' The defining characteristic of a particular existent is efficacity [i.e., the power to originate causal consequences]. Hence, 'to exist,' 'to be knowable' and 'particular existent' are synonymous terms. The absolutes are everlasting particular existents; the physical-material, the noetic and the disjunct entities are transitory particular existents. A particular existent entails substantiality (*rdzas-grub*), but does not constitute the status of being a substance (*rdzas-yod*), because the Vaibhāṣikas claim that 'absolutely real' and 'existing as substance' mean one and the same, as do 'empirically real' and 'being an index.'

A further subdivision of the ground gives (a) two truths [the empirically real and the absolutely real], (b) presence and absence of that which arouses affective states, and (c) other topics of interest.

(a) A thing has the specific characteristic of empirical reality when the idea of it can be lost when the thing in question is either physically destroyed or mentally split up. Such is a clay jug or a rosary. For, if a clay jug is smashed with a hammer, the idea of the jug is gone. Similarly, if one separates the beads of a rosary the idea of the rosary no longer obtains.

A thing has the specific characteristic of ultimate reality when the idea of it is not lost when someone attempts to destroy or mentally split up the thing in question. Such are the partless and indivisible atoms, indivisible momentary noetic events, and the three absolutes.

Thus also is stated in the *Abhidharmakośa* (VI 4):

Whatever when smashed up or split cannot
Be called the same is, like a jug or drop (of water),
But empirical truth. All else is ultimate truth.

Thus although that which is empirically true does not really exist in an absolute sense, it nevertheless exists veridically (*bden-grub*), because according to this line of thought any particular existent entails the status of veridicality (realness).

(b) Anything that is likely to favour the arousal of affective states by means of any sense-field having an outstanding sensum has the specific characteristic of the presence of that which arouses affective states. Such are the five physico-mental groups.[15] Anything that does not do so has the specific characteristic of the absence of that which arouses affective states. Such are the Truth of the Path and the absolutes. As is said in the *Abhidharmakośa*:

All constructs but the Path
Arouse affective states;
(I, 4)
Not so the Path's Truth
And the three absolutes.
(I, 5)

That which arouses affective states entails removability because the accumulation of merits and the perfection of knowledge, on the one hand, and the linking of them with the path of seeing, on the other, must be passed beyond.[16] Only the Path of Seeing does not arouse affective states. The Paths of Conscious Cultivation and of No-more-learning, each in their own way, do and do not arouse affective states. If they are the Noble Path they entail the non-arousal of affective states, but as paths in the spiritual growth of saintly people they do not do so, because these paths turn into subtler and coarser experiences in him who follows the path of conscious cultivation, and so arouse affective states.[17]

(c) Belief in substantial existence throughout the three divisions of time means that a jug, for instance, exists in its past as well as in its future [in the same way as it does now].

Although the Vaibhāṣikas recognize negation and affirmation they do not accept explicit negation ('non-existence' negation), because they claim that negation entails a 'not being this or that' negation.

The Kashmirian Vaibhāṣikas, like the Sautrāntikas, recognize the stream of the noetic as the connecting link between the cause and effect of one's actions; the other Vaibhāṣikas recognize as such a link a disjunct entity called a 'collateral' which is like an acquisition and a promissory note.

The Prāsangikas and Vaibhāṣikas claim bodily and vocal acts as pertaining to the physical-material.

The concrete, though transitory, does not perish the very moment it comes into existence, but having come into existence it lasts some time and then vanishes.

The Owner of the Objective Situation is dealt with under three heads: (a) individual, (b) the noetic, and (c) discourse.

(a) *Individual.* That which makes us talk of an individual is the mere collocation of the five psycho-somatic constituents serving as the ground to be so labelled.

The Sāṃmitīyas considered each of the five constituents as the ground, and the Kāśyapīyas accept the mind alone as the ground.

(b) *The noetic.* This works in two ways: valid and invalid.

The former is twofold: immediate apprehension and genuine and immediate inference. The former again is sensory, intellectual, and mystical. A non-referential awareness is not recognized by the Vaibhāṣikas.

Valid sensory apprehension does not fall under the noetic because the visual capacity pertains to the physical-material, which is the common basis of the physical organ, the act of seeing, and of the validity of sensory perception; and while the noetic [operating in conjunction with] the sensory capacity meets the bare fact of there being an object apart from the latter's observable qualities, it is the sensory capacity, operating from the respective physical sense organ, that sees form. The Vaibhāṣikas say that if the noetic alone were able to see, it ought to see things which are hidden from sight by walls and other impenetrable objects coming between the thing and its perception. They also claim mind and mental states to be different substances.

[The invalid forms are given below in the presentation of the Sautrāntikas' view].

(c) *Discourse.* On the whole sound is either articulate or inarticulate. The former is human speech. The latter is, for instance, the murmuring of a brook.

Both articulate and inarticulate sounds do and do not announce the presence of a sentient being. 'Announcing the presence of a sentient being,' 'conveying a meaning,' and 'making discourse' signify one and the same. So do 'non-announcement of the presence of a sentient being,' 'non-conveyance of meaning,' and 'non-formation of discourse.'

Since the Vaibhāṣikas consider the Buddha-word and the Buddhist scriptures, insofar as they are made up of linguistic elements, names, words, and letters, as a disjunct entity, there is in their line of thought no contradiction between the Buddha-word being both significant form and a disjunct entity.[18]

THE PATH

The discussion of the Path follows this pattern: the objective pole of the intentional structure, that which has to be eliminated by traversing the path, and the Path as being-itself.

The Objective Pole consists of the sixteen facets of the Four Truths: impermanence and the rest. For the Vaibhāṣikas the subtle conception of the non-existence of an absolute principle is identical with the subtle idea of the non-existence of Pure-Ego, which is the non-existence of a self-sufficient substance. From among the eighteen schools the five schools of the Sāṃmitīyas [19] do not recognize this as the subtle idea, because they acknowledge a self as being of the nature of a self-sufficient substance. None of them, however, accept the idea of the non-existence of an ultimate principle concerning the entities of reality proper, be it of the coarse or subtle kind, because they claim that the givenness of a primary factor entails its ontological ultimacy.

Traversing the Path. There are two types of incomprehension: emotively toned and non-emotively toned.

The former principally obstructs the attainment of freedom; it is the belief in an individual self and the three poisons,[20] together with their latent potentialities produced by this belief.

The latter principally prevents the attainment of omniscience; it is the four patterns of incomprehension, such as the non-emotively toned intellectual dullness, which fails to comprehend the profound and subtle doctrine of the Tathāgata.[21]

Apart from these two types of impediment the Vaibhāṣikas do not recognize the term 'impediment of the knowable.'

The Path as Being-Itself. The Path in each of the three spiritual pursuits [22] consists of a path of accumulating merits and perfecting knowledge, a path which links the former path and stage with the subsequent and central one, a path of seeing [truth], a path of consciously cultivating what has been seen, and a path of no-more-learning.

Although the Vaibhāṣikas accept this graduation, they do not recognize the transcending awareness of the ten spiritual levels.

The first fifteen moments of acceptance in knowledge are the path of seeing [truth], and the sixteenth is the path of cultivating what has been seen, a continual awareness of the path. These sixteen moments succeed one another, like goats crossing a bridge.

The Truth of the Path does not entail the status of the noetic, because the Vaibhāṣikas accept the five psycho-physical constituents, insofar as they do not arouse affective states, as the Truth of the Path.[23]

THE GOAL

A person belonging to the Śrāvaka class of beings familiarizes himself with the sixteen facets of the phase of vision, beginning with impermanence, for three or more consecutive lives, and finally, in following the Śrāvakas' path of cultivating the vision which has become a meditative concentration as solid as a diamond, he discards the possession of the veil of emotionality as something having been worn out, and realizes the status of a saint (Arhat).

A Pratyekabuddha [self-styled Buddha] of the lonely wolf type adds his view, through which he understands that there is nothing of a self as a self-sufficient substance, to the stock of merits he has accumulated during a hundred aeons or more. Whilst sitting in one place, after having had all the experiences up to the 'superior path of preparation,'[24] he realizes everything that is in between the feeling of warmth on the Path of linking [his merits and knowledge with seeing] and the Path of no-more-learning.

The Vaibhāṣikas claim that lower order saints are liable to fall from their height, because when one fails in one's rejection and attainment, one can relapse to the level of one who is tainted by worldliness but who has entered the stream [which flows] towards salvation.[25] Although they count twenty varieties of Śrāvakas and eight types of individuals, according to whether they have merely entered a certain spiritual level or are firmly established on it and enjoying its fruit, they do not recognize a person capable of discarding nine affective categories simultaneously.[26] According to them anyone who has entered or is firmly established on a certain spiritual level is a saintly person.

Bodhisattvas perfect the accumulation of merits and knowledge on the preparatory path during three 'great aeons'; then within another one hundred aeons they lay the foundation for the (thirty-two) major auspicious Buddha-marks; and in their last life, sitting under the Bodhi-tree, they conquer the

Devaputramāra in the evening; at midnight in a state of utter composure they realize the three paths of linking, seeing [truth], and cultivating the seen; and in the early morning hours just about dawn, they reach the path of no-more-learning.[27] Therefore, since the Vaibhāṣikas consider everything up to the conquest of Māra at night as belonging to the status of an ordinary person, and a Bodhisattva's three phases of linking [merits and knowledge with seeing], envisaging reality, and consciously cultivating the vision, as merely representing a state of composure, the first nine incidents of a Buddha's life are considered to be the activities of a Bodhiṣattva and the last three those of a Buddha.[28]

They claim that what is termed Dharmacakra entails the path of seeing [truth] and that when promulgated it entails the Four Truths.

They accept the seven books of the Abhidharma as the word spoken by the Buddha and this means that they are his actual words. They do not recognize eighty-four thousand topics of reality, but only eighty thousand, as is evident from the statement in the *Abhidharmakośa* (I, 25):

> The eighty thousand topics of reality
> Which the Buddha has proclaimed.

Inasmuch as the place where a Bodhiṣattva in his last life wins enlightenment is determined as being exclusively the world of sensuality, the Vaibhāṣikas do not accept the Akaniṣṭha or Ghanavyūha realms, nor do they know of a Sambhogakāya. Not only that, but they also do not recognize an aesthetically immediate awareness of all observable qualities.

The status of a saint in the three courses entails the working out of the remnant of one's Karma, because they claim that when one passes into the non-residual Nirvāṇa the stream of the noetic comes to an end like a flame that goes out. Therefore they claim that finality is found on all three courses.

Some Vaibhāṣikas say that when the Teacher passed into Nirvāṇa he did not really do so, but merely seemed to withdraw the manifestation of his form body. To say so is like wanting to have one's cake and eat it.

Although a Buddha has left behind all sorrow, there is no contradiction in saying that in him the Truth of Frustration still exists, because when all the affective states relating to the Truth of Frustration have been eliminated, the Truth of Frustration still remains to be left behind.

Although the Buddha's physical body is not the Buddha-Jewel, because the former belongs to the Buddha's physical existence and the span of life in which he endeavoured to attain enlightenment, the Vaibhāṣikas accept it as the Buddha and claim the Buddha-Jewel to be the awareness of the Buddha's mind that all disturbing affective states have been eliminated. Similarly, although the saintly disciples still subject to affective states are not the Community-Jewel, they yet form the community. The Community-Jewel is the Truth of the Path in their minds. And the Doctrine-Jewel is the Nirvāṇa of the Buddha as well as that of the Śrāvakas and Pratyekabuddhas and the Truth of the End of Frustration.

And so I conclude:

> May the young and the intelligent enjoy
> Like fresh nectar this festival of meaning
> Drawn from the ocean of the Vaibhāṣika works
> In the golden jar of my discerning mind.

Mi-Pham (1846–1914) author of *The Summary of Philosophical Systems*

FROM

THE SUMMARY OF PHILOSOPHICAL SYSTEMS

YID-BZHIN-MDZOD-KYI GRUB-MTHA' BSDUS-PA

foll. 13a.

THE SALIENT features of the Vaibhāṣikas' philosophical tenets will be dealt with under seven heads: (1) the five groupings of the knowable; (2) decay as a separate entity; (3) the substantiality of the three aspects of time; (4) an ineffable self; (5) the noetic as not being self-revealing and cognitive of an object; (6) the difference between signatum and index; and (7) an inexhaustible substance.

Their views are not correct because they are mixed with all sorts of wishful thinking.

(1) a. The five groups of the knowable:
The physical-material consists of eleven items, i.e., the four elementary functions, i.e., solidity, cohension, temperature, and movement as cause (giving rise to):
the *five* senses, i.e., sight, hearing, smell, taste, and bodily feeling as effect;
the *five* sense objects, i.e., colour, sound, taste, fragrance, and touch, and
the behaviour-trait.[29]

b. Mind as the primary factor is the six sensory consciousness which apprehend the mere object. It is claimed that they apprehend the bare haecceity.[30]

c. The mental events as the entourage of mind apprehend the characteristics of the object. There are fifty-one of them:

The five ever-present ones are: rapport, categorizing, feeling, ideation, and motivation.

The five object-determined ones are: attention, interest, inspection, intense concentration, and appreciative discrimination.

The eleven positive functions which accompany every positive attitude are: trust, carefulness, lucidity, imperturbability, decency, decorum, unattachment, non-hatred, non-deludedness, non-violence, and assiduity.

The six basic emotions are: lust, rage, arrogance, dullness, opinionatedness, and doubt.

The twenty subsidiary emotions are: anger, hostility, dissimulation, malice, jealousy, avarice, hypocrisy, dishonesty, spitefulness, pride, contempt, indecorum, delusion, overexuberance, distrust, laziness, carelessness, forgetfulness, excitability, inattentiveness.

The four variables are: drowsiness, regret, selective emphasis, and discursiveness.

Mind and mental events operate from the same basis with the same reference, observable quality, time and substance.[31]

d. There are twenty-three disjunct entities: attainment-possession, attainment of the suspension of attitudinal and functional operations, attainment of induced unconsciousness, induced unconsciousness, life, force, similarity, birth, old age, duration, transitoriness, nouns, verbs, letters, status of an ordinary person, process, distinctness, connection, quickness, sequence, time location, number, totality. It is claimed that these entities are different from the physical-material and the mental.

e. The absolute is that which is not born from causes and conditions; it consists of space, cessation of involvement due to insight, cessation of involvement independent of insight.

(2) Decay as a separate entity. There are four specific characteristics indicating the composite nature of such things as a jug. They are: being born, growing old, duration, and transitoriness. There are four subsidiary indicators of their composite transitory nature: the coming into being of the process of being born, duration of duration, the growing old of the process of aging, and the process of decaying of the decaying process. The coming into being of the process of being born brings about the actual coming into existence [of a thing]. This actual coming into existence [of the thing] brings about [the presence of the thing], totalling eight indicators. The same feature applies to the other indicators such as duration and the rest. The signatum and its specific characteristic are claimed to be different substances, just as a crow indicating [the presence of] a house [is different from the house].

(3) Since the past and future exist *substantialiter* in their own rights, the three divisions of time exist now as substances. If it is objected that this would entail the observation of the past and the future now, the Vaibhāṣikas answer that they are not seen because they are concealed through that which has ceased to exist and that which has not yet come to exist. There is a difference from the Sāṃkhya-system because the divisions of time exist as a continuity of moments.[32]

(4) The ineffable self. They claim that a self must exist as the perpetrator of acts and as the experiencer of their effects, because otherwise the relation between one's acts and their effects would not hold. Therefore, this self is neither identical with nor different from the psychophysical constituents and cannot be said to be eternal or non-eternal. While the Vātsīputrīyas and some others recognized such a self the Vaibhāṣikas proper did not do so. However, since certain sections within the Vaibāṣikas and Sautrānti-

kas recognized such a self, it has been dealt with here.

(5) The noetic is not cognitive in itself nor does it know an object. They say that non-referential awareness is not possible because that which is known cannot be the knower and while the sensory function pertaining to the physical-material apprehends the bare object because it is coupled with the mind, the noetic is like a crystal without any images and merely a selective process.

(6) The difference between the signatum and the index. They claim that when the white and red colours and the dewlap indicate an ox these three characteristics must be different substances. If they were one, act and actor would become one, which is not the case.

(7) An inexhaustible substance. This is a special form of the attainment-possession, which is an item of the disjunct entities. The fact that an act done is not exhausted, is like a promissory note. Because of its neutral character it is inexhaustible.

The critique of the above tenets:

(1) All physical-material entities [listed as] cause and effect are refutation of atoms. A trait also is not something physical-material. It is not something in itself, apart from being a label put on the mere projecting activity which lets good and bad actions by body and speech continue. While mind and mind-related substances are multiple and instantaneous, a partless point-instant is not really established and moreover is not found either outside or within. Because the knowable is not the knower there can ultimately be no self-cognitions, and there can also be no cognition of something else because no relation [between the knowable and the knower] exists, and because simultaneity and non-simultaneity are not found as cognition. The disjunct entities, too, are

mere labels for certain occurrences of body and mind, but are not substances because they are neither identical nor different from them. Furthermore the absolutes are not substances but mere labels, in view of the fact that that which is to be denied does not exist.

(2) 'Process of decaying' is a name for the fact that a perishable object such as a jar does not continue for the second self-contained moment. While it is a specific characteristic of anything concrete, like the wetness of water, if the process of decaying existed apart from the thing, the thing itself would be imperishable and the process of decaying would be fortuitous, because the thing separated from its process of decaying would be imperishable, and the decaying process would exist independently as something different from the thing. If the decaying process exists as something different from the thing, of what is it the decaying process? And for what reason is it called process of decaying? If the thing and its decay are simultaneous, the thing is not made to decay by this [alleged] process of decaying, and if they are not simultaneous, the decaying process is meaningless regardless of whether it comes earlier or later.

(3) The three divisions of time do not exist *substantialiter*. If the past as that which has ceased to be, and the future as that which is not yet, exist now, everything must be now. If one argues that the past exists merely as the characteristic of that which has ceased to be, it is a label and not a substance. 'Time' is not at all a self-sufficient substance but merely an interpretation concerning things.

(4) There is no ineffable self. [This is evident from the fact that] there is no third alternative to either identity with or difference from the psycho-physical constituents, to either a permanent or an impermanent particular existent, and that [such an ineffable

self] cannot be defined according to the four points of argumentation.[33]

(5) The noetic must be non-referential. The experience of feeling happy and so on in all its vividness, without having recourse to other cognitive means, is in common parlance called a non-referential awareness. If it did not exist, all distinctions made by the man in the street would come to naught because not a single statement concerning what is immediately experienced would be possible and the sensory function pertaining to the physical-material would not be able to cognize the object; if the noetic has no images of the objects appearing before it, the object would be imperceptible.

(6) Signatum and index do not exist as such but are mere distinctions from a practical point of view. If the fire were different from its heat it would have to be cold, and since heat which is not fire is not found anywhere, fire and heat are not different entities.

(7) The inexhaustible substance is not some other agency producing the effect of one's actions. Apart from the fact that action and effect stand in mutual relationship, a [special] substance, different from the physical-material and the mental, called 'inexhaustible substance,' cannot be validly proved. Its postulation violates the logic of the general refutation of an 'attainment-possession' and of the particular unnecessariness of such a substance.

CHAPTER THREE

THE SAUTRĀNTIKAS

WHILE IT cannot be denied that the Vaibhāṣikas contributed enormously to the subsequent development of Buddhist philosophy, the charge that their system contained considerable inadequacies is not wholly unjustified. Their main weakness lay in the field of epistemology and in what may aptly be called their substantive-substantialism, and it was here that the Sautrāntikas started with their critique.

It can easily be pointed out that the Vaibhāṣikas' theory of knowledge is merely a hypothesis, for it can never be experienced that knowledge is the product of any collision of basically neutral substances, be this collision between the instantaneous noetic and the punctiform 'atoms' or between the former and the latter's derivatives. We have a perception and immediately are aware of certain objective things, and every total state of mind seems to be diversified both qualitatively and objectively. This diversity can be expressed in the two statements 'I see a chair' and 'I feel happy.' The former seems to express *what,* and not *how,* I am perceiving, the latter *how,* and not *what,* I am feeling. Of course, words like 'seeing,' 'feeling,' and so on, as we use them, do introduce the 'fallacy of many questions,' and there also seems to exist an unbridgeable gulf between 'feeling' and 'knowing-perceiving.' This gulf certainly does not exist in Buddhist thought where 'feeling' as understood by us connotes a 'feeling judgment' and where 'knowledge' does not conflict with what we would call a 'mood' which in a certain sense is cognitive inasmuch as it constantly reveals the rough situation of which I am the centre and how it is going with me. Since knowledge is not like other phenomena in that it stands above them and interprets or illumines them all, the Sautrāntikas, taking notice of this circumstance, introduced the idea of what may literally be translated as 'self-knowledge' (*rang-rig*), a term which in course of time became misinterpreted. This was due to a purely linguistic accident. The term *rang-rig* looks formally like *gzhan-rig* which, on the anology of 'self-knowledge,' we may provisionally translate as 'other-knowledge.' But while the latter indicates such situations as expressed in statements like 'I see a chair,' or 'I am aware of something' (thus avoiding the ambiguity of the verb 'to see'), the former only refers to such a statement as 'I feel somehow' or 'I am aware somehow'; and while the latter can be stated to be a description of a non-referential event (which possibly has an objective constituent, although this event also may be 'purely subjective'), the former certainly is a referential event having both an epistemological object (the upholstery of a certain chair) and an objective constituent (a patch of a certain colour and shape). Confusion and misinterpretation set in when a possible objective constituent is equated with an epistemological object: a procedure easily prompted by the linguistic form of the term *rang-rig*. Those who do not recognize 'self-knowledge' link their rejection to the assumption that there are no non-referential events, but only referential ones, while actually it seems to be more likely that every mental state is at any moment never wholly non-referential and never wholly referential, and that both 'self-knowledge' (*rang-rig,* non-referential awareness) and 'other-knowledge' (*gzhan-rig,* referential awareness) are abstractions of a 'single event,' and these abstractions then habitually start leading an existence of their own.

'Cognizing' is a certain kind of determinable relation to an object and 'feeling towards' an object is another determinable relation. It is, however, possible to manage with only a single determinable relation to an object which may be called 'objective reference.' The difference between 'cognizing' and 'feeling towards' would in this case simply be a difference in the qualities of the term which stands at that moment in the relation of reference to an object. For instance, I may think of my wife and then love her. In both instances there is simply a certain determinate form of the general relation of reference between my mind and my wife. Since I cannot love or hate or fear anyone or anything without having an idea of him or her or the object towards which I take this attitude, it is possible and even plausible to identify a cognitive relation with the general relation of objective reference, and to suppose that the validity of this relation goes together with the fact that the event involved in this relation has at that time a certain quality which determines whether the attitude is called 'love' or 'hate' or 'fear' or whatever. On this supposition the mind (*sems*) and mental events (*sems-byung*) are no longer separate 'substances' as postulated by the Vaibhāṣikas, but are just *one* 'substance' as is claimed by the Sautrāntikas.

This interest in epistemological questions was to dominate the whole line of thought of the Sautrāntikas, who in many respects foreshadowed the subsequent mentalistic development of Indian Buddhist philosophy. There also is one other point which ought to be mentioned at this stage. The Sautrāntikas' line of thought is not one man's philosophy but comprises a variety of theories, the uniting feature being the fact that all of them are essentially related to epistemology. Because of this interest, they asserted in the realm of what is that anything that can be perceived is an object (*yul*) for the mind, and they distinguished between being 'objective' and being 'objectifiable.' To be 'objective' means that a perceptual situation has an objective constituent, and being 'objectifiable' means being capable of corresponding to the epistemological object of some referential perceptual situation. Since *everything* is in principle epistemologically objectifiable, inasmuch as everything can be thought about and is thus capable of corresponding to the epistemological object of some thought-situation, everything is 'knowable.'

The Sautrāntikas' analysis of perceptual situations led them to a re-evaluation of the so-called two truths. In order to understand the Sautrāntikas' position it will be necessary to give a rapid survey of what is implied when we speak of perceptual and cognitive situations. It is the nature of any perceptual situation that whenever it arises we claim to be in cognitive contact with something other than ourselves or our states, and this claim extends to those situations which are commonly believed to be veridical, as well as to those which are commonly held to be delusive. The two situations 'I am seeing a chair' and 'I am seeing a pink elephant' are exactly alike in having an epistemological object. The difference is that in one situation it is assumed that there also is an ontological object corresponding to the epistemological object, while in the other no such object obtains.

It is further assumed that in perceptual situations the epistemological object is of the physical kind and that its corresponding ontological object, if ever there should be one, must be a physical object.

But there also are situations which have an epistemological object of the physical kind but are not perceptual. For instance, the epistemological object of the two situations which I verbalize as 'I am seeing a jug' and 'I am thinking of a jug' is in both cases of the physical kind. Yet there is a difference; in the former case I seem to be in cognitive contact with the jug in a more direct and immediate way, while in the latter I seem to be at a distance. The perceptual situation, which may be termed 'intuitive,' is distinct by its directness from the thought-situation, which is 'discursive.' A further characteristic of a thought situation is that in it I can think of anything, regardless of whether it is held veridical or delusive in a perceptual situation.

The Sautrāntikas were clearly aware of these two kinds of cognitive situations, which we have described as 'intuitive' and 'discursive.' For them an 'intuitive' perceptual situation which common sense holds to be veridical was absolutely real, while a thought-situation was relatively real and, insofar as it was only relatively real, from the viewpoint of the absolutely real, it could even be claimed to be delusive. We shall see in a subsequent chapter that this conclusion was actually put forward by certain Buddhist philosophers. Although the trend towards considering thought-situations as delusive or relatively real was very marked, the Sautrāntikas by virtue of their penetrating analysis of cognitive situations did not commit the mistake of equating the epistemological object of a thought-situation with the latter's relative validity. The epistemological object of, say, a jug, is as real as that of a 'centaur,' but while the former fulfills the expectation of there being something denoted by the phrase 'the jug,' which forms an essential factor in a perceptual situation, and therefore is absolutely real, the latter is not so, precisely because it does not fulfill this expectation.

Due to their analysis of perceptual situations the Sautrāntikas were at once faced with the question: 'What is the relationship between the objective constituent, which accurately corresponds to the epistemological object of a perceptual situation, and the physical object which we are said to perceive in this situation?' Their answer was that there is a certain *sensum* (*rnam-pa*) which, as the objective constituent, has a certain characteristic and which stands in a certain relation to a certain physical object. By virtue of this relation the sensum is an 'appearance of' the physical object. This relation was then described as a many-one relation, that is to say, many different sensa can be appearances of one physical object, while no one sensum can be an appearance of several physical objects. According to the Sautrāntikas' view, the objective constituents of perceptual situations are particular existents of a peculiar kind; they are not literally parts of the perceived object, although they resemble physical objects as ordinarily conceived. They are more like mental states in their privacy and dependence on the mind of the observer. The full force of this implication, however, was realized by the subsequent mentalistic schools of Buddhism, who argued that the sensible form and size and distance of objective constituents was determined by the individual's predominant interests and beliefs. Nevertheless, the Sautrānikas' analysis of perceptual situations already left the existence of physical objects highly hypothetical. It was certainly a mere concession to the uncritical common-sense view, rather than a critical assessment, on the part of some Sautrāntikas when they claimed that, regardless of whether the situation is veridical or totally delusive, the situation does have an objective constituent, and that, where the situation is commonly held to be coinciding with what is assumed to be real, the objective constituent or the sensum has been created by the hypothetical object, which as the emitting region is the *dependently* necessary condition of the sensum and its specific characteristic. Where the situation is totally delusive and where there is no emitting region at all, as in visual situations such as dreams and hallucinations, it was held that the sensum was due to the *independently* necessary condition, which in either case is a living body with a suitable brain or mind.

The Sautrāntikas in this way accepted three kinds of perceptual situations: the first corresponded to what common sense holds to be a veridical situation in which the existence of an ontological object corresponding to the epistemological one is assumed; the second was of an illusory character; and the third was of a visionary or hallucinatory nature, recognized as a regular phenomenon in religious living.[1]

Inasmuch as every cognitive situation is made up of a subjective and an objective factor which together determine the particular cognition, and inasmuch as the subjective factor makes us speak of 'being aware,' while the objective factor as the epistemological object of the cognitive situation seems to be the 'appearance' (or 'semblance') of what we are aware of, the Sautrāntikas correctly epitomized the character of every cognitive situation in the words: "The subjective factor constitutes the clear experiencing; appearance [standing in the relation of] similarity [to the sensum] constitutes the epistemological object. Therefore, every cognitive situation presents itself as the difference between the subjective factor experiencing the epistemological object [and the epistemological object being experienced]." [2]

Another significant contribution towards the development of Buddhist philosophical thought by the Sautrāntikas was their critique of the Vaibhāṣikas' substantive-substantialism. The so-called 'disjunct entities,' which essentially were schemata of interpretation, were for the Vaibhāṣikas entities existing *substantialiter*, but for the Sautrāntikas they had merely a nominal existence and heuristic significance. Yet, while they were able to expose the naive assumptions of the Vaibhāṣikas' substantive-substantialism, they themselves were still hampered by their desire to retain much of what common-sense believes and, therefore, in claiming for these entities an *existence,* though only a nominal one, they failed to realize that the problem of existence, if it is one, is not solved by substituting *'subsistence'* for it. However, it was from the time of the Sautrāntikas that in Buddhist philosophy the distinction between '(particular) existents' (*dngos-po*) and 'subsistents' (*dngos-med*) was made, and while the former were transitory (*mi-rtag pa*) the latter were everlasting (*rtag-pa*).* This had important consequences for the conception of Nirvāṇa. While the Sautrāntikas agreed with the Vaibhāṣikas that it meant the cessation of phenomenal existence and could not be determined as being either this or that, they differed from them in claiming that the ultimate status of this state of extinction was that of subsistence and not of existence, because for them 'particular existent' was tautologous with 'transitoriness' and 'concreteness,' all of which was not applicable to Nirvāṇa.

Apart from contributing to and developing the logical method of philosophical inquiry, the Sautrāntikas were the first to generalize the idea of temporal sequence in a cause-effect situation. In talking about causality in Buddhism, it is of the utmost importance to be aware of the points of divergence from our ways of thinking. The conceptual framework of Buddhist associative and co-ordinative thinking was something different from the traditional European causal and nomothetic thinking. In the Buddhist universe events did not happen because of fiats issued by a supreme creator and despotic lawgiver. Nothing whatsoever has been created in the universe. Events come about because they fit into the pattern of a universe based on order, and these events cooperate in perfect freedom and not in obedience to some super-will, nor to some mathematically expressible regularity depending upon some cause which can be isolated. Causality, if such a term is ever applicable, posits an interlocking system of hierarchically fluctuating cause-factors. That is to say, the cause-

* See chart on page 38.

situation was already a 'network' of interdependent, co-existent and freely co-operating forces, and in this network at any given time any one factor may take the highest place in a hierarchy of causes and effect. The Sautrāntikas, who generalized the idea of temporal sequence, did not, however, repudiate the idea of interdependence. They merely criticized the Vaibhāṣikas' assumption of causal co-existence in the realm of the noetic. For the Vaibhāṣikas, mind and mental events were different substances existing simultaneous with each other, the one being a function of the other; for the Sautrāntikas, they were one substance; hence any total noetic situation was anteceded or followed by another noetic situation, which implies temporal sequence and not co-existence. Here again we note the pre-eminent interest in psychological and cognitive processes, which, in turn, had a moral-ethical reference. Not only did the virtues and vices, i.e., the mental attitudes, of an individual inescapably result in the endowment with which he or she began his or her subsequent phase of being, they also had their inescapable effects upon man's natural environment. Human morality remained bound up with the phenomena of non-human nature. After all, man is part of the universe. It is he who as 'causal agent' creates his world which, in turn, is a 'causal agent' creating him. This is so, because 'causality' in Buddhism is, as has been noted, an interlocking system and not a linear sequence of cause and effect.

Since no major works by Sautrāntika philosophers have been preserved in the Indian original, *The Jewel Garland*'s impartial account of their epistemological interests and their contribution to the development of Buddhist logic is particularly welcome. Furthermore, since the author clarifies the relationship of Sautrāntika thought with subsequent philosophical systems, we are enabled to see the organic development of Buddhist philosophy.

The Summary, on the other hand, singles out the assumptions which in course of time had become the target of criticism. It is also to be noted that the author links the Pratyekabuddhayāna, the spiritual pursuit of self-styled Buddhas, with the Sautrāntika philosophy. In so doing, however, he does not simply equate a philosophical system with a certain attitude towards life. Rather, since a Pratyekabuddha is superior in intelligence to a Śrāvaka but inferior to a Bodhisattva, and since the development of the subsequent philosophical systems and the emphasis on the Bodhisattva ideal coincided with the spread of the Mahāyāna, with which he is so much in favour, he had to place the Pratyekabuddhayāna in between the beginnings and the climax of philosophical speculation.

FROM

THE JEWEL GARLAND

GRUB-PA'I MTHA'I RNAM-PAR BZHAG-PA RIN-PO-CHE'I PHRENG-BA

foll. 7a ff.

IN THE PRESENTATION of the Sautrāntikas' philosophical faith there are four sections: intrinsic characteristics, schools, meaning of the name, and the contents.

CHARACTERISTICS

A Sautrāntika is a man following the Hīnayāna line of thought, recognizing self-cognition and external objects as existing in truth. The names Sautrāntika and Dṛṣṭāntika are synonymous.

SCHOOLS

There are two schools: the one following tradition and the other advocating the method of logical investigation.[3]

THE NAME

In discussing the Sautrāntikas, one also speaks separately of the Dṛṣṭāntikas because the former do not follow the Vibhāṣā but primarily rely on the Sūtras spoken by the Exalted One, while the Dṛṣṭāntikas illustrate the whole doctrine by way of analogies.

CONTENTS

There is here the triple division into the Ground, the Path, and the Goal.

THE GROUND

This is twofold: object(ive situation) and owner of the object(ive situation).

The Objective Situation. That which is cognizable has the mark of being an object, and that which is objectively given for cognition has the mark of the knowable. Hence, 'object,' 'to exist,' 'to be knowable' and 'the given' are all synonymous.

The objectively given can be listed under six pairs: (1) the two truths [empirically real and ultimately real], (2) the specific and general, (3) negation and affirmation, (4) the manifest and the hypothetical (invisible), (5) the three divisions of time, and (6) identity and difference.

(1) That which irrespective of designation and conceptualization withstands the solvent influence of critical reflection by its very presence has the mark of the ultimately real. Hence, 'particular existent,' 'ultimately real,' 'being absolutely specific,' 'transitory'; 'concrete' and 'veridical' are synonymous.

That which exists only conceptually has the mark of the relatively real. Hence, 'subsistent,' 'relatively real,' 'being general,' 'permanent,' 'absolute' and 'delusive' are synonymous.

The explanation of the two truths is as follows: 'Space as such is relatively real because it is real in the theorizing component of mind.' In this statement 'theorizing component' means discursiveness and is so spoken of because it screens the absolutely specific from immediate sight. While this is a general formulation, it has to be observed that that which is real in the theorizing component of mind does not entail its being relatively real in the strict sense of the word, because, on the one hand, a jug, for instance, having the earmark of the ultimately real, is also real in the theorizing component of mind, and, on the other, an individual self and [the idea of a] permanent sound, though real in the theorizing component of mind, have no denotation at all.

'A jug is ultimately real, because it is real in the percipient component of mind.' Here, 'percipient mind' means unerring cognition of the apparent object.

This exposition of the two truths is that of those Sautrāntikas who are similar to the Vaibhāṣikas.

(2) That which is efficacious in an unrestricted sense has the mark of the absolutely specific, as for instance a jug. That which is not so has the mark of the general, as for instance space as such.

Although such ideas as universality and peculiarity, identity and difference, disagreement and agreement, and many others may fall within the (category of) general (entities), the distinction may be made that in so doing they are not necessarily the general.

(3) That which is to be understood by the removal of what otherwise would be present has the mark of negation. It is identical with exclusion. There are two kinds: explicit and implicit negation.

That which is understood as merely the removal of what otherwise would be perceived to be present, has the mark of an explicit negation. Such is the statement: 'A Brahmin does not drink beer.'

That which allows either of negation, in retaining something of what otherwise would be perceived to be present, or of affirmation, has the mark of an implicit negation. Such is the statement: 'The fat Devadatta does not eat by day.'

That which is not to be understood by removal of what otherwise is perceived to be present, has the mark of affirmation, as for instance: '[There is] a jug.'

(4) That which is understood by immediate apprehension to be present has the mark of the manifest. 'Manifest' and 'particular existent' mean the same.

That which is to be understood to be present by genuine and immediate inference has the mark of the hypothetical (invisible). 'Hypothetical (invisible)' and 'knowable' are identical.

(5) That part of anything which breaks down the next moment after its coming into existence has the mark of the past. That part of anything which has not yet become an object in time, because of the incompleteness of the attendant conditions despite the presence of the cause for its origination, has the mark of the future. That which has come into existence and has not yet disappeared has the mark of the present.

The past and the future are everlasting; the present and a concrete thing are identical.

The Sautrāntikas also distinguish between the past of a thing and its evanescent state, and the future of a thing and its nascent state.

(6) That which is not different [from itself or something else] has the mark of identity, as for instance a jug. That which is different [from some other thing] has the mark of difference, as for instance a pillar and a jug.

While a plurality of different existents entails a differentiating-attribute pluralism, the converse does not hold true, because 'being concrete' and 'being transitory' are two differentiating-attributes, but one particular existent.

Further, although in accepting indivisible atoms and an indivisible momentary noetic the Sautrāntikas are similar to the Vaibhāṣikas, they are not so in every respect. While the Vaibhāṣikas claim that they exist and exist *substantialiter*, the Sautrāntikas do not do so.

A behaviour-trait is for the Vaibhāṣikas and the Prāsangikas something having the characteristic of the physical-material, and while the Vaibhāṣikas claim that it exists and exists *substantialiter*, the Sautrāntikas, the Yogācārins and the Svātantrikas do not accept this view.

In addition, for the Vaibhāṣikas cause and effect are simultaneous; not so for the Sautrāntikas and the other philosophical schools.

The Owner of The Objective Situation is dealt with under three heads: (1) individual self, (2) the noetic, and (3) discourse.

(1) Those who follow tradition consider the continuity of the psychosomatic constituents, as the ground for speaking of a self, and those who follow the method of logical investigation treat the intellectual process in this way.

(2) This operates in two ways: valid and invalid.

The former is twofold: immediate apprehension and genuine and immediate inference. Immediate apprehension again is fourfold: sensory, intellectual, non-referential, and mystical.

The senses, since they belong to the physical-material, cannot serve as a valid means (of cognition), because lacking the illuminating cognitiveness they are unable to make out their objects.

The invalid is fivefold: recognition, error, doubt, deliberation, and uncertainty.

Two of these are non-conceptual: immediate apprehension and uncertainty. Genuine and immediate inference, deliberation, and doubt are thoroughly conceptual.

The Sautrāntikas also claim that when the noetic encounters its object, it cognizes it together with its observable qualities. Hence mind and mental event are one substance.

(3) Intelligibility is the mark of discourse. It consists of inclusive class-words and class-member word. The former is, for instance, 'form,' and the latter 'a jug.'

A further distinction is by definition: ostensible, [as when we point out] 'the impermanence of sound'; and verbal, [as when we make the statement] 'sound is impermanent.'

THE PATH

The Objective Pole of its intentional structure is the sixteen properties of the Four Truths, such as impermanence and the others. Subtle [idea of the] non-existence of an absolute principle [concerning the entities of reality] and [idea of the] non-existence of an individual self (Pure Ego) mean the same for the Sautrāntikas, who consider the non-existence of an eternal single sovereign self as the coarse [idea of the] non-existence of a Pure Ego, and the Non-existence of a self as a self-sufficient substance as the subtle one.

That Which Has to Be Eliminated by the Path. Here the Sautrāntikas are like the Vaibhāṣikas in not recognizing the non-existence of an ultimate principle concerning (the objective) entities of reality and the impediment presented by the knowable. They differ from the Vaibhāṣikas in that they regard belief in an individual self and in emotively toned, as well as non-emotively toned, incomprehensions as mere conversational counters.

The Path in Itself. They divide the Path of the three courses into five paths, but consider all the sixteen moments of acceptance in knowledge as the path of seeing.[4] Inasmuch as an apparent object in immediate apprehension must have its absolutely specific characteristic, they do not consider the subtle [idea of the] non-existence of a self as a cognizable object on the Śrāvakas' unobstructed progress along the path of seeing.[5] This is because they consider the encounter with the elusiveness of a Pure Ego as the understanding of the subtle (idea of the) non-existence of an individual self.

THE GOAL

Except for the fact that they disclaim the possibility that a saintly sage (Arhant) can fall from his exalted status won by rejection and attainment, and that they accept the Buddha's physical form as Buddha(hood), the Santrāntikas are similar to the Vaibhāṣikas in what they consider as the methods of attaining the goal of the three courses.

Although the earlier Vaibhāṣikas and Sautrāntikas did not recognize the Mahāyāna scriptures as the Buddha-word, the later followers of these philosophical faiths are said to have done so.

To sum up:

> May logicians enjoy this banquet
> Of the secrets of those who follow
> Reason in their teaching which I have served up.
> For I have long and deeply studied logic.

FROM

THE SUMMARY OF PHILOSOPHICAL SYSTEMS

YID-BZHIN GRUB-MTHA' BSDUS-PA

foll. 15b

I

THE PHILOSOPHICAL tenets of the Sautrāntikas are, on the whole, the same as those of the Vaibhāṣikas. Their special tenets are:

1) Four generating cause-factors.
2) Appearance being [phenomenal] mind.
3) The hypothetical nature of the object.[6]
4) The spacelessness of atoms.
5) The causal efficiency of the sensory functions.
6) The disjunct entities being labels, and
7) Nirvāṇa being subsistence.

These seven topics do not constitute a correct philosophical view, because they all have the defects inherent in a view accepting particular existents.

1) The (basic) cause situation represents a mere capability of assisting [the production of] an effect; it sets up the facticity (*ngo-bo*) [of a situation]. The dominant cause-factor [in the situation] represents a mere absence of hindrances; it sets up the specificity [of a situation]. The referential cause-factor represents any object before the knowing mind. The similar-immediate cause-factor sets up a subsequent cognitive [situation] similar to the antecedent one immediately after the latter has ceased.

The basic cause situation comprises five causes (aspects): associate, [hierarchically] universal, similar, initiative, and co-existent.

Within this framework mind and mental events originate from four cause-factors; the two attainments of the suspension of attitudinal and functional operations and of induced unconsciousness do so from three, the referential cause-factor being absent; and the disjunct entities as well as the whole of the physical-material from two, the basic cause-situation and the dominant cause-factor.[7]

2) In claiming that all that appears, such as visions, illusions, and ontological objects, is actually one's mind, the Sautrāntikas are similar to those who hold *sensa* to be coinciding with what is assumed to be real.[8]

3) While there is no ontological object corresponding to what appears as a vision or an illusion, that which appears to be a real or ontological object is but a *sensum* before the mind [in the sense] that the [alleged] external object transmits a replica of itself [i.e. the *sensum*] to the mind. An object such as a jug is never actually observed. The appearance of a jug, and the place where this appearance is believed to exist, are indistinguishably hypothetical. We speak in common parlance of a cognition experiencing an object, because we are made aware of a likeness when, in the first instance, the three causal factors of object, sensory capacity, and cognition combine, and when subsequently a sensum [believed to be] an object is sensed, [which is a process] similar to the reflection in a mirror.[9]

4) Since it is irrelevant whether the atoms operate with or without intervals between them when building up the physical universe, it is further claimed that there are no spaces between them in their conglomerate. This is believed to be true either because no actual contact exists in such a conglomerate due to the absence of any intervals, or because there is no conglomerate with contact due to the fact that, although in the absence of intervals a conglomerate [is said to] occur, there is no [actual] conglomerate.[10]

5) The substance [representing] a sensory function is a capacity which can generate the appropriate sensation in a live sense organ such as the eye. It is claimed to be proved by circularity, due to the fact that the sensory awareness such as

a visual sensation arises in dependence upon this capacity, which itself has come into existence by virtue of an antecedent sensory awareness.

6) Since the disjunct entities such as origination, annihilation, and the rest are neither identical with nor different from the physical-material, the mind, and the mental events, they are postulates and mere names like a mountain or a fence.

7) The three spiritual pursuits agree that in Nirvāṇa the psychophysical constituents together with their potentialities [of re-appearing] have ceased to operate and that this cessation of the objectively given, which is like clouds disappearing in the sky, is just its indivisibility from the sphere of absolute reality. The Sautrāntikas' claim that this is just nothing is similar to that of the Vaibhāṣikas. However, the Sautrāntikas do not claim this substance, devoid of the objectively given, to have an existence in its own right.

The critique of these tenets is as follows:

1) When we examine what brings about an effect or its absence, be it by cause and effect meeting or not meeting each other or by simultaneity or non-simultaneity, by resorting to any of the four alternatives such as origination by itself [or by something else or by both alternatives together or by neither], origination ultimately does not proceed from cause-factors [postulated *ad hoc*].

2–3) If appearance is [phenomenal] mind and if an object is hypothetical, it is difficult to make a valid distinction between that which is immediately given and that which in knowledge is hypothetical. Even if an object were not hypothetical, it would not exist as a real external object, because of its apparent character.

4) If there are no spaces between the atoms, it logically follows that they coalesce into a single [atom], and if they do not touch each other or do not conglomerate, it follows equally that there are spaces between them. There is no third alternative.

5) A sensory function capacity is refuted in the ultimate sense by the refutation of its being a function, and while it suffices to say that the sensory function produces the sensory

awareness, there is no special need to label this as a capacity.

6) If the disjunct entities are nothing but postulates, the tenet of the eternalistic Vedāntic theory follows, because impermanence would not be inherent in the knowable.[11]

7) Nirvāṇa is not mere subsistence in which concrete existence has ceased. The Hīnayāna Nirvāṇa is not something absolutely ultimate, because the [intellectual] veil has not yet been torn, and Buddhahood is not discontinuity, because there is no reason that working for sentient beings should remain incomplete and that transcendent awareness [of Buddhahood] should cease.

II

The Pratyekabuddha [self-styled Buddha] is a man of medium intelligence. When by virtue of what he has learned by previous experiences, in his last life in this world, he objectively looks at what is real by means of the Pratītyasamutpāda,[12] he becomes aware of the non-existence of an individual self and of the fact that whatever is apprehendable has no reality in itself; but although he understands one and a half of what is implied by the non-existence of an ontological principle and although he achieves his goal, the saintly status of a Pratyekabuddha, he is still classified as lower than the Mahāyāna follower.

All the entities of reality, be they of the within or the without, come into existence in interrelation. Just as outwardly a sprout shoots forth from a seed, there is inwardly the concatenation from unknowing to old age and death. Motivation is the stock of karmic activity available in this life due to the presence of unknowing which has failed to become aware of what is real in a previous life. From motivation comes conscious activity, which is both the cause projecting a [future] life-form and the result of the projection. From conscious activity through the successive stages of embryonic growth, develop the psycho-physical constituents subsumed under the headings of 'four "names" and form.'[13] From here the six cognitive 'fields' related to the eye and the rest of the senses come into being, and when from this stage onwards a rapport situation has been formed in which the sense-object, the sensory function, and the sense-awareness combine, feeling follows. From feeling comes the desire, then comes the self-identification with the objective situation, and from this comes the life-form possibility with its available karmic energy; from this comes the [actual] existence in one of the six forms of life, and from and with it old age and death.

Of these twelve topics, unknowing, desire and self-identification represent emotivity; motivation and life-form possibility represent karmic activity; the remaining seven represent the mass of frustrating unsatisfactoriness. In this way, out of emotivity comes karmic activity and from this in turn comes frustration, and since from frustration emotivity and karmic activity take their origin, the concatenation leading from one life-possibility to another will revolve until this trend of unknowing has been reversed.

The meditational method of the Pratyekabuddha is as follows: He looks at a skeleton in a cremation ground and becomes aware of the fact that it has come about through death. This has been due to birth and in this way he goes back to the [original source of] unknowing. Realizing that this unknowing is abolished by a discrimination which intuitively understands the non-existence of an individual self, he applies this cognitive process to himself. By thinking of the stages in this development of old age and death from birth, the former being the quintessence of frustration, he intuitively grasps the truth of frustration. By thinking of the process by which old age and death cease to be relevant when [repeated] birth has come to an end, he arrives at the truth of the end of frustration. By thinking of how motivation and what follows arise from unknowing, the source from which frustration takes its origin, he intuitively grasps the truth of the origin of frustration. By thinking of how motivation and what follows will come to an end when unknowing has ceased to operate, he will in one session realize his goal either of a Prateyka-buddha living in a crowd [of similarly minded persons] or of a Prateykabuddha of the lonely wolf type. This is due to his realization that the essence of the truth of the path [towards the abolishment of frustration], consisting of the conscious cultivation of the idea of the non-existence of an individual self and other topics as the counter-agent of the origination of frustration, is [the development of his own] cognitive capacity.

The Pratyekabuddha type is not the last word [in spiritual development] because there are others destined for the one and ultimate course. The Pratītyasamutpāda also is nothing in itself, because origination through mutual meeting and other topics are not found anywhere. If the apprehendable is nothing real, then the apprehending [agent] also is nothing real, because the apprehendable and the apprehender are on the same level. Delighting in solitariness is not the behaviour of a highly cultured man. Ultimately, there is neither solitariness nor nonsolitariness. A mind bent on tranquility in [individual] solitude does not represent a noble intention, and since [such a] goal is not something ultimate, the Pratyekabuddha's path is an inferior one.

CHAPTER FOUR

MENTALISTIC-PHENOMENALISTIC TRENDS

THE ALMOST inevitable 'next step' from the analysis of perceptual situations as performed by the Sautrāntikas is the mentalistic view, which denies that there are external physical objects to cause our sensations and perceptions. This view is known as the Yogācāra teaching and the use of the word *yoga* here emphasizes the importance of introspective techniques. The adherents of this view are generally referred to as 'those who think that mind alone counts' (*sems-tsam-pa*). Now in Buddhist philosophical thought 'mind' (*sems*) does not mean a typical idealized mind or an actual super-mind of which all other minds would be constituents. It is therefore extremely misleading to equate this Buddhist line of thought with 'idealism,' be it of the subjective or objective variety. In order to avoid confusion, the term 'idealism,' which even in Western philosophical thought is a misnomer, will be used only when reference to ideals is involved, and when it characterizes the doctrine that the nature of the universe is such that those characteristics which are most valuable will either be present eternally, or will be manifested in even greater intensity and wider extent as time goes on. In contradistinction, the term 'mentalism' will be used when the view is expresed that the relatively permanent conditions of interrelated sensa are minds. Furthermore, since the Buddhist term for 'mind' (*sems*) is wider in scope than what may be called 'a particular mind-entity,' according to the systems which use it, the word 'mind' must be understood not only as a symbol for such a particular entity, but also as a symbol for the particular experience which, in those persons who have had it, has brought forth the peculiar response expressed in the proposition that 'mind alone counts' (*sems-tsam*). Consequently, it will be necessary to restrict the use of the term 'mentalism' even further, and to employ it only when epistemological problems are involved.

Before proceeding with the mentalistic system, it will be useful to give a rapid survey of the terms used for what we call 'mind.' It will have been observed from the foregoing chapters that Buddhism developed a functional, rather than a static, interpretation of mind, and described it by three different terms: *sems, yid,* and *rnam-*(*par*) *shes-*(*pa*). Of these terms, the last one denotes man's perceptions; the middle one the co-ordination of the data of his senses and his 'thoughts.' The first one describes man's responsiveness and indicates the fact that all awareness is intentional or relational, from a subjective pole to an object of some sort; in other words, it names the bipolar structure of immediate experience. While the Vaibhāṣikas had emphasized the intentional or relational and referential character of this responsiveness (*sems*), the Sautrāntikas drew attention to the fact that there also is a nonreferential aspect to mind. Consequently the structure of 'mind' in Buddhist philosophy can be shown diagrammatically as follows:

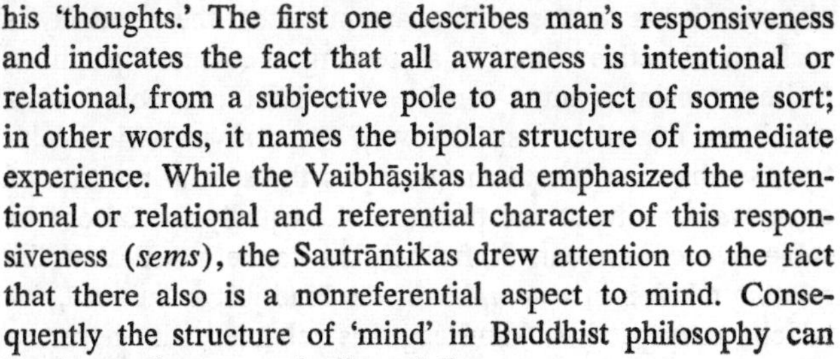

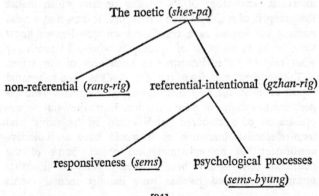

All schools of Buddhism accepted this structure of mind except that the Vaibhāṣikas and Prāsangikas did not recognize the non-referential aspect. The former probably based their attitude upon their object-orientated analysis of perceptual and cognitive situations, while the latter must be accused of either having confused *in*spection with *intro*spection, or having demanded of introspection something which no one would demand of inspection.

The mentalists claimed that we can and do have introspective knowledge of such situations as sensing a coloured patch or feeling a pain. The Prāsangikas at once objected that in such cases when we try to *intro*spect this situation we merely *in*spect the coloured patch or the pain itself. Against their objection it has to be said that, assuming that there actually is such an objective situation as sensing a coloured patch or feeling a pain, it must consist of at least two constituents which are related in a specific way by an asymmetrical relation, so that one constituent occupies the special position of *objective* constituent and the other the equally special one of subjective constituent. It further has to be noted that the relating relation in a *complex* of the kind just mentioned, for which introspective knowledge is claimed, is never a constituent of this complex in the same way as the terms are. The complex itself *is* the objective situation of sensing a coloured patch or feeling a pain, and we have direct and non-inferential knowledge of its relating relation which makes this complex of such and such a structure. If, however, we did nothing but inspect each constituent we would never know them to be constituents of a complex whole. So much for what may be called introspective knowledge of our states.

Taking their cue from the Sautrāntikas' non-referential aspect of mind, the mentalists developed it into aesthetic experience *simpliciter* or pure sensation. Here, the intuitive apprehension of a coloured patch would be 'objective' and 'non-referential' inasmuch as it would have an objective constituent but no epistemological object. Some of the mentalists seem to have been inclined to hold the view that apparently coloured patches were literally mental events which, on the basis of this view, would be both non-objective and non-referential in the same way as a feeling as such would be. Such an event would then be 'purely subjective.' A natural outcome of the mentalists' position of emphasizing the non-referential character of 'mind' was the distinction between being 'epistemologically objectifiable' as developed and discussed by the Sautrāntikas, and being 'psychologically objectifiable,' which means to be capable of being an objective constituent of some objective mental situation. If, as some of the mentalists seem to have believed, a coloured patch is a non-objective mental event, it nevertheless becomes an objective constituent of a mental situation whenever it is sensed or used for perceiving.

In course of time the mentalists were accused of upholding pure subjectivism and of being unable to go beyond it. They certainly advocated causal subjectivity by which anything is defined as subjective when it is assumed to have as a necessary condition of its being the occurrence of a percipient event. The conclusion that anything generated by a percipient (mental) event is ipso facto mental does not follow, as the critics of the mentalists have pointed out. For a thing is *not* proved to be mental in any ordinary sense, even if it is proved that the sole necessary conditions of its existence are mental. Although the mentalists claimed causal subjectivity, they did not subscribe to existential subjectivity by which is implied that anything that owes its being to a percipient event occurring in me, exists only *for* me (solipsism). It is logically possible that even if the occurrence of a percipient event is essential for the generation of its character as a particular, the latter may persist after its perception has ceased.

The situation is complicated still further by the fact that the mentalists were divided as to whether what we perceive or sense and feel is veridical or delusive. The term used to denote that which we directly sense and are aware of is *rnam-pa,* which admits of various terms in English, those of 'observable quality,' 'particular character' and 'sensum' being the most accurate ones. These sensa are not essences, timeless and ingenerative entities, but particular data; not universals characterizing particular existents, but attributes of the 'object,' which must be understood as being capable of having particulars as attributes. This is possible when the 'object' is itself not another concrete particular, but an 'event'—a region of space at a given time. In other words, the particular or character which is my sensum (*rnam-pa*), though generated by the percipient event in me, exists at the present time 'out there' in a certain determinate region of space at a certain determinate time, and, insofar as this is the case, may be credited with an attributive objectivity or veridicalness.

A number of theories of perception are mentioned in this context in the indigenous works, but it is extremely difficult to extract some definite and distinctive meaning out of them and to relate them to similar theories in Western philosophies, because their initial intentions had already become problematic by the time that they were codified and transmitted in the Tibetan works summarizing the main trends of Buddhist philosophy. Only in this way can the fact be accounted for that under one and the same title quite divergent views are enumerated, some of which certainly could never have been proposed by the mentalists. The following remarks, therefore, do not pretend to be more than tentative propositions about Buddhist problems of perception.

One of the major problems seems to have involved the question whether my perceptual datum, e.g., red, is or is not a duplicate or representation of a character or observable quality of the 'object,' but *is* just that character itself. Another problem seemingly dealt with the fact that not all experiences with which we are acquainted are sensations. There are images, thoughts, feelings, pleasures, and pains. The ways in which a man becomes acquainted with colours, sounds, smells, or pains need not involve his being sensitive in any other way than that he be capable of simple detection or inspection of such things. This in effect would explain the having of sensations as the *not* having any sensations (there being no sensa/sensation). Lastly, perception seems to have been recognized as a unique pattern of relationships, qualities, and properties that cannot be broken up without being altered at the same time.

Whatever the various theories may have specifically implied, the obvious difficulties that attach to the problem of the veridicalness and attributive objectivity of sensa are not solved by declaring the latter to be delusive, as was done by some mentalists. First of all, inasmuch as sensa are assumed to owe their being to a percipient event and hence are 'causally subjective' and, in all probability, also 'existentially subjective' it is rather unlikely, if not impossible, that the one constituent should be delusive while the other is and remains veridical. Furthermore, this type of reasoning seems to be prepared to admit in advance that there is an absurdity inherent in the very idea of knowledge and then, in order to escape the implications, invokes an Absolute Mind of which it is said that its knowing is not subject to the infirmities of ordinary human knowing.

Here two types developed, a weaker one which attempted to preserve some semblance of what is ordinarily understood by perception, and a stronger, absolutistic one. Whatever the validity or fallacy of their epistemological theories may have been, there can be no doubt that these two types paved the way to a new conception of ontology and of metaphysics.

Although in a certain sense the mentalists did not escape subjectivism, they greatly contributed to a genetic theory of mind, developing the idea of a 'substratum awareness,' a stratum of being (*kun-gzhi*) which has been interpreted in different ways by two of the four major traditions in Tibet, the rNying-ma-pas and the dGe-lugs-pas. The latter took this stratum to be a homogenous interiority, capable of retaining structures and their modifications (*bag-chags*). Its status was both '(existentially) uncompromised' and '(ethically) neutral' yet it was being disrupted by a thrust of consciousness to its object in a sort of *cogito* which is still prereflective. In this upsurge the stratum loses its status of being 'uncompromised' and also of being 'neutral' although it does not become '(ethically) positive' or 'negative.' In other words, it becomes 'individuated' and the background of all subsequent reflective conscious activity. There are thus two consciousnesses involved: a reflective consciousness-*of* and a consciousness reflected-*on*. This is to say, while every consciousness is a consciousness *of* something, it is not a thetic consciousness of itself, and explicit positing of itself; it rather remains a non-positional consciousness (of) itself. But in this upsurge of consciousness to its object it constitutes an other as the 'real' I; i.e., the non-positional consciousness is presented in an act to a consciousness-*of*, as having a certain noematic objective sense which is claimed to be 'the self.' This act initiates a 'compromised mind' because the mind's initial status has become disintegrated and has been robbed of its integrity. It is now a real *cogito* whose status is 'dimmed,' 'obscured,' 'compromised' (*bsgribs*) due to its evolving egoness. But insofar as this status is just the *being* of consciousness it is still 'neutral.' Only by entering the habitual reflective and cognitive levels it makes itself experienced as ethically varied ('good' and 'evil').

It is quite obvious that the *kun-gzhi* was treated both as a process of becoming conscious-*of* and as a stratum of being, the difference between epistemology and metaphysics was not clearly in focus.

The rNying-ma-pas must be credited with having clarified this problem and having made a singular contribution to the development of Buddhist philosophy. For them there exists in man a faculty which is capable of discerning the ultimate, and in order to be able to discern the ultimate, man must, in some way, partake of the ultimate. The latter is known by its Indian designation *dharmakāya* (*chos-sku*) and the faculty that is capable of discerning it is known as *rig-pa*, which is best translated by 'aesthetic experience' or 'intrinsic perception,' as it refers to the apprehension of the full intrinsic perceptual being *and* value of the object or field, and brings into action, in a specific way, the total being of the percipient. It is contrasted with ordinary perception (*sems*) which is essentially a means to a metaperceptual end. The nature of man as a partaker in the absolute is known as his 'constitutional ability to become enlightened' which, as it were, acts as a mediator between man's absolute nature and his individual nature of a conscious and perceptual being. It is this latter nature that is tied up with the *kun-gzhi* inasmuch as 'being a (human) being' is tantamount to 'being compromised'; man is a 'fallen' being, not from the fact that he has committed such and such a sin, but simply because he has 'fallen,' 'gone astray' into the world, into the midst of things. More properly speaking, a man *qua* man represents a continuously on-going act of 'falling' or going astray. The *kun-gzhi* therefore is an '(existentially) compromising' force, even when it is still '(ethically) neutral.' It is 'compromising' by the very fact that it forms the basis of the experientially initiated potentialities of experience which operate through every sense and by means of which an individual's animate organism becomes the most immediate actualization of his or her volitional activity and of emotional habits.

Viewing the rNying-ma-pas' fully developed conception of the *kun-gzhi* as a whole, it is evident that it is an extremely complex one and that it developed from the reflective observation of the continuously on-going embodiment of the flux of mental life. In other words, first of all we have the *kun-gzhi* as the phenomenon of a continuously on-going act of going astray. This act has no 'beginning' because it is the functionality of the *kun-gzhi* and because there is no 'before.' The going astray implies a process of singling out, which gives the individual the experience of 'my body' and 'me-as-acting'; this experience is tied up with some kind of 'feeling' which is both 'perceiving' and 'emotionally active and reactive' (*bag-chags*). The disclosure of my 'being active' focuses attention on the individual's body as an orientational centre in relation to which the world and its multiple objects are organized. Lastly, an individual's being is a synthetically organized system of what is commonly spoken of as body and mind.

The growing interest in metaphysics, which characterized the whole mentalistic movement, carried forward the attempt to bridge the gulf between the wordly and the transworldly, to blend the sensible with the supersensible, the human with the transcendental or, as the Tantras would say, the divine. In passing it may be noted that the mentalistic movement was the motivating power behind the flowering of Buddhist art which is the embodiment of the fundamental ideas, concepts, and values in metaphysics.

Metaphysical considerations are prominent in the mentalists' assumption of three 'absolutely specific constitutive principles':

1. The 'notional-conceptual' corresponds to what we would call a formal sign whose whole function is a meaning, a signifying of something else to a knowing power, particularly in a conversational setting. Its hallmark is universality, because it is impossible for us to say or think about anything without using formal signs or concepts that are universal. Thus, the jug in front of me is conceived of as a jug, made of clay, brown in colour, fragile, etc. Yet the notion 'jug' does not apply just to this particular jug, but to any and all jugs, and the same is true of any other notions such as 'brown in colour,' 'fragile,' 'in front of me' and so on. Further, we must have the concept "jug" in order to become aware of a jug, but it is not necessary to be aware of the concept 'jug' in order to become aware of what it signifies, its *significatum*. "Apart from merely being a tag (a being of reason) used and created by apprehending something while verbalizing a non-ideal universality, the notional-conceptual is not something having an ontological status; it is like a sky-flower having no essence." [1] Since formal signs are nothing but meanings or intentions, it is possible to distinguish between first and second intentions. This is to say, the jug as it is in itself is an object of first intention, while the jug as it is in a condition of being known or of being an object before the mind is an object of second intention.

The nature of the notional-conceptual may be restated in the following way which would account for its being conceived as an absolutely specific constitutive principle. If I express a feeling with a word, the word is meant to be an indication of the reality which evokes within myself, let us say, the power of my loving. The *word* 'love' is meant to be a symbol for the *fact* 'love,' but as soon as it is spoken it tends to assume a life of its own, it becomes a 'reality.' Consequently I come under the spell of the illusion that the saying of this word is the equivalent of the experience, and soon I say the word and feel nothing, except the *thought* of love which the word expresses. All this is a complete deviation from intrinsic perception.

2. The 'relative' refers to certain experiences or 'states' with which everyone of us is familiar, but which our language can only describe by the stimulus which produces these states. This is because human language developed from references to what are believed to be the concrete things around us, but not from what goes on in referring to them. There are no words which at the same time cover the within and the without. Only indirectly can we say 'the state which would occur if a person saw a jug.' It is precisely this state that is indicated by 'the relative,' not the relation that holds between two terms or connects two events. It is a state in which subject and object are given together, because subject *qua* subject means to 'function,' and to 'function' means to 'relate' oneself to an object which is given, together with the subject, as the possibility of positive and negative judgments. To relate oneself to something means that the subject is constantly varying its relation to the object, but while the subject-object relation is unequivocal, its functionality reveals the plurality of objects. "Mountains, wells, plots of land, houses, residences and other 'objects' of the world, as well as the sentient beings as the 'subjects' therein, seem to each of us at every moment to be mutually apart and distant from each other, and this is the mode of things appearing as objects external to the observer. However, since this mode of appearing is itself not something empirically verifiable, objects external to the observer do not exist [apart from functionality]. What then is the mode of being or of existing of mountains, wells, houses, sentient beings and so on, which constitutes 'the relative'? When the eye sees a figure, the ear hears a sound, the nose smells a fragrance, the tongue tastes a flavour, the skin feels a touch, and

the mind thinks a thought, the noetic (*shes-pa*) performing all these activities is like a crystal, shining in all the colours with which it comes into contact. In this sense the 'relative' exists really, being one substance, one fact and one state in the same way as the dream-consciousness and the house we dream of are one event." [2]

3. The 'ideally absolute' is said to rest on the 'relative' in in the sense that the former is the presential value of the latter. It is therefore not something above or behind the 'relative,' but the 'relative' in its aesthetic immediacy from which further intellectual and other abstractions may in turn be made. Still there is a difference between the 'relative' and the 'ideally absolute,' which can best be illustrated by what happens in and characterizes aesthetic experience. Here, it is necessary to distinguish between (a) aesthetic experience *simpliciter* as it exists only at the first instant in consciousness, distinguishing within itself the aesthetically valid from the aesthetcally invalid, and (b) aesthetic experience enriched by other experiences which have been put back into the crucible from which aesthetic experience emerges and upon which aesthetic intuition imposes its presential value. Thus in the moment of the validity or enjoyment of our aesthetic intuition of, say, a jar (the 'ideally absolute'), we can apprehend it aesthetically as a jar (the 'relative'). In other words, when a man looks at a jar, he has both aesthetic and intellectual activity, but he usually does not make a clear intellectual abstraction from aesthetic experience, put it back into the crucible, and then become clearly aware of a new intellectually clarified object. Rather he tends to contaminate his experience with the superficial fictions of some practical concern (the 'notional-conceptual'), which are characteristic of what may be termed 'ordinary' perception as contrasted with the richness and liveliness of aesthetic awareness. In ordinary perception a man uses perception as a means to a metaperceptual end, rather than as an end in itself.

From this account we are now in a position to understand the mentalists' definition of the three absolutely specific characteristics and their interaction:

"The 'ideally absolute' is the [aesthetic] content of the process of unerringly [and aesthetically] apprehending the phenomenal, that is, the 'relative' and the 'notional-conceptual' as well as its presential value in its own right. It is the [convincing] knowledge that the appearance of whatever constitutes the 'relative' and the awareness which makes the presential value [in the 'relative'] self-manifesting, exist as one event; and it is the intuitive awareness that any perceptual phenomenon of the 'relative,' although it appears as an external object, does not so exist as an object of practical concern, [as regards which] its *negandum* becomes the fiction of negation and that which cannot be negated by any means whatsoever, although it is merely postulated by words and concepts, that of affirmation." [3]

Both the 'ideally absolute' and the 'relative' are said to be real in an ultimate sense, while the 'notional-conceptual' is stated not to be so. This is to say that only the 'ideally absolute' and the 'relative' are significant as a means of self-growth, because as aesthetic experience they create an affection for appreciation and contemplation as against possessiveness, cultivate a sense of worth and dignity by changing things into the intrinsically interesting and intrinsically valuable. The Tantras express this by saying that the whole world is a divine (intrinsically valuable) mansion and every sentient being therein a god or goddess (an intrinsically dignified being). It is this aesthetic perception that sharply curtails the sensory, intuitive, imaginative, emotional, and intellectual processes in the interest of some ulterior end. While aesthetic perception allows a new freedom to these processes, so that they may attain their own ends and develop themselves as fully as possible, 'ordinary' perception is more likely to destroy the possibility of growth than to further it, and hence is of no significance at all. The emphasis on the aesthetic element is related to the rich world of art which is intimately linked with the mentalist movement in Buddhist philosophy. From a purely philosophical point of view the mentalists initiated a metaphysics which did not claim to reveal truths about a world that lies beyond the reach of the senses and hence nowhere; rather were they concerned with how to deal with what happens here and now, how to get the things of the world into perspective.

The fact that as metaphysicians the Buddhist mentalists saw the world in a new way and in unusual lights accounts for their drawing unusual and new conclusions in the sphere of conduct. Their conclusions constituted an essential part of the premises on which they were based. The mentalists were convinced that knowledge, Buddhahood, was a basic factor, pervading the whole world of man and the whole nature of man. To the extent an individual approximated to his very foundation of being, different 'types' were recognized. Some of them were closer to their real being, others were less so. In course of time the so-called 'cut-off' type, which at first had been considered to comprise those who would never realize their Buddha-nature, was reinterpreted as referring to those who would need a long time to grow up to be human. This re-interpretation was due to both logical and humane considerations. If every individual is capable of realizing Buddhahood because every individual is a potential Buddha, then the assumption that some will not be able to realize their true being is self-contradictory; and if every individual is a potential Buddha, then this very fact constitutes his value and thus his ultimate value cannot be disputed.

The conviction in the ultimate Buddhahood of man has found its expression in the idea of Three Kāyas. It is tempting to see in them metaphysical principles and to misunderstand their logical character in viewing them as basic premises or in concretizing them, as is evident from their lexical (and hence utterly misleading) translations by 'bodies.' The three Kāyas are value-experiences and principles of interpretation.

The Dharmakāya refers to the presence of Buddhahood as a possibility of actual being. It is a model of possible actuality; therefore, unless the very possibility of such being can be concretely envisioned, there can be no actual and concrete grasp of the essential realities with which a person growing up to Buddhahood is concerned. Logically, also, the Dharmakāya is not only prior to the other Kāyas, but also is the structural process taking shape in the concrete. As process it is known as Dharmajñānakāya;[4] viewed ontologically it becomes the Svābhāvikakāya.

The Sambhogakāya is empathetic Buddhahood. It brings into prominence the factors of imagination and feeling. In this empathetic state the tendencies on which the perception of Buddhahood is based are not merely noted cognitively but also performed imaginatively by the percipient. Such imaginative and affective appreciation of the significance of Buddhahood is similar to the best aesthetic experience as a means of apprehending most vividly what is there for intrinsic, value-sustained perception. In this state the percipient allows himself to be transformed by the object's (Buddhahood's) intrinsic value and being, which is the aim of aesthetic experience. To this end empathy is a vitalizing factor.

The Nirmāṇakāya is embodied Buddhahood. This means that an individual becomes the concrete actualization of Buddhahood. The individual 'expresses' Buddhahood, as speech expresses thought, in an originatory way; the individual is both the 'expression' and the 'expressed.' In other words, Buddhahood, absolute in itself (*dharmakāya*), manifests (expresses) itself in the body-proper of an individual, and is manifested (expressed) by the animatedness of the body-proper of an individual, and is manifested (expressed) by the animatedness of the body-proper (*nirmāṇakāya*).

Both *The Jewel Garland* and *The Summary* agree in presenting the mentalistic-phenomenalistic trends in Buddhist philosophy as the continuation of the epistemological interests of the earlier systems both in India and Tibet. They also bring out the renewed interest in metaphysics, but they differ in its interpretation. *The Jewel Garland* remains the 'traditionalist,' merely re-stating the more or less generally accepted Indian position; *The Summary* clearly distinguishes between epistemology and metaphysics. Historically speaking, it was metaphysics that enabled Buddhism to spread to China, Korea, and Japan.

FROM

THE JEWEL GARLAND

GRUB-PA'I MTHA'I RNAM-PAR BZHAG-PA RIN-PO-CHE'I PHRENG-BA

foll. 9a ff.

IN THE PRESENTATION of the mentalists' philosophical faith there are four sections: intrinsic characteristics, schools, meaning of the name, and contents.

CHARACTERISTICS

A mentalist is a man who, following the insiders' philosophical faith, does not recognize the existence of external objects, but considers that which fits into the world-order to be veridical.

SCHOOLS

There are two schools: (i) those who claim sensa to be veridical and (ii) those who consider them to be delusive.

That is to say, there is a dispute as to whether the sensum is veridical or delusive when one says that there is an appearance of blue as blue for the eye perceiving a patch of blue. Those who claim that sensa are veridical assert that when the eye perceives a patch of blue, there is the blue as it appears, but those who consider sensa to be delusive say that when the eye perceives a patch of blue, there is no such blue as appearing blue. So far so good.

However, while both parties, whether they consider sensa to be veridical or delusive, agree that when the eye perceives a patch of blue there is an appearance of blue and this seems to be an external object, those who claim sensa to be veridical attribute their appearance as an external object to the working of un-knowing, but not so the appearance of blue as blue and the appearance of blue as the epistemological object of the perceptual situation. Therefore, among the mentalists those who claim the epistmological object of the perceptual situation to have literally all the qualities it seems to display have the mark of considering sensa to be true, while those who do not do so have the mark of considering sensa to be delusive.

(i) There are three varieties in the assumption of sensa being veridical. They are defined and described as (a) an equal number of what we considered to be subjective and objective factors; (b) the two halves of one egg; and (c) the non-duality of the multiple.

However, scholars do not agree as to what is specifically meant by this triple distinction.

Gung-ru rgyal-mtshan bzang-po [5] says in his *Dbu-ma'i stong-mthun* that when one sees the multicoloured surface of a butterfly's wing there come from the object as many impulses as there are colours, as for instance blue and yellow and so on; and on the part of the subject there originate as many true sensations as there are impulses of blue and yellow and so on. This is what is meant by (a) an equal number of what are subjective and objective constituents.[6] Then, while there come from the object as many impulses as there are colours, these impulses do not turn into sensation, in other words (b) the two halves of one egg.[7] Lastly, when there do not come from the object as many impulses as there are colours, but only one impulse of multicolouredness, and when on the part of the subject there are not only no sensations of the various colours such as blue and yellow, but also no sensation of multicolouredness, this is (c) the non-duality of the multiple.[8]

Drung-chen legs-pa bzang-po and Paṇ-chen Bsod-nams grags-pa, as well as others, say that just as the yellow and the blue appearing in the perception of multicolouredness are different entities, so also the perception process in the perception of multicolouredness is constituted of different entities, in other words (a) an equal number of subjective and objective constituents. Thus although the blue and the perception of this blue are both of the nature of the noetic, to hold them to be different entities is what is meant by (b) the two halves of one egg. Lastly, just as the blue and the yellow in a multicoloured patch are one entity, so also the two sub-perceptions of the blue and the yellow in the perception of multicolouredness are but one process, in other words, (c) the non-duality of the multiple.

The *Grub-mtha' chen-mo* states: When one looks at a multicoloured patch there arise simultaneously suitable perceptions equal in number to the colours, as, for instance, blue and yellow and so on, in a multicoloured patch.[9] There is in other words (a) an equal number of the subjective and objective constituents. Then, although the blue and the perception of this blue follow each other, when considered analytically, they are one process, considered integratively, and this is what is meant by (b) the two halves of one egg.[10] Lastly, when in looking at a multicoloured patch one declares that there is no simultaneous origination of suitable perceptions equal in number to the colours such as blue and yellow and so on, found in the multicoloured patch, but declares instead that the single vision of multicolouredness is the perception of blue and yellow and so on in this multicoloured patch, this is (c) the non-duality of the multiple.[11]

One may choose any view one likes.

Among those who accept an equal number of the subjective and objective constituents, there are those who recognize eight awarenesses and those who acknowledge six.[12] Among those who claim the nonduality of the multiple, there are some who accept six awarenesses and some who speak of only one awareness.

(ii) Those who consider sensa to be delusive form two groups: maculate and immaculate.

The former are those who claim that the mind *qua* mind [13] is vitiated by the experientially initiated potentialities of experience due to the working of un-knowing.

The latter are those who assert that this is not so in any way.

Further, while the maculate state that although on a Buddha's level there is no un-knowing, yet appearance remains deviant, the immaculate declare that since there is no un-knowing there is also no deviant appearance.[14]

Lastly, there are the two groups of those who follow tradition, and those who follow the logical method. The former follow the Five Divisions of the *Yogācārabhūmi*, and the latter the Seven Treatises on Logic.[15]

The Name

A mentalist derives his name from the fact that he claims the whole of entitative reality to be solely of the nature of experience. Hence he is also called an experientialist. Another name for him is Yogācāra because he uses his experience as a basis in following the Path of mysticism.

Contents

There is here the triple division into Ground, the Path, and the Goal.

THE GROUND

The Objective Situation. Everything knowable is, the mentalists claim, subsumable under three absolutely specific constitutive principles:

The relative or everything concrete;
The ideally absolute or everything ultimate; and
The notional-conceptual or everything else.

Although these three absolutely specific constitutive principles are claimed to be self-evident and *sui generis,* there is a difference as to their being or not being real (significant). The notional-conceptual is declared not to be real, but the relation and the ideally absolute are said to be so.

That which exists as the dichotomizing activity of mind, though not being ultimately real, has the mark of the notional-conceptual. It is twofold: pluralistic and postulational. The former is the knowable. The latter is the postulate of an absolute status for a self and for the entities of reality other than the self.

That which arises in dependence upon causes and conditions and is the reason for the ideally absolute has the mark of the relation. This also is twofold: pure and impure. The former is a saintly person's continual awareness and a Buddha's auspicious marks.[16] The latter is the organized body-mind with its arousal of affective states.

Suchness to which applies no postulate of an ultimate principle, be it of a self or of entities other than the self, has the mark of the ideally absolute. This, too, is twofold: incontrovertible and unchanging. The former is a saintly person's composure awareness. The latter is ultimacy.

Although the incontrovertible is stated to be the ideally absolute, it is not so [in the true sense of the word] because as the intentional object of the pure path through which every fog surrounding reality is abolished, it is not finality.[17]

The knowable can also be divided into the relatively real and the ultimately real.

That which one arrives at by means of valid propositional investigation has the mark of the relatively real. Hence, 'being delusive,' 'relatively real' and 'denotatively-designatively-propositionally true' are synonymous.

That which one arrives at by means of valid philosophical investigation has the mark of the ultimately true. Hence, 'nothingness,' [18] 'reality,' 'the ideally absolute,' 'being ultimately real,' 'real finality' and 'suchness' are synonymous.

Although that which is ultimately real entails existence by virtue of its being what it is, that which is relatively real does not do so, because the relative exists by virtue of its being what it is, while the notional-conceptual does not do so.

That which is delusive need not necessarily be a delusion, because that which is relative is delusive but not a delusion.

As regards the three divisions of time and explicit negation, the Sautrāntikas, mentalists, and Svātantrika-Mādhyamikas are of one opinion.

The five constituents, such as form and the others,[19] do not exist as external objects; they are born from the material of the inner [i.e. private] noetic through the power of the experientially initiated potentialities of experience implanted by a special act inherent in the substratum-awareness.[20]

According to those who accept sensa to be true, the five constituents, such as colour, form and the others, do not exist as external objects but as objective constituents of perceptual situations. According to those who consider sensa to be delusive these five constituents also do not exist as objective constituents of perceptual situations, because then there ought to be an external object.

The Owner of the Objective Situation. Those who follow tradition accept the substratum-awareness as the self. This is because they recognize eight awarenesses. Those who follow the logical method of investigation accept the co-ordinating and abstractive processes as that which is to be called a self.

The substratum-awareness is as regards its internal experientially initiated potentialities of experience (existentially and ethically) neutral, but is disturbed and divided by the 'constant' which as a primary factor [in cognitive life] is accompanied by five ever-present function patterns as its assistants.[21] Further, as regards its status of being either 'compromised' or 'uncompromised,' it is 'compromised' and non-neutral; and since it is found in him who is utterly without merits, it is not ethically positive, and since it is also found in the higher spheres, it is at the same time not ethically negative.[22]

The affectively toned mind is, in its reference to the substratum-awareness, the ego-idea, (essentially) compromised and (ethically) neutral.

The other six perceptive and co-ordinating-abstractive processes follow the general classification.

The mentalists recognize immediate apprehension and genuine and immediate inference as valid means of cognition and accept four kinds of immediate apprehension. Non-referential awareness and mystic perceptions entail non-errant cognition. Those who accept sensa to be true claim that the perception of a patch of blue by an ordinary person is a non-errant cognition; those who consider sensa to be delusive claim that sensory perception by an ordinary person entails an errant cognition, while his abstractive perception may be errant or non-errant.

THE PATH

The Objective Pole of its intentional structure is the sixteen properties of the Four Truths.[23] And while the non-existence of a self as an eternal, single, and sovereign principle constitutes the coarse aspect of the non-existence of an absolute principle, the non-existence of a self as a self-sufficient substance is the subtle one; the non-existence of perception and the perceived content as different substances, as well as the non-existence of the tendency towards dichotomization as something existing in and by itself, are considered by the mentalists as the subtle aspect of the non-existence of an absolute principle relating to the entities of reality other than the self. But neither of the two types of the subtle aspects of the non-existence of an absolute principle, which they recognize as nothingness, is necessary as far as nothingness is concerned, because for them the Truth of the End of all Misery and Nirvāṇa are also nothingness.

Furthermore, everything concrete is self-evident and substantial; everything absolute is self-evident and factual.

That which has to be eliminated by the Path are wishfulness and emotivity and intellectual fog.

The former is the belief in a self, both in its coarser and subtler form, together with its latent potentiality; the six primary and the twenty secondary affective patterns.[24]

The latter is the belief in the absolute status of the entities of reality other than the self, together with its latent potentiality.

Bodhisattvas are primarily concerned with the elimination of the intellectual fog, not with that of wishfulness and emotivity. For the adherents of the Hīnayāna it is the opposite.

The Path as Being-Itself. Each of the three courses into which the path is divided consists of a path of preparation, of linking the previous stage with the subsequent and central one, of seeing truth, of attending to the truth seen, and of no-more-learning. In Mahāyāna ten spiritual levels are recognized in addition.

THE REALIZATION OF THE GOAL

A confirmed Hīnayānist is primarily concerned with the contemplation of the ideally absolute as it relates to the non-existence of an absolute principle as a self. When he has become thoroughly acquainted with this ideal, by means of a meditative concentration as solid as a diamond which is the Hīnayāna path of attending to the truth seen, simultaneously with the elimination of all wishfulness and emotivity he realizes the goal of a Hīnayāna saint. As there is not the slightest difference between Śrāvakas and Pratyekabuddhas as regards that which has to be attended to, namely, the non-existence of an absolute principle, and as regards that which has to be overcome, that is, wishfulness and emotivity, the two groups divide into the eight categories of those who have entered and those who are firmly established on and deriving the benefit of a certain Hīnayāna spiritual level; but inasmuch as a Pratyekabuddha has to work out his salvation on the level of the world of sensuality, there is no division into twenty types of saintly people.[25] However, this is not to say that there is no difference between Śrāvakas and Pratyekabuddhas. The point is whether the accumulation of merits extends over a hundred aeons or not, and whether there is accordingly a higher or lower level of the goal.

Those who follow tradition claim that a Hīnayāna saint merely passes away and does not set out on the Mahāyāna path: only an enlightened saint does so. To do so is possible when alive but not later, because they claim that finality can be found in all three courses.

Those who follow the logical method declare that a Hīnayāna saint enters the Mahāyāna path, because finality is claimed to exist only on one course.

Mahāyānists are primarily concerned with the contemplation of the ideally absolute as it relates to the non-existence of an absolute principle relating to the entities of reality other than the self. Having experienced this ideal in connection with their accumulation of merits and knowledge through three 'incalculable' aeons,[26] they ascend the ten spiritual levels and travel the five paths successively; by the obstacle-removing path of their continuous concentration they eliminate their intellectual fog as well as their wishfulness and emotivity, and in the Akaniṣṭha heaven they realize the Pure Existence most excellent in both rejection and attainment and sufficient unto itself, and the two Form-patterns,[27] most excellent in their activity which benefits others.

Some people who follow the *Abhidharmasamuccaya* declare that the Buddhahood is attainable on the human level.

The mentalists declare the Buddha-word to be explicit and suggestive, because the first two discourses as detailed in the *Dgongs-'grel*[28] are considered to be suggestive and the last one explicit.

The mentalists profess the Mahāyānist philosophical faith by upholding the following axioms: (i) Nirvāṇa is triple (a) while physical life still lasts, (b) when it has been thrown off, and (c) is nonpredicable. (ii) The Buddha-pattern is threefold: Dharmakāya, Sambhogakāya, and Nirmāṇakāya. (iii) Dharmakāya is twofold: Svābhāvikakāya and Jñāna(dharma)kāya. (iv) Svābhāvikakāya also is twofold: 'pure in being-itself' and 'pure as regards the removal of incidental stains.'[29]

To sum up:

May the judicious long enjoy
This dissertation on the faith
Philosophical of those who follow mankind's
Leader, speaking of experientiality.

FROM

THE SUMMARY OF PHILOSOPHICAL SYSTEMS

YID-BZHIN-MDZOD-KYI GRUB-MTHA' BSDUS-PA

foll. 18b ff.

THE MENTALISTS claim that all entities of reality are subsumed under mere experience, and that the cognitive event devoid of both an objective and a subjective determinant exists really in an absolute sense.

There is a common philosophical position adopted by mentalists and a specific one which depends on their acceptance of sensa as either veridical or delusive.

COMMON PHILOSOPHICAL POSITION

The common position of all the branches of this school is that the noetic, insofar as it is not divided into an objective and subjective determinant factor, is a non-referential, self-luminous event existing really in an absolute sense, while the notional-conceptual, the relative, and the ideally absolute are three absolutely specific constituent principles which define all entities of reality.

This philosophy, in brief, comprises the reality of the given, the method of acting, and the goal realized.

THE REALITY OF THE GIVEN

This comprises (a) 'types of persons' as the auspicious foundation [of philosophical-spiritual life], (b) five basic topics as the operational ground for philosophical looking, and (c) the two kinds of the non-existence of an ontological principle as the operational ground for meditative (self-) development.

(a) It is claimed that there are three types exemplary of the three spiritual courses, as well as an undecided type and a 'cut-off' type.

(b) The physical-material realm: Although external objects do not actually exist as inert things, there is an appearance of objects existing externally by virtue of the maturation of the experientially initiated potentialities of experience in the substratum [of all experiences], and the status of external objects is claimed to be like horses and elephants in dreams.

The mind: It comprises six sensory functions, an emotively-toned ego-consciousness, and a substratum—eight facets in all.

Of these the substratum is the basis of the experientially initiated potentialities of experience and becomes aware of the mere haecceity of an object. It forms a series of homogenous instants. It divides into a maturation and a germinal part, both of which constitute a mutual cause-effect relationship. It is essentially-existentially 'compromised,' but ethically neutral. It is attended by the five ever–present functions such as rapport and the rest.[30] Its objective reference, the world as a container and the sentient beings as the latter's content, is indistinct and taken broadly.

Therefore the seven [remaining] aspects of mind, together with their attendant functions, do not originate from their own series [of instants]; it is rather that a potentiality, by which a subsequent experience similar to the previous one is effected, pervades the substratum and originates with each instant of the substratum like the shadow of a jar. Since this forms the basis of the motivating power of Saṃsāra as well as the ethically positive, negative, and neutral aspects of all concrete reality, together with the cognition-groupings, it is called the substratum of the various experientially initiated potentialities of experience.

The Buddhahood of man, pure in itself, and the immanent metaphysical reality, is the real substratum because it is not apart from the qualities of Nirvāṇa, the uncreated, and [its] facticity.

In the philosophy under consideration 'substratum' is used

in the sense of the sum total of the experientially initiated potentialities of experience forming the basis of Saṃsāra.

The emotively-toned ego-consciousness takes the substratum as its self. Accompanied by nine features such as the belief in a self, it is present in every phase of mental life except the concentration on the noble path and the attainment of the cessation of phenomenal existence.

The six functional cognitions are the ones which are so well known.[31]

The mental events attending the mind: they are the fifty-one events discussed in a previous section.[32]

The twenty-three disjunct entities are merely second intentions and do not exist *substantialiter.*

In addition to the three [commonly accepted] absolutes the mentalists add three others so that they accept a total of six. The three others are (i) the unconditional suchness of the non-existence of [the two types of] an ontological principle, (ii) the stable cessation when in this suchness-absolute the entities of the world of sensuality do not arise, and (iii) the cessation of ideas and feelings when in this suchness-absolute the seven cognition factors do not arise. Five are classified according to what specifically is absent in the suchness-ultimate.

In addition to all these differentiating items they accept three absolutely specific constitutive principles: the *notional-conceptual* is that which apart from being a postulate has no specific characteristic of its own. It is everything that allows us to speak intelligibly about what appears in the duality of subject and object and about what we become involved with. The *relative* is that which comes into existence in dependence upon causes and conditions. It is the noetic as it manifests itself in various pure and impure appearances by virtue of various experientially initiated potentialities of experience. The *ideally absolute* is that which remains when the relative has been divested of everything fictional as the notional-conceptual. It is present as that which is by nature devoid of the two types of an ontological principle.

The notional-conceptual is twofold: (a) hypothetical, i.e., that which is objectively impossible but postulated by mind *ad hoc,* as, for instance, an ontological status for a self or for the entities other than the self, and (b) delusory, i.e., that which, though non-existent, appears before a mind, as, for instance, a double moon and the like. An illusion, a vision, and whatever can be named are all of this nature.

The relative is twofold: (a) an impure one in which a world-bound mind and its attendant functions are concerned with (ordinary) objects, and (b) a pure one in which a world-transcending mind with its attendant functions at its subsequent [aesthetic *post*-immediate] stage is concerned with the unfolding of the Buddha realms and so on.

The ideally absolute is twofold: (a) unchanging or the suchness of the objective situation and (b) incontrovertible or the primordial awareness of the owner of the objective situation.

In this system the physical-material, twenty-three mental events beginning with rapport, and suchness exist as substances, while twenty-nine mental events beginning with care, all disjunct entities, space, and the five [types of] cessation exist as labels. Moreover, the relative as partaking in authentic reality and the ideally absolute as authentic reality are claimed to be ultimately real, while the notional is relatively real. Therefore all the statements in the Sūtras to the effect that all the entities of reality have no nature of their own are made in view of the objects conceived of and postulated as [constituting] the (aesthetically) apprehendable object and the (aesthetically) apprehending subject; while of the three absolutely specific constituent principles the notional-conceptual has no essence whatsoever, the relative no self-originated essence, and the ideally absolute no particular-thing-essence; the quintessence of Buddhahood is claimed to be nothing other than this mentalism, because the noetic in its mere self-illuminingness is undeniable due to its being the source of Saṃsāra and Nirvāṇa.

(c) Meditative (self-) development means to make the individual mind enter the non-referential sphere which is free from the ontological principle of a self and from any ontological principle belonging to what is other than the self, i.e., the (aesthetically) apprehendable object and the (aesthetically) apprehending subject.

THE METHOD OF ACTING

The method of acting is to practice the six 'perfections' [33] for a period of three 'incalculable' aeons with reference to the countless beings who are a mere series of mind-instants which is conceived as 'sentient being.'

THE GOAL REALIZED

Goal attainment is an awareness incomprehensible [by a fiction-ridden mind]; it is due to a change in attitude, beautified by limitless Buddha-fields, Buddha-existences and Buddha-activities.

The critique of the above tenets:

While it will be readily admitted that external objects do not really exist, the existence of the noetic is not *eo ipso* guaranteed, because on the apparent level as expressed in propositions it equals existence, and in the presence of the ultimately real it equals nonexistence, due to its not being veridical.

A type is not something self-existent, because the noetic is not self-existent. There cannot be any 'cut-off' type because any person is capable of change by such conditions as intelligence and dullness and so on; because mind being naturally resplendent, its accidental blemishes can be removed; and because nothing is ever lost by resorting to the pure counter-agents.

The relative is not [independently] real since it has originated from conditions, and likewise the substratum, being a series of instants, is not a real solid stream and therefore has not the slightest essence, because its objective inference, its 'seeds,' and all its maturations are multiple.

In the same way the emotively toned ego-consciousness and the six sensory functions and all the cessations are mutually related and merely interdependent, and therefore are not found in any way as real [independent] entities.

Specific Subdivisions

Although there are two groups distinguished according to whether they claim *sensa* to be either coincident with what is assumed to be real (verdical) or delusive, in their assumption that whatever appears as an external object is the inner noetic itself, neither can be said to have understood the problem properly, and each merely propounds his private opinion, because they [both agree in saying] that consciousness is self-illumining and really existent.

SENSA ARE VERIDICAL

In this group the Brahmin Śankarānanda and others claim that what appears as the (aesthetically) apprehendable part [in the cognitive process] is the mere facticity of the noetic in its act of (aesthetically) apprehending, and since [the noetic] is illuming and cognitive, [object-cognition] is like the experience of pleasure and pain.

There are three kinds of interpretation offered by this group: (a) the separateness of the noetic and the sensa, (b) an equal number of sensa [and (aesthetic) apprehensions], and (c) the non-duality of the multiple.

(a) While the appearance of such genuine objects of knowledge, such as mountains and so on, may be noetic, that which appears as the (aesthetically) apprehendable part and that which appears as the (aesthetically) apprehending part of the noetic are different in the same way as are the white and the yellow in a boiled egg. Since it is believed that the appearance of blue and the perception of this appearance of blue are veridical as two aspects in a straightforward way, those who hold this view are also referred to as 'the two halves of an egg.'

(b) Just as one can account for a large number of *sensa*, so one can also account for a large number of (aesthetic) apprehensions. It is therefore claimed that two (or more) sensa cannot appear in a single apprehending noetic because the five fingers as five apprehensions are veridical, but not as one apprehension.

(c) It is claimed that although many appearances such as blue and yellow appear in a single noetic [moment] the noetic in being one is veridical.

The problem in this line of thought is that when one determines the external object as the noetic by the [latter's] characteristics of illumination and cognition, the [predication of] 'cognizable particular existent' and 'being merely cognizable' equally applies when it is assumed that there are external objects. That the object *is* the illuminating and cognizing noetic is not established by asserting *as* fact what *has* to be established as fact. Even if one asserts that indeed it is the noetic which is illumining and cognizing, by pointing out that [the assumption of a] 'relation' in the case of the simultaneity of the cognizable object and the cognizing act [by the subject], and [the assumption of] 'similarity' in the case of the non-simultaneity of the cognizable object and the cognizing act [by the subject] are both untenable, then it still has not been established that the apparent object is identical with the noetic, which is claimed to be coinciding with what is assumed to be real, even if [by this procedure] the existence of external objects should have been proved to be delusive. The following may serve as an illustration: even if it is established that the reflection of the face in the mirror is not the face, it still is not the mirror.

Moreover, (a) in the case of those who hold 'the two halves of an egg' theory, it has to be noted that if the existence of an external object is delusive, it follows that the noetic, being one with it, also must be delusive, or, if it is veridical, it must be found as an object just as it appears. If then there exists a noetic appearing as an external object, but different from the inner (aesthetically) apprehending noetic, several consequences follow, all of them militating against [this claim]: consciousness must be objectively found outside the body [which it animates]; colours and so on belong literally to the mind; mountains and so on must be cognitive of us, and just as there are many different appearances at one and the same time so also many minds must be present in one individual. This is so because if consciousness is veridical each appearance of an object is a noetic.

(b) In the case of those who believe in 'an equal number of the (aesthetically) apprehendable and the (aesthetically) apprehending [events]', the following has to be noted: the concrete appearance [of something] which is [said] to be at one and the same time seen as something multicoloured would break down, because each apprehension would be different [from the other] and as such veridical. In the same way as there is the idea of the being of many people, because taken in itself no one being is something else, so also something multiple can appear instantaneously in the noetic, because the noetic is not really existing as a multiple of different things, even if it is not one when there is the appearance of something multiple.

(c) In the case of those who assert the non-duality of the multiple, it has to be pointed out that if one designates as one that which appears as many, the designation of the five colours and so on as many breaks down, because there is no other means of asserting a difference than this very appearance as the many. Therefore, even if it is appropriate to speak of merely one perception in connection with the sensing of something multi-coloured, yet it is not really one because it is applied to what is the many.

For this reason there are other fallacies involved if, apart from making propositions about what appears, appearance is claimed to be something. [On such reasoning] a Buddha and an ordinary sentient being would be one and the same because a sentient being appears as a Buddha and, if something appearing as something else is really this other thing, everything then would be everything else, so that a blazing fire would be real water.

Therefore, if the problem is thoroughly investigated, it is important to realize that precisely because of the fact that both the object and the noetic are not veridical, the object and the noetic may appear in various ways as subject and object, but do not so exist really.

SENSA ARE DELUSIVE

The thesis that sensa are delusive is held by the teacher Dharmottara and others. It is claimed that what appears as an external object is neither an external object nor the noetic, but merely a hallucination just like hairs in the air, due to the power of un-knowing, and that the noetic is devoid of sensa or observable qualities, like a bright crystal.

(a) Those who hold that the noetic is sullied, claim that, as long as there is the operation of mind, consciousness exists really in an ultimate sense as eight group-patterns, and since even on the Buddha-level there is the distinct appearance of the world and the beings in it, sensa (observable qualities) are not contradictory, although they do not exist really.

(b) Those who accept an immaculate nature of the mind, the 'purists,' claim that, as long as there is the working of the mind, the noetic with its even incidental group-patterns is relatively real, and that the substratum-awareness in its ultimate nature called the 'genuine noetic' is ultimately real because this substratum neither increases nor decreases and has no (aesthetic) apprehensions unsuited [to its nature]. It is further claimed that if there does not appear anything else but mind [itself] and this mind is felt as being free from all sensa and as devoid of any thought-constructions, because on the Buddha-level the experientially initiated potentialities of experience have ceased, just as the dream-images have stopped when one wakes up, then the presence [of this mind] as pure sensation (mere self-awareness) and self-luminousness is the Dharmakāya. What appears out of its sustaining power as the omniscience concerning the world and the beings therein, on the part of those to be led, although not existing as some particular existent, and as the proclamation of the Dharma and the enactment of the Buddha acts, is the Rūpakāya.[34]

While their claim that whatever appears as an external object is unreal may be endorsed, their statement that consciousness is real is inadmissible. Although on the side of error[35] there is the appearance of the noetic as the owner of the objective situation, as there also is appearance of an objective situation, neither the noetic as owner nor what is owned by it is found if investigated, nor is there in the last analysis any non-referential awareness found. If then the noetic is [said] to exist because it is felt, by the same argument the objective situation [should be said to] exist.

Mind and mental events, constituting the realm of the relative, are nowhere found when one searches for them, any more than the notional is found, so also the substratum does not exist, just as one does not find the incidental seven group-patterns when one investigates them.

CHAPTER FIVE

THE MĀDHYAMIKAS

As THE ANALYSIS of the preceding philosophical trends has shown, at the centre of each system there lay a certain intuition and imaginative picture from which the philosopher started and to which he constantly returned. Thus, at the centre of the Vaibhāṣikas' and Sautrāntikas' systems lies the picture of reality as a vast assemblage of substances of variable duration, entering into various combinations which constitute our phenomenal world. Similarly the Yogācārins envisaged reality as the operation of *a* or *the* mind. Because of the misleading way in which the main contentions concerning 'material' and 'mental' substances were commonly formulated, it is tempting to see in Buddhist philosophy something like materialism and idealism comparable with traditional Western philosophies. The point to note is that none of the Buddhist philosophies conceived of matter or mind as names either of something palpable and familiar, or of a remote kind of stuff which is not accessible to immediate experience. What these philosophers actually wanted to say was that things had to be taken in a certain way if we were to make sense of them. None of them ever claimed to be able to reveal truths about a world which lay beyond the reach of the senses or experience. The Vaibhāṣikas at the one end of the philosophical spectrum and the Yogācārins at the other, therefore, were not so much expounding an account of what there is, as offering a thesis about the proper way to take things. The key proposition of these two, apparently so divergent, lines of thought might be put as follows: it is out of the question that there should be anything that cannot be satisfactorily explained in substantival terms, regardless of whether these terms imply materiality or mentality. Such a proposition is not a factual thesis of any sort. It is merely the claim to be able to get into perspective, or to understand, things and events with which everyone either is or could be familiar, and it is also the desire to urge upon us a point of view which maintains that it alone has the answer.

Another point to note is that the above systems attempted to be both descriptive and explanatory; they professed to cover both *what* there is and *why* it takes the form it does. It is here that the confusion between (supposed) facts and their interpretation entered. The metaphysical principles of materiality on the one hand, and of mentality on the other, tended to be mistaken for basic premises on which other assertions were to be based. It was not clearly realized that no amount of scrutiny of the evidence can establish a principle of such unrestricted generality. It was also not seen that the decisive factor in interpretative, metaphysical thinking is not the premises the philosopher starts from, but the principles of interpretation he brings to bear. Each of us confronts the same world, but each differs from the other in his way of taking it. The basic judgments of a metaphysical thinker derive from some particular type of experience, e.g., intellectual, aesthetic, or moral, which seems to provide a clue towards developing a philosophical attitude or 'world perspective.' The impetus to the development of a particular interpretaion comes from an experience which gives rise to a sense of importance which, in turn, imposes a perspective and thereby rises above the level of merely cataloguing items of reality. It was an interest in the nature of metaphysical thought that gave rise to the Mādhyamika philosophies.

The Svātantrikas

There are two major divisions within the Mādhyamika movement: the Prāsangikas and the Svātantrikas. The former may be said to represent a more radical type of metaphysician, the latter a more moderate one. Inasmuch as in metaphysical thinking the premises from which a philosopher starts are less decisive than the way in which he interprets things, it is only natural that, as we can see in the case of the

Svātantrikas who accept the Sautrāntika premises and the Svātantrikas who accept those of the Yogācārins, the Svātantrikas divide into Sautrāntika-Mādhyamika-Svātantrikas and Yogācāra-Mādhyamika-Svātantrikas. Although metaphysics is neither deductive nor inductive, metaphysical thinkers make constant use of deductive inference. It was by drawing attention to the constitutive conditions of valid inference which they considered absolute or categorical, i.e., not to be deduced from further truths nor to be established empirically even if experience suggests them, that they styled themselves Svātantrikas ('independents').

What the Mādhyamika-Svātantrikas wanted to emphasize was that all human experience, inasmuch as it is experience and not mere propositions or the like, is an insight into reality, an awareness of coherence which is not its own authentication of reality, but reality itself. Insofar as it is reality, it is not a 'presentation,' which in the Mādhyamikas' terminology is 'error' in the special sense of 'error' itself being quite real. This is evident from their interpretation of the 'two truths,' which basically is a development of inherent implications of the two truths. The distinction into 'higher' (absolute) and 'lower' (conventional) means that 'truth' is a matter of criticism. That is to say, truth (absolute) is the experience of a satisfied critical imagination, while truth (conventional) is the lack of this satisfied imagination manifesting itself in various degrees. At what we may call the lowest level we have that which is described as an illusion as, for instance, the water in a mirage. By this it is meant that we do not see the reflection of the sky on the pavement of a highway across a stratum of hot air as the sky's reflection but as a pool of water, and therefore do not see it as we *ought* to see it. A little further critical investigation should make it clear that this view is itself an illusion. It assumes naively that the water in a river is the real or standard water and, at the same time, this view fails to realize that in a world where perceptions occur under varied and varying conditions, a standardized way of seeing things is nothing but a useful convention.

Still there is a conceivably higher stage of awareness in

which this 'ought' proves itself to be doubtful. If a man were under all circumstances immediately conscious of the medium of vision and of its effect upon the image of the object, he would immediately be able to see the precise effect of substituting any other medium. He would be like a skilled musician who can play in one key what is written in another without transcribing the score (of what there is into what there ought to be). For him one key is as good as another, just as for a perceptive person one medium is as good as another. The only thing he must not do is mixing the keys or the media. The real difficulty then would be in conveying experience. Without experience what the Mādhyamikas have to say remains a mere form of words, a series of pictures. Therefore a critique of the Mādhyamika-Svātantrikas' views often does not penetrate to the core, which is unassailable because as experience it is reality itself; the critique falls short because it merely deals with the periphery, the use of picture-language. In their attempt to convey their experience the Svātantrikas had to use pictures which seem to 'represent' their object necessarily and inevitably, but without the activity of imagination (which is an image-making power) a picture is not a picture and 'represents' nothing. To say that the universe is of an apparitional nature is to use picture-language, but such a use does not validate the naive assumption that pictures are somehow natural conveyors of knowledge. The fact that the 'presentation' of the experience is liable to be distorted by what we have termed the mixing of keys and media, and that 'presentation' becomes open to critique which, like the presentation it attacks, is not the experience, is therefore subject to further critique.

In continuing and developing the metaphysical trend in Buddhist philosophy, the Mādhyamikas as a whole realized that it is impossible to have a metaphysics which asks whether ideas expressed in such a system are true 'of reality,' because there is no relation between this system of thought and a reality outside it. Consequently they insisted on coherence and self-consistency, rather than on correspondence, especially since we can only be aware of anything to the extent that we know it through the interpretative forms of our experience. This realization prompted them to throw over the 'thing'-concept because, as a matter of fact, we have no warrant for supposing any relation of representation or likeness between the interpretative and symbolic forms of thought and things-in-themselves, which by definition fall outside experience. Still, the Mādhyamika-Svātantrikas preserved the notion of 'things,' although they, too, did not assume any view as to the intrinsic nature of a 'thing' which might be anything. They needed this concept of 'things' as a testimony to the conviction that as living persons they were concerned with something besides a mere nexus of logical relations. They were concerned with understanding how conceptual interpretations arise out of a background of 'responsive' activities. Such 'things' by their impingement on us produce certain types of responsive activities. We may say that our perceptual experience is a kind of 'projection' of events in our environmental world (external as well as internal), preserving, in spite of its distortion, some sort of variation concomitant with its differential conditions in the environment. Here we touch upon the central problem of Buddhism, that of self-development without a prejudged nature of the self. The vision of the Mādhyamika-Svātantika does not provide a premise on which to build; it rather suggests an interpretative scheme in which 'things' are concepts drawn by analogy from interpretations of experience. 'Things' are therefore hypotheses symbolizing a possible way in which events may be connected and are drawn from types of relations which are intelligible due to their having occurred in familiar settings. In the process of self-development I become aware not of objects ('things') but projects, of myself as I am going to be, and I recognize the projecting act as my own. In uncritical being, that is, where no self-development is attempted, I am always involved in my projects which are never without alternatives, or, as the texts declare, there is always something that directly or indirectly arouses affective states which have a disrupting effect upon the individual. But to state the matter so is already a step in the direction of detachment and non-involvement, of an unrestricted perspective and authentic being, that is, satisfied critical imagination. The technique is first to bring one's biased and hence distorted project clearly before one's eyes or, in psychological terms, to tackle the disturbing affect-situation and in the cognition of this situation for what it is, to be freed from it. In practise this often may mean to resort to the antidote of the affect-situation, as when a person overcomes his feeling of hatred by one of love. But the antidote is itself an indirect affect-situation, hence the distinction between the immediately present affect-situation and its 'purification,' both of which have to be depleted of their power if ever authentic being is to be realized. Over and above, in being aware of my projects, I am also aware of myself projecting, that is, I can distinguish between my projects and myself conceiving and judging them. These acts can be manifested clearly and sharply by so-called second intentions, and no range of being is closed to such apprehension. It is when that which divides man at the very root of his being has lost its power to do so by an awareness that any object or 'project' (*gzung*) must involve a subject and 'acts of projection' (*'dzin*) of some kind ('conceptualizing' and 'reifying') that the unrestricted perspective or enlightenment is realized. In this process perception plays an important role, and the Svātantrikas divided ordinary perception as it operates in the conventional setting of an individual's world into two kinds. The more common one involves the beliefs we have about the common-sense objects and, for this reason, is a means to a metaperceptual end. It is harnessed to these metaperceptual ends and reduced to an extremely economical recording of qualities and events significant for these specific ends. The other is not concerned with such metaperceptual ends and is essentially a means to the apprehension of the full intrinsic perceptual being and value of the object freed from specific practical connections and considerations. It may be called aesthetic perception whose main aim is the elaboration of intrinsic perception, which then may turn into 'absolute' perception in which the critical examination has been satisfied, as pointed out above.

Intrinsic or aesthetic perception is important for self-development, as it fosters appreciation as against possessiveness and exploitation. Thereby it extends the value range and provides a vision of human purpose in an ideal embodiment that can serve as a guide for both personal and group life. Such an ideal embodiment is The Buddha, whether he is envisaged as the Absolute, that is, an absolute value, or as a means to change things and persons into the intrinsically interesting and intrinsically fine and noble, or whether a human being is seen as the embodiment of Buddhahood and thereby is given dignity. Aesthetic perception has both a spiritual and cultural value.

Undoubtedly, the greatest Buddhist thinkers in India belonged to the Svātantrika group within the Mādhyamika movement. This is clearly brought out both by *The Jewel Garland* and *The Summary*. By linking the Svātantrika philosophers with the various trends in philosophical thought and thus revealing the ever growing richness of Buddhist philosophy, these two authors clarify many problems that beset a student of Buddhist philosophy. Usually passed over in silence or dismissed with a few non-committal words because the original works are either lost in their Sanskrit version or merely preserved in fragments, the Svātantrika philosophy is here dealt with as a whole and, in the case of *The Summary*, critically assessed.

FROM

THE JEWEL GARLAND

GRUB-PA'I MTHA'I RNAM-PAR BZHAG-PA RIN-PO-CHE'I PHRENG-BA

foll. 12a

IN THE PRESENTATION of the philosophical faith of the Mādhyamikas who disclaim the existence of anything as such,[1] there are four sections: intrinsic characteristics, meaning of the name (Mādhyamika), divisions, and explanation of each division.

A Mādhyamika is a follower of the insiders' philosophical faith and claims that not so much as an atom of anything really exists.

The Mādhyamika derives his name from the fact that he avoids the extremes of eternalism and nihilism. He is also called a person who rejects any form of ontology, because he declares that of the entities of reality not one can be said to have an essence that is veridical (*bden-grub*).

The Mādhyamikas divide into Svātantrikas and Prāsangikas. The Svātantrika line of thought will be discussed here; (the Prāsangika system, on page 141, following the discussion of the Prāsangikas in the text).

CHARACTERISTICS

A Svātantrika is one who accepts by way of propositions that things exist by virtue of a constitutive principle through which they are what they are.

THE NAME

He is called a Mādhyamika-Svātantrika because he refutes

the thesis that things exist in truth by resorting to a logically appropriate form which satisfies three self-evident principles.[2]

Schools

There are two schools: Yogācāra-Mādhyamika-Svātantrikas and Sautrāntika-Mādhyamika-Svātantrikas.

The former do not recognize external objects, only a self-validating (non-referential) awareness. A representative of this school is, for instance, Śāntarakṣita.

The latter do not recognize a self-validating (non-referential) awareness, but accept external objects as existing by virtue of a constitutive principle through which they are what they are. A representative of this line of thought is, for instance, Bhāvaviveka.

A further explanation of these school-names is that the Yogācāra (Mādhyamika-Svātantrikas) are similar to the mentalists in what they define as the ground, and that the Sautrāntika (Mādhyamika-Svātantrikas) are similar to the Sautrāntikas in accepting that external objects are built up of atoms.

The Yogācāras are twofold inasmuch as they are similar either to those who claim sensa to be veridical or to those who consider them delusive. The former are represented by Śāntarakṣita, Kamalaśīla and Ārya-Vimuktasena; the latter by the teacher Haribhadra, Jetari, and Lavapa. Among the latter Jetari is similar to those who consider sensa to be delusive and mentality maculate, and Lavapa to those who consider the former delusive and the latter immaculate.

Contents of the Philosophical Faith of the Yogācāra–Mādhyamika-Svātantrikas

THE GROUND

The ground is twofold: object(ive situation) and owner of the object(ive situation).

The Objective Situation. The Yogācāras claim that the

given entails existence by virtue of a constitutive principle through which it is what it is, because one will find, if only one seeks, that which has been signified as this or that. Hence, to 'exist by virtue of being-itself,' 'by virtue of a constitutive principle through which something is what it is,' 'by virtue of its presence,' and 'being self-evident' are synonymous.

The knowable is further divided into the ultimately and the conventionally real. That which is understood in a manner in which all duality has been subsided, through the valid cognitive means of immediate apprehension in all its immediacy, has the mark of the ultimately real. That which is understood in a dual manner by the same valid cognitive means of immediate apprehension, has the mark of the conventionally real. An example of the former is the perception of jug apart from the belief that it really exists. The latter is the (common) awareness of a jug.[3]

The ultimately real is further divided into sixteen types of nothingness which can be subsumed under four headings.[4]

The conventionally real is divided into the commonly accepted as conventionally real and the mistakenly accepted as conventionally real. Ordinary water is an example of the former. The water in a mirage is an example of the latter.

According to this line of thought the noetic entails the status of being conventionally real as commonly accepted.

The Owner of the Objective Situation. In taking the coordinating and abstractive processes as the ground for what is designated by the term 'self,' and in recognizing six awarenesses while rejecting a substratum-awareness and an affectively toned mind, both schools of the Svātantrikas are alike.

Immediate apprehension and genuine and immediate inference are valid cognitive means. Immediate apprehension is fourfold: sensory, abstractive, non-referential and self-validating, and mystic. The latter two types, the Yogācāras claim, entail non-errant cognition.

As they do not accept that objects exist externally, a patch of blue and the immediate awareness of it are of the same stuff.

THE PATH

The Path is dealt with under three heads: the objective pole of its intentional structure, that which has to be eliminated by the path, and the path as being-the-path.

The Objective Pole. This is the non-existence of a self as an eternal, single, and sovereign principle, the coarse aspect of the non-existence of any absolute principle; the non-existence of valid perception and the perceived content as being of different materials, the coarse aspect of the postulate of an absolute principle concerning the entities of realities other than the self; and the non-existence of things existing in truth, the subtle aspect.

Traversing the Path. Belief in the absolute status of the self is for them wishfulness and emotivity, and belief in the absolute status of the entities of reality other than the self is intellectual fog. The latter is of two kinds: *coarse,* insofar as it is the belief that the objective and the subjective are of different material; and *subtle,* insofar as it is the belief that the psychophysical constituents and other entities of reality exist in truth.

Path as Being-Itself. They accept fifteen paths, five for each spiritual pursuit.[5] In particular, they declare that a Pratyekabuddha's obstacle-removing path and free progress must be of the nature of perception and of the perceived content as not constituting different materials.

THE GOAL

Since a Pratyekabuddha is primarily concerned with the elimination of the coarse intellectual impediment, the distinction into eight types of those who have entered and are firmly established on a spiritual level is not accepted for his class, although it is recognized to hold good for the Śrāvakas.

Confirmed Śrāvakas are primarily concerned with cultivating the view which realizes that there is no absolute status of a self. Then, finally, by means of a diamond-like concentration which is their path of attending to the seen, they attain the goal of a Śrāvakas saint, simultaneously with the complete elimination of wishfulness and emotivity.

Confirmed Pratyekabuddhas are mainly concerned with cultivating the view which realizes that the objective and subjective are not of different material; and finally by means of a diamond-like concentration, which is their path of attending to the seen, they reach the goal of a Pratyekabuddha saint, simultaneously with the complete elimination of all wishfulness and emotivity as well as with that of the coarse intellectual impediment.

The Hīnayāna Nirvāṇa is twofold: residual and non-residual. The former is one in which something of the misery conditioned by former actions and affective states is still present. The latter is a state which is free from such misery.

Being a Śrāvaka or a Pratyekabuddha saint entails setting out on the Mahāyāna path, because it is claimed that finality is found only on one course. Therefore, according to this line of thought, there are higher and lower goals, owing to differences in what is to be rejected and attained by Pratyekabuddhas and Śrāvakas.

Confirmed Mahāyānists develop an enlightened attitude. By means of the 'teaching continuity concentration,' the phase of the Great Preparatory Path, they plainly hear the instructions from the manifestation of the most sublime reality.[6] When they take the message of these instructions to heart and an attention-born discriminating-appreciating awareness relating to nothingness is first born in them, they are transported to the path linking them with the vision of truth. With the onset of the feeling of warmth they diminish the power of what is believed to be an object and to arouse affective states directly, keeping clearly before their eyes the affect-arousing nature which they can get rid of by seeing its true nature. When this feeling of warmth reaches its peak-value they diminish the power of what is believed to be an object and believed to counteract the arousal of affective states, keeping clearly before their eyes the affect-countering nature which also they have to get rid of by seeing its true nature. When a state of patient acceptance has been reached they diminish the power of the subjective, the concretizing acts and judgments. And when the climax of this process is reached they diminish the power of the subjective consisting in conceptualizing acts and judgments, keeping clearly before their eyes these powers that they can get rid of by seeing their true nature. These four phases of warmth, peak-value, patient acceptance, and climax are respectively known as 'light-attainment concentration,' 'light-effulgence concentration,' 'concentration through which suchness is partly entered' and 'obstacle-removing concentration.' At the very end of the last phase when the obstacle-removing aspect of the path of seeing has been entered, the notional wishfulness and emotivity, as well as the potentialities of the one hundred and eight types of intellectual impediments that can be got rid of by attending to the truth seen, are eliminated one after the other. Finally, having simultaneously eliminated the coexistent wishfulness and intellectual impediment by pursuing the continuous obstacle-removing path, they realize the goal of being certain to attain supreme enlightenment the very next moment.

While they declared that 'Mahāyāna Nirvāṇa' and 'Nirvāṇa about which nothing can be predicated' mean the same and that the Buddhahood-pattern is fourfold, Ārya-Vimuktasena and Haribhadra disagreed about the manifestation of these four patterns.[7]

The Buddha-word is for them suggestive and explicit. Those Sūtras, which mainly deal with the exposition of the conventionally real, are suggestive, while those that mainly deal with the elucidation of the ultimately real are explicit. The first division of the Buddha's teaching, as detailed in the *Dgongs-'grel,* is suggestive; the middle and last ones are both suggestive and explicit.

Contents of the Philosophical Faith of the Sautrāntika-Mādhyamika-Svātantrikas

The Ground

Except for the fact that they accept external objects but do not recognize a self-validating non-referential awareness, their conception of what is described as the ground is on the whole the same as that of the previous philosophers.

THE PATH

The peculiar features here are that, as far as confirmed Śrāvakas and Pratyekabuddhas are concerned, they disclaim an intuitive understanding of the fact that the entities of reality have no absolute status and, since they also do not accept an awareness which understands that the subjective and objective are not of different material, they do not recognize the conceptualizing process which believes in external objects as the intellectual fog.

THE GOAL

Since for both Śrāvakas and Pratyekabuddhas there is no differentiation into the subtler and coarser aspects of what has to be eliminated, namely, wishfulness and emotivity, and of what has to be attained, the understanding of the non-existence of a self as an ultimate principle, the division into those who have entered and those who are firmly established on a certain spiritual level holds for both.

Confirmed Mahāyānists eliminate wishfulness and intellectual impediments successively and, as is stated in the *Madhyamakahṛdayavṛtti Tarkajvālā,* it is with the attainment of the eighth spiritual level that wishfulness and emotivity are completely eliminated.

However, unlike the Prāsangikas, they do not admit that unless wishfulness and emotivity have been abolished the elimination of the intellectual fog cannot be attempted.

Apart from these minor differences, their conception of the ground, the path, and the goal is similar to that of the Yogācāra-Mādhyamika-Svātantrikas.

To sum up:

May the learned appreciate this sober
Dissertation on the differences
Of the Svātantrikas' philosophy which recognizes
Things to be what-they-are, though not so to exist in truth.

FROM

THE SUMMARY OF PHILOSOPHICAL SYSTEMS

YID-BZHIN-MDZOD-KYI GRUB-MTHA' BSDUS-PA

foll. 22b sq.

THE MĀDHYAMIKA-SVĀTANTRIKAS, by assigning all entities of reality to two truths, demolish all arguments such as that these entities can be established as having true existence in themselves but no existence as assumed by common sense. Nevertheless, in spite of their profound analysis of appearance as encountered by common sense, those who represent the earlier and the later philosophies, deviate from the calm of Reality, because they give too much credit to the maze of their judgments.

THE EARLIER SVĀTANTRIKAS

The earlier Svātantrikas are (a) those who hold everything to be an apparition, and (b) those who hold appearance and nothingness to be separate entities.

(a) The former are represented by the teacher Samudramegha and others. They declare that all entities participate in the two truths by having no essence, only an apparitional nature. Since the appearance of the common-sense world is unreal and like an apparition, and since the ultimate, though nothing as such, does not cease appearing as the interdependence [of causes and conditions constituting our common-sense world], it is by the accumulation of the two requisites, which are like an apparition, that the goal or enlightenment, which is like an apparition, is attained; and while this apparitional [reality] as such forever remains what it is, it is through an [equally] apparitional activity that care is taken of the needs of the apparition-like sentient beings. Therefore, through the interrelation of causes and conditions, all appearance is like an apparition, that is to say, deviant appearance is an apparition, and translucently incessant appearance, in view of the fact that the proliferation into an apparent object before an error-free awareness has stopped, is an apparition. In brief, the whole of the ground, the path and the goal is like an apparition.

The critique is that since they do not pass beyond the maze of their postulates which make the ultimate originate and fade like an apparition and imply that an apparition resists any further attempt to analyse it, their conception cannot be the Buddha's ultimate meaning.

(b) Those who hold appearance and nothingness to be separate entities are represented by the teacher Śrīgupta and others. Because ultimately nothing whatsoever is found, to speak of an illusion has no foundation. Jars and other objects of knowledge in the conventional way are not [such a] nothingness, because they appear to be efficacious and are true enough. In the ultimate analysis they are nothing because nothing whatsoever is found. Therefore the ultimate resists any further analysis, the conventional does not, and hence the thing and its predicates do not, coincide; otherwise the ultimate would be as transitory as the conventional, and, in the same way that the ultimate does not originate and come to an end, the conventional would not. Therefore, appearance or the conventional as something qualified and nothingness or the ultimate as something in itself are found only in relation to each other.

In dividing the conventional into erroneous and reliable, the earlier Svātantrikas are like the later ones.

The critique: A nothingness which is not an appearance cannot partake of the two truths, because if there is nothing to appear before someone there is no observable quality at all, and even the conventional would become non-existent like the horn of a hare. One also does not find appearance apart from nothingness, because when one examines whatever appears it is not found [as an entity]. If the ultimate is not something that can be investigated by becoming an appearance, it cannot be something that can be understood. If it can be investigated and expressed in words, it must appear with observable qualities. If not, it cannot be comprehended. The ineffable is not similar to it, because it transcends the extremes of either appearance or nothingness.

If [this postulated] nothingness is to be envisaged apart from appearance, something impossible is demanded. The meditation on a nothingness different from appearance is not the path, because it is unable to abolish the obscurations, and also cannot serve as the agent that abolishes them. When one gets angry at an enemy, it is of no use to know that the sky is nothing. The so-called 'nothingness' is not found anywhere, because whatever becomes an object before the mind in space and time has observable qualities.

The Later Svātantrikas

The later Svātantrikas are represented by Jñānagarbha, Śāntarakṣita, Kamalaśīla, and others.

Although the ultimate and ever-present reality is beyond all judgments, because the ultimate conceived of as apparition and as mere nothing does not withstand a critical investigation, it is assumed that the things as they incidentally appear to common-sense have their essence and are incontestible, but when critically investigated they do not in the least exist in truth, hence their nothingness and nominal ultimacy are on the same level. Accepting this thesis they establish their own theory and refute others by means of syllogisms [whose elements] they consider to be constituted by themselves. Also accepting origination from something other, as was done by the previous systems, they distinguish between a true conventional which is efficacious, as for instance the moon in the sky, and an illusory conventional which is not so efficacious, as for instance two moons. Further, the illusory conventional exists until the pure levels of spirituality have been reached. In the post-concentrative state of the spiritually advanced, one speaks of a 'pure world.' Knowing the two truths not to be contradictory, they accumulate the two prerequisites and realize the two Kāyas.[8]

The critique: Ultimately the true conventional as well as the illusory conventional are of the same level, both owing their origin to causes and conditions. If one examines the appearance as an object, the statement that, because of its similarity with the non-existing, the object exists by its essence, is merely to use a label in the joy of making judgments. On closer inspection nothing of this sort is found. Origination from something else is similar to origination from itself, because both turn out to be impossible when properly investigated. If they say there is an origination from something else dissimilar to this, though found in common sense, the answer is that when one examines whether such a common-sense object as the seed and the sprout originate, or do not originate, by themselves or from others, one cannot find anything of this sort, because apart from it one cannot postulate an origination from something else ultimate.

Then how does a sprout come from the seed in common-sense conception? The appearance of a sprout as effect coming from the seed as the cause in an infallible progression must be accepted as origination by relations, but the four alternatives need not be accepted.[9]

Inasmuch as these alternatives need not be accepted, the mere appearance of thing originating in relation [to causes and conditions] has no essence whatsoever even in common sense, and inasmuch as all such judgments as self-origination, origination by something else, origination and non-origination are all erroneous, there is no need to accept any of them.

Further, when one examines whatever appears, it is never found as such, and likewise the ultimate also is not found, because if there is no appearance, there is also no nothingness. Both being identical in the sense of not being found apart from being labels, the division into two truths exists only mentally, and not in actuality. Inasmuch as even the most subtle analysis of appearance, postulated by the demands of a philosophical thesis, becomes the cause of an irreversible subtle judgment, one must enter the 'initially pure,' the great middle where all appearance is pure from the beginning because the fallacies of reason have never entered the fact of self-sameness.

The Prāsangikas

While all the philosophical movements discussed so far tried to 'explain' reality, rather than merely to interpret it, and in this attempt at explanation were forced to set up various hypotheses, the Prāsangikas abandoned the temptation to explain and were pre-eminently concerned with pointing out the inherent shakiness of every postulate. Their main target was the notion of 'existence' with its implicit assumption of the thingness of what is claimed to exist. 'Things,' as we have seen, are hypotheses symbolizing possible ways in which events may be connected, but precisely because of their being hypotheses there is no need to introduce a distinction between veridical and delusive aspects which are but concretizations into things of what at best are possibilities. This does not mean that there is no difference between veridical and delusive situations. The difference is purely pragmatic, not existential. Similarly, there is no need to distinguish between the absolute and its conceptual presence. Such a distinction, far from being invalid, merely tends to reduce the absolute to a concrete entity which then would have to be 'explained' in one way or another. Such an explanation would involve the acceptance of a thesis as a basic premise on which other assertions can be based. It is obvious from this critique of the other schools that for the Prāsangikas philosophy was a movement and that they attempted to keep the philosophical spirit alive. The high praise that traditionally has been bestowed on the Prāsangikas is due to their radical objection against any kind of reductionism. In order to point out the fallaciousness of any determinate thesis, they developed a formidable technique of argumentation which was designed to pull the rug from under the opponent's feet.

The significance of the Prāsangikas as critics and opponents of the reductionist trend in philosophizing lasted until they themselves succumbed to the temptation of accepting certain premises. It is well nigh impossible to say when this happened. But it did happen, as we can learn from rGyal-tshab's statement that the Prāsangikas accepted and rejected four theses respectively. "Concerning the ground they [the Prāsangikas] do not accept, even propositionally, (1) the idea of a substratum and (2) the idea of a thing-as-such, but recognize (i) external objects; concerning the path they do not accept (3) categorical conditions and (4) self-validating non-referential cognitions, in the intuitive perception of the absolute, but recognize (ii) the disposal of the two kinds of obscuration [emotional and intellectual] and (iii) the apprehension by both Śrāvakas and Pratyekabuddhas of the non-essence character of what there is; and concerning the goal they recognize that (iv) the Buddhas have an awareness of reality as it is manifested." [10]

Although the Prāsangikas are claimed to represent the climax of Buddhist philosophy, this does not mean that the development of Buddhist philosophy has come to an end. On the contrary, the movement from the Vaibhāṣikas to the Prāsangikas is merely the preparatory step from 'speculative philosophy' to 'philosophy lived individually.' This step is possible because Buddhist philosophy has never been purely speculative. The subsequent development is due to a shift in emphasis.

While the Prāsangikas are traditionally held to represent the climax of Buddhist philosophy. Mi-pham 'Jam-dbyangs rnam-rgyal rgya-mtsho makes it abundantly clear that they merely represent the climax of Buddhist epistemology and that the next step in the philosophical quest is the one from epistemology to Being. Therefore he is the only one who deals with Tantrism in his *Summary,* while *The Jewel Garland* lets philosophy end here with epistemology.

FROM

THE JEWEL GARLAND

GRUB-PA'I MTHA'I RNAM-PAS BZHAG-PA RIN-PO-CHE'I PHRENZA-BA

foll. 14a ff.

THE ELUCIDATION of the Prāsangikas' philosophical faith comprises three sections: intrinsic characteristics, meaning of the name, and the contents.

CHARACTERISTICS

A Prāsangika is a person who absolutely denies the notion of an essence and who does not accept that things exist by virtue of a constitutive principle through which they are what they are, even in a nominal sense.

Representatives of this line of thought are Buddhapālita, Candrakīrti, and Śāntideva.

THE NAME

A Prāsangika is so called because he claims that a judgment of perception as regards what is under consideration comes about in a person merely by epistemic conditions.

CONTENTS

The contents are arranged according to the Ground, the Path, and the Goal.

THE GROUND

They claim that the given does not exist by virtue of a constitutive principle through which it is what it is, because in recognizing the given as entailing a being merely postulated by conceptuality, they refute by the word 'merely' existence by what-something-is. Thus, 'the given,' 'being an object' and 'being knowable' mean the same. This can be divided into (a) the manifest and the invisible and into (a) the two truths.

(a) That which can be understood by direct experience independent of an argument has the mark of the manifest. 'Immediately experienceable,' 'manifest,' 'sensory object' and 'not invisible' are different terms meaning the same thing. Examples are: form, sound, fragrance, flavour, and touch. That which can be understood dependently on a reason or argument has the mark of the non-manifest. 'Non-manifest,' 'not immediately experienceable' and 'inferential' are different terms meaning the same thing. Examples are such propositions as 'Sound is impermanent' and 'Sound has nothing to do with a pure Ego.'

In this line of thought 'manifest' and 'non-manifest' as well as 'the three factors in cognition' are mutually contradictory.[11]

(b) That which is obtained through the instrument of knowledge investigating the denotative-designative is this instrument turned towards itself and has the mark of the conventionally true, as, for instance, a jug. There is no distinction into the veridically conventionally true and the delusively conventionally true. For to be conventionally true means to be non-veridical and this must be delusive.

However, as far as common sense goes the distinction into a veridical and a delusive aspect of the conventionally true holds good, because in this context a coloured patch [as immediately apprehended] is veridical, while mirror-images are delusive. Yet the common-sense veridical does not entail existence as such, because coloured patches [and so on believed to] exist in truth are precisely this common-sense veridical.

That which is obtained through the instrument of knowledge thrusting into the ultimate is this instrument turned towards itself and has the mark of the ultimately true, as for instance a jug not existing as such by a constitutive principle. A likely distinction within the ultimately true is dealt with in the same way as in the preceding instance.

Further, the past, the future, and that which has been destroyed are considered as particular existents;[12] also, external objects are recognized because the subjective and objective are claimed to be different facts.

The owner of the objective situation is dealt with in the following way. Inasmuch as the mere index 'I' relating to either four or five psycho-somatic constituents as the contents of the indexing is the reason for the assumption of a self, this self entails the status of being a disjunct entity.

There are valid and invalid cognitive means. The former comprise immediate apprehension and genuine and immediate inference. The first of these is sensory, abstractive and intuitive. A self-validating non-referential awareness is not recognized. Sensory perception of sentient beings entails errant noeticness, while intuitive apprehension is both errant and non-errant. It is non-errant when it is of the nature of composure not arousing affective states, but as an ordinary being's intuitive apprehension of the subtle impermanence it is errant, and this is so because it is an ordinary being's noetic act.[13]

Recognition entails valid immediate apprehension because the second moment in the judgment that understands sound to be impermanent is the immediate validity turned concept, and the second moment of sensory perception is immediate validity not turned into a concept.

Judgments of perception are fourfold: existential, metaphorical, comparative, and doctrinal.[14]

Although judgments of perception are wrong as regards the nature of the content, this error does not contradict comprehension; the judgment that sound is impermanent is wrong as regards the nature of the impermanent sound [i.e., believing it to exist in truth], but it does comprehend what is meant by it.

Dichotomic noeticness entails its immediate self-manifestation because the act of conceiving sound to be permanent is its immediate self-manifestation; and the noetic entails its own projection because such fictitious entities as a hare's horns or a permanent sound are its own knowable projects.[15]

THE PATH

The objective pole of its intentional structure is the non-existence of a self as a self-sufficient substance, which is the coarse aspect of such non-existence, and the non-existence of a self existing in truth, which is its subtle aspect. The two subtle aspects of the idea of the non-existence of an absolute principle, the one of a self and the other of the entities of reality other than the self, are distinguished from each other by way of the referent and not by what is to be negated concerning them. This is because, in the case of an individual self, the negation of it as existing in truth is the subtle aspect of the non-existence of an individual self, and in the case of the psycho-somatic constituents and the other entities of reality apart from the self, the negation of them as existing in truth is the subtle aspect of the non-existence of these entities. Therefore, since the distinction between a coarse and subtle aspect does not apply to these two subtle forms of the non-existence of an ultimate principle, the one of an individual self and the other of the entities of reality other than the self, they consider this existential mode [of not existing in truth] as finality.

That Which Has to Be Eliminated by the Path. The subtle and coarse beliefs in a self, together with their latent potentialities as well as the three affective behaviour patterns [16] set up by these beliefs and their latent potentialities, are considered as wishfulness and emotivity, because the Prāsangikas declare that the belief in something existing in truth, and the error of the subject-object dichotomy due to this tendency, as well as the belief in the two truths as different facts, are intellectual fog.

The Path as Being-the-path. Each of the three courses has five paths. The ten levels of spirituality in Mahāyāna are like those detailed in the *Daśabhūmikasūtra.*

The three courses do not have different modes of discriminating-appreciating awareness, because it is held that being a saintly person entails the immediate apprehension and understanding of the non-existence of an absolute principle concerning the entities of reality.

REALIZING THE GOAL

The Realization of the Hīnayāna Goal. Confirmed Hīnayānists cultivate in a limited way the viewpoint of the non-existence of an absolute principle. Then, simultaneously with the elimination of the belief that truth exists as such, together with the latent potentiality of this belief, through a diamond-like meditative concentration, which is their path of attending to the truth seen, they realize their enlightenment.

While the Mādhyamika-Svātantrikas and those before them claimed that before attaining the non-residual Nirvāṇa one must have reached the residual one, in this [the Prāsangikas'] line of thought the non-residual Nirvāṇa must be realized before the residual one.[17]

The division into those who have entered and are firmly established on a spiritual level of Śrāvakas and Pratyekabuddhas is not recognized, because it is claimed that belonging to any of their eight types entails the status of being a saintly person.

The Realization of the Mahāyāna Goal of Enlightenment. Bodhisattvas cultivate the vision into which the postulate of an ultimate principle does not enter, in infinite ways and in an extensive manner. Without having eliminated wishfulness and emotivity they do not attempt to remove the intellectual fog. This starts from the eighth spiritual level. Bodhisattvas who have not previously travelled the lower paths eliminate wishfulness and emotivity on reaching the eighth level. Lastly, by the continual obstacle-removing path, simultaneously with the elimination of the intellectual fog, they come to the citadel of the four patterns of Buddhahood. According to them Nirvāṇa and the Truth of the End of all Misery entail the status of absolute truth.

From among the three discourses as stated in the *Dgongs-'grel,* the first and the last one are suggestive, because they do not teach nothingness directly; the middle discourse is explicit, because the *Prajñāpāramitāhṛdayasūtra* deals with it explicitly.

The most conspicuous character of a Prāsangika is that by means of relativistic arguments he rejects all outer and inner entities as existing by a constitutive principle through which they are what they are. Moreover, he can put forward his ideas straightforwardly without being forced to hypostatize such words (indices) as bondage and liberation, cause and effect, the knowable and the knowing and so on, inasmuch as a word in common use is itself a mere stipulation.

There are nowadays certain people who are puffed up by this sublime philosophical view and who declare that the things that appear are but errant appearance. In this way dismissing them as non-existent like a barren woman's son they consider their lack of insight as the supreme experience. These people do not taste the flavour of the Prāsangikas' philosophical faith.

Therefore, those who have seen all the precious things of this world to be but a pool of fire and whose concern is freedom should discard all wrong views which are patched up to look respectable, and should enjoy the cream of all philosophical faiths, the Prāsangika doctrine.

Who can fathom the great ocean of the faiths of those without and within [the fold],
The playground of men clear in mind who enjoy the countless streams of diverse views;
The huge waves [of that ocean] frighten [all] those of little mind; its depth is hard
To penetrate with words of meaning planted in philosophy's golden soil.
But here and now a man may find a jewelled garland
Of sayings that are significant when he sets sail
In a boat wafted by the wind of appropriate effort
To the centre of the ocean of faiths philosophical.

If one of the greatest scholars wants to celebrate
A festival of sayings that are significant,

The young and bright should at once repeat this precis
Of the faiths of those within and without [the fold].

If people of their learning proud
Study not the teachings deeply,
But only make a show for their gain and honour,
How can they make good use of their precious lives?
The sun of significant sayings by scholars critical
Causes the night-flower of evil teachings to close [its petals],
But lets the lotuses of pure philosophy
Unfold [theirs] in splendour wonderful.

This (short) explanation of the various faiths philosophical
Embodying the essence of Indian and Tibetan sages,
Has not been composed from jealousy of rivals
But to nurture understanding in my peers.

The good that comes from such endeavour
Surpasses the full moon in splendour;
It leads all beings from the mire of evil views.
May they for e'er breathe freely on the proper path.

FROM

THE SUMMARY OF PHILOSOPHICAL SYSTEMS

YID-BZHIN-MDZOD-KYI GRUB-MTHA' BSDUS-PA

foll. 24b ff.

THE PEAK of epistemological courses is the Prāsangikas, the real essence of the ultimate meaning of the Buddha's message. They dispense with all judgments such as existence, non-existence, being (this or that), and not-being (this or that).

That which is ultimately not found as some thing or other and is beyond the reach of the intellect, is existentially present as the absolute indivisibility of the [two] truths, pure from the beginning. Without presenting any theory about it of their own, the Prāsangikas demolish all other theories concerning its substantival existence by exposing the [fallacies of the] implications of these theories. In this way all that exists in appearance originates merely in relations; entities come about in relations; and non-entities are postulated in relations.

Thus all entities subsumed under relational existence have no essence, for if they had an essence they would not originate in relations, but because they originate in relations there is not so much of anything which could be found as an identity or difference and of origination by any of the four alternatives. It is by way of things not existing in truth, but being like an apparition and devoid of the slightest trace of permanence or annihilation, that the Prāsangikas 'absolutize' the incidental way and the ultimate goal. In order to establish the non–existence of an essence they use five syllogisms named (a) *gcig-du bral,* (b) *rdo-rje gzegs-ma,* (c) *yod med skye bral,* (d) *don-byed 'gog-pa,* and (e) *rten-'brel chen-po.*

(a) That which appears as a thing implies that it does not exist as a thing or a non-entity, because, just like the reflexion of the moon in water, it is neither one nor many.

(b) Anything in the manner in which it appears has no essence, because it does not come about through itself, by something else, by both together, or without any cause, like a dream. If it came about by itself, there would be no need for its coming about and it would be useless; if it came about from something else, anything could come about from anything; and if from both, there would be at once the fallacy of both alternatives; and if without a cause, there would never be any appearance and prerequisite, for a result would have been absent. Since the growth of a sprout from a seed is merely relational, the seed and the sprout not being found as either something identical or different, seed or sprout does not refer to anything.

(c) The variety of what appears as things has no essence, because whatever is not an entity is free from origination. Because that which exists has already come into existence, it follows that it does not come into existence, and since non-existence is contrary to existence, it cannot become existence.

(d) The knowable is not found as a thing because it is not efficacious. An (instantaneous) moment cannot act in this way because it has already ceased when it would start acting, and a series cannot do so because the idea of a series and of an (instantaneous) moment contradict each other.

(e) Mere appearance is not a thing because it is relational, like a mirror-image. Moreover, if a thing had an essence, it would not come about in relations, because the thing *is* already.

That which comes about in relation [to causes and conditions] entails its nothingness. Just as from the time that an apparitional horse and elephant make their appearance they are nothing but horse or elephant and are not found as something coarse or subtle, so also that which incontestibly appears by causes and conditions appears while being nothing, and if investigated, is not found anywhere and need not be accepted.

Further there are three syllogisms by which the four possibilities of eternity and imperishableness, change and no-change are refuted.

(a) That which merely appears does not exist as a substance, because it does not exist as either a thing past or not past. If the jug existed as something past, it would be past in either case of existence or non-existence. It is not past when it exists, because this is contrary to the past, and when it does not exist it need not be past. It also does not exist as imperishable or eternal, because it is momentary.

(b) That which merely appears is not a substance, because it neither changes nor does not change. If a thing would change, an old man should become a youth, and change itself should be either eternal or non-eternal, but it is not found when properly investigated. If it did not change, a young man could not become an old man.

(c) If birth, age, duration, and disappearance come about gradually they cannot be fully present in a single moment, and if they come about at one and the same time they would fall under the contradiction that birth and death, as well as age and youth, come about simultaneously. This fallacy has already been discussed in the dissertation on the Śrāvakas.

Thus, being certain that no entity whatsoever has any essence, one has to demolish all judgments concerning an essence in all one's actions and to remain in utter all-alikeness. Even so, without denying appearance in the ordinary way, the Ground is the two truths, the Path that of the two requisites, and the goal that of the two Kāyas.[18]

THE GROUND

While neither the object before the ordinary mind nor the object of transcendent awareness beyond the ordinary mind is found as an essence in their facticity, the two truths are interpreted in such a way that appearance in the ordinary sense is not false as far as the errant mind goes, and that the ultimate to be achieved, as well as the path and the goal, are not false. The reason is that what does not pass beyond the ordinary mind does not withstand a critique, while that which does so is beyond all reference. The inadmissibility of its withstanding a critique has been refuted before.

Both [truths] are not found separately, the thing and its nature are the same and beyond judgments and beyond mind and characteristics.

When one posits the two truths, that which is in conformity with worldly use and which appears as an object to the senses when they are unimpaired is the true conventional, but what appears before the senses impaired, like the vision of hairs in a certain eye-disease, is an illusory conventional.

THE PATH

The Path is, ordinarily, the practice of the six perfections and, ultimately, the meditation on the unity of radiant light and transcendent awareness.

The method of the practice of concentration is to sit cross-legged and first to take refuge and to develop an enlightened attitude; then, with a mind utterly relaxed to remain, without the fluctuations of mentation, in a steady radiant brilliancy, in a realm into which no dichotomic thought enters as there is no thinking of and about anything whatsoever, such activity having been cut off, as it were, by the vision of reality; when thereby all referential perceptual situations have faded away because there is neither affirmation nor negation in a mind engaged in meditation devoid of external objects and of the projects before a mind and acts of projection, then perceptiveness, internally freed from judgmental activity due to the cessation of the operations of the phenomenal mind and its mental events, becomes the contemplation of radiancy as individual intrinsic perception. In the post-concentrative stage one engages in the accumulation of the merits on behalf of the beings who are like an apparition, without attachment and involvement.

THE GOAL

When finally the ten levels have been scaled and the cause of Saṃsāra, i.e., the mind and the mental events with their experientially initiated potentialities of experience, has come to rest and is submerged in the ultimate, the Dharmakāya as the unity of knowledge and its field, as well as the two form patterns deriving from it,[19] spontaneously act for the welfare of the world.

While it does not follow that the Prāsangika does not hold any thesis and yet accepts everything observable, there is this difference concerning the existential mode of what is beyond judgments in concentration and of the appearance of differentiation in the post-concentrative state: while the former is not concerned with holding any thesis, the latter is so concerned, as can be known from the *rNam-dbye rigs-mdzod*.

In this way the epistemological varieties of the Mahāyāna have been discussed.

CHAPTER SIX

THE MEANING OF TANTRA AND THE SUPERIORITY OF TANTRISM

EVER SINCE the word 'Tantra' found its way into the English language in A.D. 1799, it has remained a name for certain literary documents recording an inner, mental-spiritual growth which is expressed in ritual and other forms of human life. Since the language of these documents is highly figurative, it can be dangerously misleading, particularly when one no longer knows what it means. This happens when the tradition is broken or when someone conversant with it is not specific. Therefore, unless we are constantly aware of the metaphorical character of the language and are prepared to recognize its psychological significance and to accept it as symbolic, almost all that the Tantras say is easily misunderstood, misrepresented, and highly vulnerable. It is easy for the skeptic to refute the literalist and expose his fallacies and inadequacies. Why, then, in view of their psychological significance, should the Tantras use misleading objective terms instead of employing a simple and unambiguous psychological language? The very fact that the Tantric terms are not found elsewhere goes far to prove that the linguistic symbols do not stand for certain things and psychological states, as do the words 'dog' and 'pleasure,' but for vivid experiences whose content is of such a far-reaching nature as to make all other terms seem limited to the agreed meaning and so utterly inadequate. Apart from being terms for experiences they also serve by means of their specific affectability to lead people to, and finally to evoke within them, these very experiences which those who have had them consider to be the most worthwhile. As a name for a certain kind of literary work, only one aspect of the use of the word Tantra has been specified and therefore the question 'What is the meaning of Tantra?' remains pertinent. However, framing the question in this manner is liable to ambiguity, because we may ask something about the word 'Tantra' itself, or about the thing it stands for. In answering the former we can either report what other people already mean by it as, for instance, when we continue using this word as a name for some literary documents; or we state what we are going to mean by this word. The latter is usually done in order to point out which of the several meanings we are going to use on this occasion or to make the existing meaning more precise. It is by stipulating a meaning for the word 'Tantra' that the ways of the Hindus and Buddhists part, the former defining it as 'systematization' and the latter as 'continuity' and 'integration.' Both these definitions are interpretations of the Sanskrit word *prabandha* by which Tantra has been explained in the *Guhyasamāja,* which is considered to be the oldest available Tantra (as literary work) in Buddhism. There we read:

> " 'Tantra' is continuity, and this is threefold:
> Ground, Actuality, and Inalienableness." [1]

This definition of Tantra has been widely accepted and it gives us a clue to what was understood by it in Buddhist circles.

The second definition of Tantra as 'integration' is a kind of 'lexical' interpretation in the sense that dictionaries, as a rule, report the meanings attached to different words by the users of a language. By 'integration' we understand the welding into a unity of different features and processes that are present in the development of the personality. And so it was in this sense that *tantra/prabandha* was defined by Rong-zom Chos-kyi dpal bzang-po who in his day (he was a contemporary of Mar-pa, A.D. 1012–1088) was an outstanding linguist or, more precisely, Sanskritist.[2]

The definition of 'Tantra' as 'continuity,' however, has superseded its definition as 'integration' without obliterating the latter. Still, 'Tantra' cannot be rendered adequately by a single concept; it requires multiple definition. This has been done by Klong-chen rab-'byams-pa (A.D. 1308–1363) whose personality and penetrating insight have overshadowed vast regions of Tibetan Buddhism. His words are:

> "Tantra in its mere fact of being (*ngo-bo*) *means* the great mystery of the presence (*gnas*) of intrinsic perception (*rig-pa*) and its determining operation. It is pervasive and one cannot add to or detract from it. Its definition indicates certain action patterns, that is to say, one speaks of Tantra because (that for which it stands) assigns a certain action pattern to man and because it is pervasive, without break, and continuous. Its division is twofold: (a) its actuality or Tantra-as-such (*don-gyi rgyud*) and (b) the literary works pointing out the former.
>
> "(a) This is man's spirituality (*sems-nyid*) radiant in itself and free from the corruption of thought-constructions. That is to say, one speaks of Tantra because it is always present in everyone, because it is the pattern of Buddhahood, and because it has the characteristic of the awakening process of realizing Buddhahood.
>
> "(b) The literary works speak about the presence [of this spirituality, Tantra], and explain it by linguistic symbols. In those works in which the Developing Stage is the predominant theme, emphasis is laid on the instrumental nature [of Tantra]; where the Fulfilment Stage ranks foremost, on a heightened sense of appreciation; where both are of equal distribution, on non-duality or unity [of the process]; and where all this is being transcended, the very core of Utter Perfection and Completion is the subject-matter.
>
> "The range of each class is as follows: Where the Developing Stage is emphasized, ten procedures are indicated: initiation and commitment; the [visualization of the] deity and the chanting of its mantra; the arrange-

ment of the *maṇḍala* and the ritual worship; meditative concentration and the behaviour mode [deriving from it]; action [on behalf of others out of this behaviour mode] and perseverance in an attitude of 'looking' [at things].[3] Where the Fulfilment Stage ranks foremost eight features are involved: unbiased perspective and goal realization; behaviour and creative imagination; mentation and aesthetic awareness; aesthetic feeling and communication. Where the unity of the Developing and Fulfilment Stages is the subject-matter, all the above eighteen procedures are necessary. In the realm of Utter Perfection and Completion the Fulfilment Stage is of primary importance, and it is subdivided into a lower one which has to do with the gradation into structuring, motility, and creativity,[4] all of which implies concrete imagery, and a superior one which deals with the empathetic activity of realizing the primordial transcendent awareness as a radiant light. Here [in our system] the superior stage is meant, which implies initiation and commitment, the traversing of the path of self-development and the feeling of certainty as well as the realization of the goal.

"A simile for Tantra is texture: out of the many strands of the weft and the warp a piece of cloth is woven. Similarly by different explanations one arrives at a single notion.

"Its suitability is that it indicates that which is in each of us. Moreover, since by means of verbal symbols it elucidates the presence [of Tantra] unambiguously and thereby enables us to apprehend it directly, it is defined as 'Tantra.' "[5]

Klong-chen rab-'byams-pa defines 'Tantra' as something in us. The preposition 'in,' however, must not mislead us into believing ourselves to be a container of some sort. Rather, as living and sentient beings we are in our totality the instrument of experience viewing itself in its activity. It is only later, through a curious twist of consciousness, that we begin to disown the mere fact of being aesthetically aware, and by selecting one segment of our vision and converting it into some particular object, we give it a status of its own. This then creates a host of new problems which remain unresolvable because they have lost all connection with their source.

It is difficult for us to think in terms other than consciousness. This word covers a wide range of meanings and is used in a vague and flimsy sense, as when it is made the condition and concomitant of all feeling, thought, sensation, and volition, including the recognition by the knowing subject of its own acts, cognitions, and affections. But, as Klong-chen rab-'byams-pa points out, 'Tantra' is more than such subjective consciousness. It is an awareness in comparison with which consciousness, the ordinary world of mind, looks like a corruption. But when we define Tantra by 'spirituality' (*sems-nyid*), we must again be careful not to conceive of it as an immanent universal mind, as might be suggested by the connection this word has with 'spirit' which again is used to cover many meanings. Unfortunately all such terms as spirit, soul, and mind are used in a very loose manner in all European languages and while 'mind' is often restricted to meaning 'intellect,' 'spirit' is made to mark a distinction from matter. None of these connotations are of any help in clarifying the concept 'Tantra.' On the other hand, the insistence on Tantra being something which we ordinarily would call mental or, very loosely, a mind, does not simply imply the idealist's doctrine that *esse* is *percipi* or that mind makes nature. All that can be said is that every form that reality assumes for us has its ground within mind, and that insofar as mind in this neutral sense expresses itself through a body behaving and acting in certain ways, this body *is* the mind. Thus, Tantra may be said to be the cognitive absoluteness in man's Being-as-such and his body-mind without in any way referring to a special theory about it as such or about any of its components.

One other point has to be noted. Throughout the modern epoch of thought the tendency has been to move away from the process of sensation. Devices, rhetorical or otherwise, have been developed which appeal to reason rather than sensibility. In the wake of this tendency, philosophy, which once was a comprehensive science involving sensation and imagination, feeling and thinking, has been relegated and restricted to semantic or logical activity. The result is that many of us have lost the capacity of understanding that, apart from an intellectual apprehension of the world, there is another one which yields truths just as valuable and valid. This is the aesthetic apprehension or intrinsic perception by the artist, the poet, and the seer, whose words are a commentary on a vision rather than a futile attempt to establish a system of supposedly universal truths over and beyond man's cognitive and sensible capacity, or to reduce the latter to some preconceived scheme demanding the exclusion of everything which the propounder of this scheme is unable to fathom. Aesthetic awareness is certainly subjective in the sense that it must be 'felt,' experienced by the apprehending subject, but it is not 'merely subjective' in the widely held sense of the phrase as being a passing personal whim. Beyond its subjective accessibility as a vividly moving experience the aesthetic fact is the matrix from which all conscious life emerges.

What reality looks like depends entirely on where the beholder stands when he makes his observation—whether his temperament induces him more to an active or to a contemplative patterning of his life. But each temperament, by virtue of its being an action pattern, enables man to overcome his narrow-mindedness and to expand the range of his vision and aesthetic appreciation which, ultimately, is the meaning of the realization of Buddhahood. Such action patterns have no fixed frontiers, but have an inherent elasticity, as a result of which man is able to grow in mental stature, to experience a transformation and transfiguration of the world and the beings he perceives therein, as well as to find new horizons and perspectives. All this helps to clarify the meaning of 'Tantra' because it entitles us to identify it with that aesthetic activity of mind which constitutes our first mode of awareness of reality, the ground of all we think and do.

Aesthetic experience belongs to the core of man's Being; it is more fundamental than any intellectual experience. Being basic to man's striving, it is the *terminus a quo,* enlightenment being the *terminus ad quem* which is nevertheless permanently grounded in aesthetic experience. Inasmuch as every experience is a living process, it is not reducible to anything else. Only when we study this process, where we are ourselves the primary elements of our own enquiry, is it on a subsequent, reflective level that we speak of experience either as a process or as a product which, when communicated to others, may become a guide to a new experience as a process. In this way, experience may be more concisely described, not defined, as the formative principle of life itself; formative insofar as it applies to itself and informative as it assists formativeness. This double aspect is clearly brought out by Klong-chen rab-'byams-pa when he continues analyzing the meaning of Tantra:

> "Tantra as such implies formativeness and actuality. The former is the aesthetic awareness and the instruction which makes us 'feel' its significance. It may further be subdivided into Tantra as formative principle and Tantra as informative aid. The former, concerning its facticity, is the all-encompassing aesthetic fact of experience, enlightenment. It is a formative principle since it is its own subject, the foundation of aesthetic apprehension, and the principle of freedom. When analyzed it is 'nothing' (*stong-pa*) and 'irradiative' (*gsal-ba*). 'Nothing' means that it is ever present in utter freedom from concretizations, because every aesthetic fact is devoid of substantiality and determinate characteristics. 'Irradiative' means that, being 'nothing,' it does not turn into a nihilistic nothing [which just is not] but that its lustre radiates in the aura of the five kinds of awareness [through which the images or idea of things are 'felt']; that warmth, coolness, lightness, and wideness are present in their own rights in the five primary constituents [of the phenomenal world], and that it engulfs the aesthetic cognition by the brightness of compassion shining forth in incessant creativity. And so Tantra is formativeness because it is the encompassing nature of primordial and

> transcending noeticness as aesthetic awareness (*rig-pa*), irradiativeness and nothingness present in all sentient beings." [6]

Awareness is not given us for its own sake but in order that we may act. However absorbing the aesthetic vision may be, it tends to become expressed. Aesthetic activity, as a vital necessity, is not the attempt to grasp reality as a whole, but the crystallization, out of the amorphous mass of feeling and sensation, of forms that are significant for man's further growth. This is why the Buddhist division of man's development into a starting point, a path, and a goal reveals the utmost significance of this development. In view of the ambiguity of the term experience, we may equate the starting point or the ground with the aesthetic fact, the path with the aesthetic experience as the unfolding of the aesthetic fact ever present in us, and the goal with the matured aesthetic awareness that enables man to act in a world of values.

This division into a starting point or ground, a path, and a goal is the next point discussed by Klong-chen rab-'byams-pa.

> "Tantra as actuality means starting point, path, and goal. The very fact of its being is the trinity of nothingness, translucency, and aesthetic awareness as ground, path, and goal. Its definition is its actuality as all-encompassingness and Buddhahood realization. It is subdivided into ground, essence, and quintessence.
>
> "*Ground* is the primordial transcendent aesthetic awareness as [the trinity of] fact, actuality, and responsiveness. That is to say, since the fact of its being is its transcendence, no such predication as 'unknowing' obtains, nor has there ever been a straying away from it. Its actuality is its givenness, the translucency of aesthetic appreciation in a [multicolored] halo of light. Its responsiveness is its all-encompassingness, incessant in making experience and judgment possible and ever present as the origin of either Saṃsāra or Nirvāṇa.
>
> "*Essence* is the triple gradation of aesthetic appreciation, having become the essence, as it were, in our hearts,

and since it manifests itself as the four lamps in the aesthetic appearance of the ground, which is the existential dynamics of [that] ground, it is the direct vision of the four vistas of the path.

"*Quintessence* is the maturation into the goal of the experience of the aesthetic appearance before the aesthetic awareness.

"Moreover, since the fact of its being is nothing as such it cannot be concretized into something having distinct features; since belief in eternity does not apply it is not found as a concrete substance; and since this nothingness manifests as aesthetic appearance in its own right, it is not some nihilistic nothing [which just is not]. Inasmuch as the indivisibility of nothingness and translucency is the quintessence of aesthetic awareness and since this has matured into its highest vividness, one speaks of the condensation [of the essence] into the quintessence." [7]

After discussing certain factors in connection with the goal attainment, Klong-chen rab-'byams-pa sums up:

"How do these three [factors of starting-point, path, and goal] come [to be considered as] Tantra?

To define Tantra as ground (or starting-point) means that one is justified to call this situation as 'ancestress' or 'ground' because all Buddhas and sentient beings originate from it. And it is all the more reasonable to speak of it as ground because it is on this nature (*rgyud/tantra*) as foundation that through intuitive understanding one hastens to the status (*rgyud*) of a Buddha, but, by failing in this understanding, to that of an ordinary being.

"Tantra as formative principle participates in the ground. Since formativeness is the foundation of that which is under consideration, the very ground [of Being] becomes Tantra as formativeness. As every Buddha or ordinary sentient being has started from this ground, aesthetic experience, Tantra is continuity because it upholds the status of each. By making a vivid experience of it, the intuitive understanding of the real results and the feeling of freedom is its own consequence or goal.

"Since such intuitive understanding does not come about unless it is taught by a competent Guru who elucidates what it is all about, this elucidation is termed Tantra as information. As this information continues from one person to the other, one speaks of the elucidation of formativeness. Through such elucidation aesthetic vision results, and then the feeling of freedom. If it is argued that Tantra does not exist because it is not found anywhere, the answer is that such is not the case. It is quite appropriate to label that which is under consideration as Tantra-as-such, because apart from it there is no continuity of the aesthetic experience.

"Tantra as essence is intrinsic perception (*rig-pa*), because when in aesthetic experience the thing-in-itself is directly seen, the continuity of Nirvāṇa is upheld, while when in the absence of a Guru's instruction no such vision obtains, continuity in Saṃsāra is guaranteed."

"Tantra is said to blossom because anyone who sees the 'four lamps' [8] and has an intuitive understanding belongs to a type of man who is immediately aware of the thing-in-itself, while he who does not so understand continues in a pattern of karmic action and reaction and emotional instability."

"Tantra as quintessence is the crystallization of the essence into the quintessence when one experiences it vividly. It is Tantra because through the vision of the aesthetically present in aesthetic appreciation one does not become involved in the triple world." [9]

These multiple definitions of Tantra by Klong-chen rab-'byams-pa are rather illuminating. They reveal clearly that Tantra is coterminous with man's Being, not something standing in a special relation to it. So we dare not put a limit to the diversity of its aspects. This, however, makes it extremely difficult, if not impossible, to render the word 'Tantra' by any one concept in English, while on the other hand, the retention of the original term is misleading because of its fixed usage as the name for a class of literary work. We will simply have to use many terms, and, in each specific case, paraphrase it.

Two features are most conspicuous from the above analysis. The one emphasizes the cognitive character, the other the existentiality of that which is designated 'Tantra.' Both features are closely interrelated, for awarenes is at the core of man's Being. More specifically, awareness ranges from the aesthetic fact or experience as the first instant of mental activity and as the matrix of all other cognitions, through a disentanglement of the aesthetic experience from the 'ordinary' and confused manner of cognition, to the mature and pure aesthetic experience which is known as 'enlightenment,' a persisting in an intuitive attitude. This progression, which is often called a 'way up,' represents a certain continuity. Similarly, when the disentanglement of the aesthetic experience is not attempted or turns out to have been unsuccessful, a 'way down' is taken, which marks the continuation of the status of an 'ordinary' being who becomes more and more involved in the maze of his presuppositions and thought-constructions.

Existentially, 'Tantra' is the essential and absolutely individual nature of man as a constant possibility, not as something that can be reduced to some entity or other or be defined by rational concepts. In this respect man, whether he is or becomes a Buddha or is and remains an 'ordinary' being, *is* his possibilities in the light of which he has to decide what to become. Such a decision, which may be made in a moment or gradually induced, is ultimately grounded in man's freedom, which again is present as a possibility, not as a fact, in the concrete human situation.

Man's Being *qua* being, Tantra, is nothing as such. Yet this nothing radiates into every phase of his concrete being. It is the indivisibility of nothingness or, more precisely, being as nothing, and of illuminatingness that gives man his distinct human nature of compassion which is both existential and cognitive. This is not by accident because awareness is primarily this Being *qua* being in its knowledge about itself.

However, it is the nature of awareness to be intentional in structure even before it divides into a 'subjective' and 'objective' pole of what we call an ordinary conscious experience. In this specific case, awareness, synonymous with Being *qua* being, is an encounter with itself, though not in the sense that a concrete mind knows itself as a concrete object in intellectual reflection. So in aesthetic experience we may say that that of which we are aesthetically aware, before we are aesthetically aware of it, is nothing. But this nothing, as the texts again and again assert, is not an absolute nothing which just is not. It is a dynamic nothing which, when we are aesthetically aware of it, has already been given a form and so resides in the vividly present and its meaning. This basic nothing is termed 'ancestress' which is a verbal symbol for pure transcendence. In the fine arts this nothing is represented as a female figure whose color depends on the interpretation given to the nothingness of transcendence. This conception of the ground of man's Being as female has important consequences for the whole attitude of Buddhism. It recognizes the female principle in the nature of things as valid in its own right and attributes to it an inspiring and emotionally moving character of friendliness, tenderness, and intimacy, the greatest one being the union of two lovers. This recurrent theme in Tibetan painting is therefore a symbol of aesthetic awareness in which inspiration and appreciation have become united in wedlock. That which from the viewpoint of intellectual reflection is nothing as such and unlimited, is not viewed with horror as in Greek thought,[10] and its symbolic representation in the human female form lets the transcendent and the divine remain near man, who becomes the center of this-worldliness and otherworldliness.

In discussing the 'formative' and 'informative' character of Tantra and in countering the objection that no such thing as 'Tantra' can be found in the concrete, Klong-chen rab-'byams-pa deals with the problem of being and the distinction between the real or actual and the possible within the unity of being. The real and the possible coincide in the sense that, inasmuch as Being *qua* being is not limited like some entity of reality, possibility belongs to and is included in being, so that possibility is itself the real and any distincton can have only a functional character. That is to say, at any moment the individual has to act in a certain way. This he does in view of his projects and his future, which means that possibility becomes an actuality. Another point to note is that Being and awareness are conterminous, and just as Being is both fact and possibility so also awareness oscillates between these two poles and *is* both of them. Thus there is, existentially, no other Being apart from Being *qua* being and, epistemologically, there is no awareness other than the aesthetic one. Everything else is to be conceived of as a mode of Being and awareness. The unity of Being-awareness is already present in man as the ground of his being and his cognitions, and at the same time this unity is aimed at as a goal. The latter is pursued through what is called Tantra as 'formativeness.' On the one hand, formativeness follows its own course within the framework of being and, on the other, it can be aroused by 'information' which also pertains to the framework of being. Inasmuch as the formative process as goal-directed striving varies from individual to individual, each person, as it were, follows his own destiny. In speaking of Tantra as destiny, however, we must not consider it as a force acting from outside on the individual; destiny is man's Being in its dynamics. In this sense formativeness is closely related to information which starts formativeness on the way on which fact and possibility intermingle. In order to be effective information must take into account the specific temperament of the individual to be informed. This is clearly reflected in the importance attached to the Guru-disciple relationship.[11] Certainly, a man of aesthetic or poetic temperament and sensibility needs a different guidance and treatment than the one who is suffering from the disease of conforming to public opinion as part of a herd. Information thus becomes the communication of Being. But Being is beyond words and irreducible to any of the categories of thought. And yet words are the most needed instruments in communication. The question therefore is how to get out of this dilemma. The answer is given by the peculiar language of the Tantras. Their 'informative' character turns out to be an appeal to man's possible Being; it does not address itself to the intellect which fails to make aware of his possibilities and, instead of teaching him the art of living, reduces him to an emotionally starved machine-minder. The wealth of psychological information contained in the Tantras is therefore never a science of psychology. It always addresses itself to man's uniqueness in being a living being, and not a theoretical schema.

In this communication which occurs between two individuals who pursue their aims, each in his own way, within a pattern of unity, each can blossom forth as his own individual essence, because Being is present in both at least in bud. And when this bud has grown into a full flower there is still aesthetic activity, richer in comparison to what it was before and untrammelled by the defects of logical reflection and ratiocination, the hallmarks of involvement in worldliness.

Because of the complexity of what is involved in that which is referred to by the word 'Tantra,' it is understandable that most indigenous Tibetan works, dealing with the legacy of the Indian philosophical systems and their interpretation or alleged misinterpretation by native scholars, are reluctant to deal with the Tantras, although they all admit that the Tantras are the climax of Buddhist thought. At the same time they insist these works can be understood only after thorough study of the epistemological problems discussed in the Sūtras. The latter are, indeed, a prerequisite for training the aspirant's mind in clear and critical thinking. But basically they are mere abstractions from the horizon of the individual's life-world which has to do with meanings and encompasses all that we can know by feeling, thought, imagination, and other natural powers. It is this kind of 'felt' knowledge, of 'intuitive imagination' that is of primary importance in the Tantras. Such knowledge is 'existential' rather than abstractive-postulational. This is so because here we deal with life as it is or can be lived in the concrete, and from which we cannot become detached in order to gaze at it as an external lifeless object, due to the fact that we are living it as we think. Consequently, the Tantras, which represent a living Buddhism, are inaccessible to the traditional methods of rationalism and positivism.

It is easy to see why the Tantras are unanimously acclaimed as being superior to the Sūtras (*lakṣanayāna*). In the latter the individual's gaze is primarily directed towards an external 'objective' item or system (*lakṣana*) into which the individual also tries to fit himself. This, of course, is impossible because of the incommensurable character of the individual's 'subjective' component. It is the objectivist's fallacy to use the term 'subjective' to refer to that which is as yet not clearly understood but eventually will become a dead counter in an objective universe (whatever the objectivist may mean by it). This objectivistic trend is patent in the Sūtras and the philosophical systems derived from them, which always speak of 'the objective situation' (*yul*) and 'the owner of the objective situation' (*yul-can*) as constituting the objective basis (*gzhi*), and as different from the 'path,' which is man's process of realizing integration (*lam*) and the attainment of the goal (*'bras-bu*) varying according to the initial premises. The Tantras, on the other hand, see that the 'subjective' component is an overarching reality, having a structure of its own and resisting any attempt to reduce it to an objectivistic counter. It is a wider horizon from which the 'objective' and the 'subjective' as irreconcilable opposites have been abstracted. The Tantras realize that 'being-a-subject' is not the same as 'being-this-or-that-subject,' which is but another way of seeing man as an object and of ignoring his life-world. Being-a-subject is tantamount to 'functioning,' that is, to relate oneself to something as one's object. This means that the subject as subject takes a certain attitude towards the object which it 'thinks' to be this or that. The object as such also is not merely 'postulated,' but is co-present with the subject as the presupposition of every possible judgment which results in this-or-that-subject dealing with this-or-that-object.

While all accounts of the Tantras tally in assigning the teaching of the highest value to them, Mi-pham 'Jam-dbyangs rnam-rgyal rgya-mtsho specifically and clearly elucidates the character of this value. He states that whatever appears to us is a cipher (*dag-pa*), an enigmatic sign which man interprets when contemplating it. This interpretation can proceed in a reductive way. It then leads to the meaninglessness and absurdity of man and the world, the favorite theme of Western existentialism. Or it can proceed constructively. Then it retains the vividness and mystery of appearance and leads to meaningfulness and authentic being, the topic of Tantric thought.

However, the phenomenal as a presence rather than as a logical construction is not something divorced from absolute self-same Being, which we usually tend to conceive as something behind and above the phenomenal, somewhere beyond the conflicting opposites. In man's life-world the absolute and the phenomenal are indivisible. The consequence of this way of thinking for the concrete life of the individual is that, since any empirical 'fact' can become, or is already by nature, a cipher through which the absolute shines forth and from which it is never wholly distinct, there is nothing to be 'accepted' or 'rejected.' Acceptance and rejection belong to the realm of abstractions constituting the various systems (scientific, philosophical, religious), belonging to the life-world but not being it. As long as we try to build up a meaningful life-world from the abstract perspectives of the specialized disciplines, such as epistemology discussed at length in the Sūtras, we follow the *hetuyāna* which thus is a cause-factor (*hetu*) in finding a meaning for ourselves, but when the life-world with its global interpretations guiding our different styles of life is in the foreground of our thoughts, we follow the *phalayāna* because here the goal (*phala*) is made the guiding principle in our actions and thoughts. In other words, the *hetu-* or *lakṣaṇayāna* gives us a useful perspective on things and on certain aspects of ourselves, as the criticism of the *ātman*-theory shows, but it leaves out a good deal—the meaning of life and of our own being. This omission is made up by the Tantras.

FROM

THE SUMMARY OF PHILOSOPHICAL SYSTEMS

YID-BZHIN MDZOD-KYI GRUB-MTHA' BSDUS-PA

foll. 27a ff.

AFTER THIS DISCUSSION of the objectively orientated disciplines (*lakṣaṇayāna*) forming the incentive [for further study (*hetuyāna*)] in the Mahāyāna, the Adamantine Course of the Guhyamantra, which is the culmination, will be discussed.

First of all, although the latter is in many special ways superior to the teaching contained in the objectively orientated disciplines, its nature can be stated concisely as follows:

In the *hetuyāna* it is claimed that the goal of Buddhahood is reached after a long time because man's natural disposition or potentiality of Buddhahood, present as a seed, must be developed through the accumulation [of knowledge and merits] as contributory cause-factors. Hence cause and effect are considered as following each other. In the Adamantine Course, man's spiritual nature which is an actual irradiative light and which is immanently present as his value, [as pervasive as] celestial space, is made the starting point [seemingly] to be purified. That from which it has to be cleansed is the aggregate of the eight perceptive functions [12] together with their apparent objects, constituting the actuality of Saṃsāra, which is like clouds. When this [impurity] has been quickly removed by the profound processes of the initiatory empowerments and the Developing and Fulfilment Stages constituting the purificatory acts, likened to the wind [dispersing the clouds], the real foundation of human existence, or Buddhahood, shining forth directly, is realized in a short time. In view of this fact we speak of the axiom of the indivisibility of cause and effect.

Although both disciplines (*hetuyāna* and *phalayāna*) are identical in purpose, the realization of the goal of Buddhahood, the methods differ. While the objectively orientated disciplines are not sure about the fact that the appearance constituting Saṃsāra is in itself a meaningful cipher and a divine *maṇḍala* and that the absolute is indivisible from the actuality (of Saṃsāra), they adopt a viewpoint of acceptance and rejection. In the Mantra discipline, on the other hand, everything is known to be indivisible in its truth (reality) of cipher and absoluteness. Since here we are [spontaneously] without [deliberating between] acceptance and rejection, cause and effect, the perspective is unbiased. In addition, since in the objectively orientated disciplines we are concerned with acceptance and rejection, it is not possible to take all and everything as a friendly helper when pursuing our path of spiritual development. In the Mantra discipline, however, there are many methods and hence it is profounder concerning goal realization. Because of this, the objectively orientated disciplines have nothing easy to offer, while the Mantra discipline has. [Lastly], since such a profound path is suited only for persons of highest intellectual acumen, the Mantra discipline is particularly superior.

Moreover, the indivisibility of cause and effect implies that in the Anuttarayoga the irradiative clarity of mind and the perfection of Being is everpresent without effort. In any case, while the Kriyāyoga is superior to the Sūtras in being less uncertain [about reality], from among the six Tantras each subsequent one is superior to the preceding one by becoming less and less uncertain.[13]

For all these reasons, the path of development as outlined in the Sūtras is called *hetuyāna* [a course in which we are impelled to move]; but while the goal is pre-existent in living our development which constitutes the cause of Buddhahood, it is in the Mantra discipline that the goal which consists of the three existentials (as principles of interpretation) is made the path, by virtue of their being the most excellent and appropriate means [of developing our style of life]. Hence we speak of a course in which the goal is ever-present (*phalayāna*) and [what in a temporal setting is spoken of as] goal-attainment is won in a short time.

In this specific Guhyamantra there are four kinds of Tantra possessing the greatest value. This fourfold division is due to such differences as the four classes of society, the gradation in intellectual acumen, and the intensity of emotional impairments.[14]

CHAPTER SEVEN
THE LOWER TANTRAS

KRIYĀTANTRA

THE TECHNICAL TERM Kriyātantra is a compound of the two Sanskrit words *kriyā,* 'action,' and *tantra,* which admits of multiple interpretations as pointed out above. According to Klong-chen rab-'byams-pa, *kriyā* indicates the emphasis on man's behavior and activity as it expresses itself in deeds, words, and thoughts; and *tantra* refers to the explanation man's behaviour has found in the various commentaries on the Tantras (literary works). This interpretation of *Kriyātantra* is highly significant, because its author realized that man's behaviour is not merely the observable sum total of the dissectory classification into bodily, verbal, and mental acts, but the perceptible manifestation of the otherwise hidden and secret order which makes the human organism an acting centre through which man's 'inwardness,' his humanism is 'externalized.' The significance of Kriyātantra, which initiates the subsequent stages for man's quest for meaning, is that it opens up a new perspective from which man is enabled to see himself as a living being rather than as a theoretical postulate. In following the direction illumined by this new insight man is on his way to the source of his very Being. He realizes as never before that the system 'man,' circumscribed by bodily, verbal, and mental acts, is part of a guiding system of a higher order and that man's actions are but the end-phases of an essentially creative, in the last analysis self-creative, process.

This creative superstructure is referred to by language in such terms as 'spiritual' and 'divine.' But language tends to concretize its own creations into an immaterial something which then is believed to pervade man's organism in some mysterious way and to persist after the latter's death. It is one of the peculiarities of language that it veils when it reveals; it draws attention to the secret of life and at the same time compels us to look away from it. Another peculiarity is the evaluative aspect conveyed by language. The divine, the spiritual is 'higher' and 'purer' and the ordinary beings in their ordinary world are 'fallen' and 'impure.' A third peculiarity of language is that it endows its creations with anthropomorphic features: the divine becomes a person who, as a rule, is not much different from ordinary man except for exhibiting more of the 'same stuff' of which man is constituted. This myth-making tendency then leads to all sorts of fictional systems, philosophical, religious, political. However, when the attempt is made to see man as a living being in his totality and not in the fragmentary reductions of the various analytical disciplines, it soon will be realized that however far man may have moved away from the all-sustaining life-stream he is still part of it and can retrieve his lost wealth of being alive. Seeing himself as impure he feels he can be 'purified,' and feeling himself 'fettered' he dimly assumes that he can be 'freed.' Freedom has been unanimously declared to be the goal of all striving. But it has to be noted that freedom is never a *thing* as are those other things with which man deals in his life. If freedom were such an attainable 'thing' it would constitute a contradiction in itself because it would be as much a fetter as the 'things' which are believed to fetter man. Freedom is the very life process which flows vigorously when it does not allow itself to be sidetracked into shallow areas. Viewed superficially the life-stream finally seems to come to a dead end, but actually the stream is more like a pendulum swinging between two poles. The one, rightly called death, is the enervating process of reification, the world of things as dead counters in a predominantly rationalistic framework; the other is a peak value which enables man to see his same old world in the light of values, intrinsically rather than superficially and externally. These two poles form an indivisible whole in which attention can be directed either way. While our ordinary world of phenomena may seem to be sullied and in need of purification, the ultimate is yet in and with it and constitutes the possibility of understanding reality as such. The process of understanding is a kind of drama enacted in the inner forum of thought. Actions take place between persons conceived and modeled after the social context, where different degrees of intimacy prevail. The lowest level of intimacy is represented by the relation between master and servant, the unreserved submission to the rule of power. While slavish servitude may certainly be implied, particularly when this relation is modeled after a slave society context, there is present also a certain readiness for service, often with the *arrière pensée* of becoming like the master in one's god or gods to whom one pledges oneself to render service. The possibility of choice is implied by the various *yi-dams,* the tutelary deities on 'whom one's mind is fixed.'

The analysis of the relation between master and servant, given by the Buddhists, is highly significant as it avoids the fallacy of absolutizing one term in this relationship. The Buddhists clearly saw that in any relationship both terms are relative to each other, and that in their togetherness each one finds its partner and limit in the other. Togetherness is what we mean by being; being means to exist, to be exposed to something and expose oneself to something, to stand in mutual interaction. While everything that is, is thus relative to something that equally is, Being itself is not relative to anything. It is not subordinate to or contained in the relativity of all that is, but is this very relativity. In other words, the relativity of what there is is not itself relative. The absoluteness of Being-as-such and the relativity of what there is do not contradict each other but are factually one and the same, 'the indivisibility of the Two Truths.'

The relativity of what there is, essentially is a process of becoming, which in its self-manifestation is awe-inspiring and therefore deserves the qualification of 'divine.' It is this relativity of what there is or becomes in its absoluteness of Being-as-such, that Klong-chen rab-'byams-pa sums up in the words: "In knowing that in the relative world of phenomena all that appears is of the nature of six divine powers, and by conceiving of the god of one's choice as the embodiment of original awareness and as master, and of oneself as a being committed to him and a servant, one deals in the ultimate sense with the unborn Absolute, the Radiant Light." [1]

Readiness for service not only implies complete submission; it also as 'representative' action imitates the master or god. Representation in this sense presupposes observation which may completely absorb the agent's attention so that the importance of concrete activity or 'enactment' is more or less reduced to merely imaginary processes. Due to the ambivalence of what is meant by doing-observing, different interpretations of the six divine powers (*lha drug*) in the Kriyātantra have been offered.

Mi-pham 'Jam-dbyangs rnam-rgyal rgya-mtsho and many others favored an epistemological interpretation, but Klong-chen rab-'byams-pa offers an 'existential' one in which the divine powers operate freely. Freedom, as has been shown, is not a thing, but an existential category, commensurate with Being-as-such. While Being-as-such is the relativity of all that is as mutually relative, freedom is the absoluteness of this Being-as-such. It operates as an open dimension and as aesthetic transparency in all that is. That is to say, Being-as-such appears as being this and that, though not as a correlate to an unknowable thing-in-itself (Kant) nor as a semblance (Plato), but in the form of impressions which are distortions of an identical thing by the observer. As a presence with an open dimension, appearance is felt to be of divine quality. Speaking in terms of perception, things which ordinarily are seen and realized in physical space are now envisaged as determined by intensities or values of colour, sound, and meaning. This shift in perspective does not involve seeing something as another *thing,* rather an educated looking which comes as a gradual achievement and enrichment.

In the realm of human existence man's Being (which can be analyzed as his activity manifested by body, speech, and mind as end-terms of a self-creative process and as this process itself) is no longer 'observed' as a physical object or material thing (to conceive of him as a mental being is equally postulational), but experienced aesthetically. Klong-chen rab-'byams-pa gives the following account:

> "Appearance as aesthetic presence (*lha'i sku*) is luminous like an apparition and is not tied up in the postulates of singularity and plurality. Appearance is the open dimension of aesthetic form-colour."
>
> "Communication (*gsung*) making use of the elements of speech is luminous in its presence as being sound and continues like the reverberations of an echo and thus is the open texture of word-elements."
>
> "Responsiveness (*thugs*) by relating itself to the symbol-creations is luminous in its attentiveness, concentration, and empathy; it is the freedom of discursive thought as creative imagination."
>
> "Since aesthetic progression and regression is luminous in the colour intensities of the aesthetic presence, progression and regression is the open dimension of light experience, whereby the elements of speech are resolved in original awareness."
>
> "Since luminosity, the aesthetic onset, affects one's residence and clothes, whatever appears is transformed into a palatial mansion."
>
> "The open dimension or animatedness by original awareness is luminously present in the world of becoming, since it is the absolute whereby that which has to be purified is resolved in pure awareness." [2]

The aesthetic experience induced by this shift in perspective gradually gains in depth, and ultimately can lead to the enlightenment as an abiding peak experience.

CARYĀTANTRA

While the Kriyātantra implies and emphasizes the relation between man and the divine power or powers as essentially one of servitude which very often borders on the imitation of these powers, the *Caryātantra* interprets this relation on a different level which is an advance on the previous one. The literal meaning of the term Caryātantra refers to man's behaviour (*caryā*) as exemplary rather than imitative. Those associated in any relationship may well be friends, and thus the divine power, felt and concretized as a god who is accepted in the compact, is a friend. This friendship with the god or gods not only awakens, but also deepens, the sense of the likeness between god and man. Moreover, friendship is built on trust, and therefore excludes fear. It does not necessarily replace service, but service is rendered freely and there is mutual respect. For this reason another term for this type of Tantra is *Uba-tantra* which is the Tibetan modification of the Sanskrit term *Ubhaya-tantra* referring to 'both' (*ubhaya*) aspects, service and friendship, with its feeling of intimacy.

YOGATANTRA

Friendship which in spite of its attendant feeling of intimacy still implies separateness can precisely because of this feeling of intimacy develop in such a way as to bring about the feeling of identity in which the last trace of separateness is eliminated. This stage is the subject matter of the *Yogatantra*. It is effected by intensifying and giving priority to creative imagination (*sgom*) which acts as a process of transfiguration by means of symbols which reveal their significance as possible modes of coordinating various experiences. Ritual acts by body and speech are of secondary importance, although they are not absent, and fluctuations of attention between acts and imagination and vice versa are possible. The important points to note in this connection is that action must originate in contemplation and represents its expression in the temporal world. Action must be action inspired by insight.

The imaginative process, which is of particular importance, is described in terms of an existential analysis whereby an experience of an intellectual and spiritual nature is elucidated by images taken from sensory experiences. This process of creative imagination implies a judicious application of the appreciative-discriminative function of the mind [3] which can operate either in a spontaneous, non-referential way or, more frequently, in a referential one. Either way is conducive to a purified concentration which prevents the mind from disintegrating, as is customary, into its own fictions, and in this state of disintegration failing to recognize them as its own creations. The desired state of concentration and integration is induced and later on stabilized by five 'intuitions,' each of which is an 'awakening' from a static world of postulates to a dynamic one of live values. The symbolic character of what happens in this process is evident from the different interpretations that have been offered by various authors. For it is the nature of symbolism that it conceals as well as reveals, and becomes deflected as it passes through the prisms of individual temperament and predisposition.

These intuition-awakenings have a profound noetic quality. The knowledge involved is acquired not much by way of observation, although it is present as 'intuition,' but rather by way of participation, of being 'awake.' Such intuition-awakenings are existential perceptions of the Absolute which lights up the phenomenal world in a new vision. The contemplative here gains a consciousness of being that which he knows and knowing that which he is.

Klong-chen rab-'byams-pa explains the various intuition-awakenings as follows:

> "The awakening from intuiting sun and moon (on) a throne means imaginative attention to sun and moon in the centre of a lotus flower as symbols of the actuality of fitness of action and of intelligence.
>
> The awakening from intuiting the characteristic of (spiritually) cognitive responsiveness is imaginative attention to such emblems as a sceptre, a jewel, a lotus flower, a sword, and a wheel as symbols of respective action patterns.
>
> The awakening from intuiting the perfected shape is the immediate presence of any of the divine powers such as Vairocana or the others, having crystalized out of their emblems, symbolic of their respective activities.
>
> The awakening from intuiting letters as elements of communication is the imaginative attention to the chain of vowels and consonants filling the sky resoundingly as

communications by the various divine powers, symbolic of the 'turning of the wheel' of the great mystery.

The awakening from intuiting ultimate purity in [the felt vision of] Vajrasattva is to seal [one's being] by four seals when we as persons committed have become fused with awareness-being, and to be spiritually sustained in authentic being, communication, and responsiveness. This is symbolic of the non-duality of the reaches of awareness and awareness-as-such.

These five intuition-awakenings act as indications that the five 'excellencies' in the Akaniṣṭha realm emerge at the time a person is becoming an enlightened one."[4]

Inasmuch as perception plays a significant role in all phases of man's life the use of symbols as a device for making man more perceptive can hardly be underestimated. In order to perceive more fully and to be able to see more and more aspects of the many-sidedness of any given fact, it is necessary to overcome the tendency to classify, to compare, to need, to use, to abstract. Useful as abstracting may be, it also falsifies in the sense that we no longer see the object as it is but make of it what we wish it to be within a certain system. The moment we do so we have cut ourselves off from the possibility of seeing anything as it really is. To perceive anything as it is in its intrinsic uniqueness is to perceive it aesthetically and empathically. In contrast with ordinary cognitions and reactions which proceed under the aegis of suitability for ego-centred purposes, aesthetic and empathic perception is complete in itself and needs nothing else. It is felt as being intrinsically true, good, and beautiful. The percept is seen as a unique instance and also is felt as such. The symbol for this experience is the lotus flower which, though growing from the mud in a pond, is not sullied but shines in singular beauty. Its purity is, therefore, to continue the symbol language, a suitable basis on which sun and moon, the two illuminating bodies, can come together. Moreover, there are lotus flowers which bloom when the sun shines and others which bloom when the moon shines. In this way even the lotus flowers have individual preferences, but if we perceive the lotus flower as a flower we no longer classify. Similarly, man also exhibits certain preferences; he may be more of a contemplative or of an active type, but seen as man he is the sole member of his class in whom fitness of action (*thabs*) and intelligence (*shes-rab*) unite. 'Intelligence' in Buddhism is analytical and appreciative and, in particular, is the ability to perceive what may be called the 'open dimension' of everything perceived and which cannot be reduced to something well-defined and narrowly circumscribed. Trying to reduce it would be tantamount to making it something other than it is, something else *like* it, and yet something different from *it* itself. 'Intelligence' in the Buddhist sense is an undemanding rather than a demanding perception. Each perception, however undemanding it may be, entails a reaction to it and each reaction to a perception bears on further perceptions. This facet is referred to by the term 'fitness of action' which is not naive expediency, that is, to do what seems obvious, easy, or convenient, but action which preserves the values perceived directly.

Attention to undemanding perception makes it perceived and reacted to as if it were in itself 'out there,' as if it were a perception of a reality almost independent of man and persisting beyond his own being. It is as if a person becomes exposed to his deepest source of being, and this exposure after the initial receptivity of inspiration gives way to activity in certain patterns. This is what is meant by responsiveness which again expresses itself at first symbolically whereby the 'I-Thou' monism becomes a greater likelihood. Here the symbol of the sceptre, ordinarily associated with the ruler of a country, indicates that man's actions and reactions will be determined by the centre of his personality and will be no longer at the mercy of peripheral occurrences; the jewel suggests the enrichment of the personality; the lotus flower his purity; the sword his capacity to cut the fetters that tie him to a world of bondage which is but the product of his limited and self-centred vision; and the wheel the irradiation of what is felt and known to be the peak value into every level of his being.

These emerging patterns impress themselves more and more

in concrete forms as immediately felt presences (*sku*) which are expressions of a drama within the person that has been thrown into sensory form. The relation between the emblems intuited on the previous stage and their felt presences on the new level may be compared with the one that holds between simplicity of motif and complexity of expression as the enactment (*mdzad*) of what the felt presence stands for.[5]

Cognitive responsiveness is, in the last analysis, indivisible from existence which is an act, or, to put it differently, to be is to be sensitive and to respond, and to be sensitive means to be in communication with what is responded to. Communication occurs mostly by words consisting of vowels and consonants. But communication, in the true sense of the word, is quite different from the deafening clamour of mere verbiage. It has to do with meaning and in conveying meaning it touches the very core of man's being. The presence felt (*sku*) communicates (*gsung*) cognitively (*thugs*) and what it communicates is the sense of the great mystery of being. To awaken man to this mystery has been termed the 'turning of the wheel,' which must not be confused with the promulgation of a set of propositions.

To the extent that perception becomes more receptive and less interfering, it loses its ego-centredness, and Being becomes the centering point. It seems as if a kind of dynamic parallelism between the within and the without is operating and leading to a fusion of what seems to be polar extremes. This is to say that, as Being is the focal point around which the perceptive experience is organized, so also does the person concurrently come closer to his own Being. Each makes the other more possible. This feeling of being *part* of the unity one perceives (as man becomes more integrated and unified, he tends to be able to see more unity in the world), of the essential purity that one appreciates, is technically termed Vajrasattra (*rdo-rje sems-dpa'*). *Vajra* (*rdo-rje*), 'sceptre,' has always been a symbol of indestructibility and firmness, and *sattva,* 'being,' but interpreted by the Tibetan sages as 'mind-strength,' indicates that man's source of his individual being is 'mind.' In philosophical terms this is to say that in

Vajrasattva both the absolute and relative fuse, that the perceiver and the perceived are identified.

The new centre, Vajrasattva, is both static and dynamic. In its static aspect it is existence, communication, and cognitive responsiveness, the sustaining source of man's actual being which is an act. The dynamic aspect is termed 'sealing.' That is to say, existence as such (*Mahāmudrā*) seals man's existence in the world, in the sense that he is no longer a 'cog in the machine' but recognized and accepted for what he is in his fulness, richness and complexity. Communication as such (*Dharmamudrā*) seals his being-with-others, in the sense that he has to communicate something valuable instead of pouring out meaningless verbiage. Responsiveness as such (*Samayamudrā*) seals his 'thoughts' by making him 'think' of others as values, as gods and goddesses, as religious language expresses it, which means to perceive another human being in his Being, as if he were the whole of what there is to be perceived. Similarly, the world is to be 'thought' of as a celestial mansion, rather than as a means-object. Lastly, perception as such (*Karmamudrā*), symbolized in the text by the emanation and reabsorption of light rays, 'seals' by being a shifting process in which the fluctuations of attention remain strictly *within* the perception moving from one perfection to another.

As compared with ordinary perception, by means of which the characteristics of things are realized as 'qualities' that 'qualify' them for metaperceptual ends, aesthetic or value perception realizes the characteristics of things in 'aspects' that 'animate' them, whereby they are perceived in their own rights as having an intrinsic value of their own. The transition from one kind of perception to the other, which is the aim of the Yogatantra, seems to be like entering another world, more beautiful, more perfect, more sublime. It is called the Akaniṣṭha realm and, like the ordinary life world, has five constituents termed 'excellencies' (*phun-sum-tshogs*) because each is replete with its own values.

Although perception, ordinary or intrinsic, may seem to come naturally, it is actually a learning process which presupposes a teacher-disciple relationship. Moreover, it occurs at a given place and time and is continuous and complex rather than momentary and separate. The perceptual world therefore comprises a teacher, a place, an audience, a time, and a continuous complexity. In intrinsic perception one sees the 'excellencies' which Rong-zom Chos-kyi dpal bzang-po explains as follows:

> "Excellency of teacher: this is the sublime Samantabhadra (All-good), the lordliness of absolute existence, communication, and sensitive responsiveness of all the Tathāgatas of the ten regions and the four times,[6] that teaches the true nature of all that is, not an individual who may embody the Buddha-awareness.
>
> Excellency of place: this is the endless Akaniṣṭha realm, the actuality of enlightenment which is the quintessence of all the citadels of Reality, not what is separated into the pure spheres (of Bodhisattvas) and the impure spheres (of ordinary beings).
>
> Excellency of audience: this is the self-manifestation of primordial awareness in its indivisibility of the tainted and the untainted as something not different from enlightenment, not one's own pure and impure aspects.
>
> Excellency of time: this is existence, communication, and sensitive responsiveness as the Ghanavyūha-ornament in the self-same sphere (of reality) throughout the four times, not the divisions of time such as moments and seconds, or time thought about, time not thought about or time beyond thought.
>
> Excellency of continuous complexity: this is the actuality of becoming completely aware of the fact that whatever has been termed Saṃsāra and Nirvāṇa has been an indivisible unity from the very beginning; it is not the (continuity) of cause and effect depending on necessity and friends."[7]

In these statements picturesque, if not mythological, language has been used. The reason is obvious: ordinary language is concerned with material from the phenomena of common experience, but here an attempt is made to express valuable experiences of meaning. In this case it is obvious that the literal meaning is not adequate to the subject of the statements, for in talking of the 'teacher' (and the other points as well) it both affirms and negates. It negates because it talks about a subject which does *not* belong in any plain sense to the realm of everyday events in the universe; it affirms because it talks about not one of many things but 'one' and 'alone.' Most significant is the fact, which has been psychologically verified over and again, that the experience which language attempts to convey, is only good and never evil, beautiful and never ugly, encompassing space and time, rather than being caught up in the ravages of (ordinary) time and the confines of (cagelike) space.

FROM

THE SUMMARY OF PHILOSOPHICAL SYSTEMS

YID-BZHIN-MDZOD-KYI GRUB-MTHA' BSDUS-PA

foll. 28a ff.

IN THE KRIYĀTANTRA great stress is laid on the observance of outer ablutions, ritual purity, and other ritual actions by body and speech. The divine power, who as a god is the embodiment of primordial awareness, is considered to confer favours like a master, while the individual committed to his service receives these benefits like a servant. It is claimed that thereby temporal and lasting realizations are achieved.

Here, too, one distinguishes between perspective, creative imagination, conduct, and their fruition.

Although all phenomena are ultimately the same in their actuality which is the indivisibility of the truths of appearance and nothingness, in our relative world, supreme divine being becomes the embodiment of primordial awareness in which the radiancy of the evidence of being is directly present in its nature of being free from any defects and in being replete with all values in highest perfection. And so it is considered to be like a master because he confers temporal and lasting benefits on us, who receive them like his servants. Since we are not yet perfect as regards our real being and are shrouded in the veils [of unknowing and emotional instability], we feel ourselves dependent upon [such a] god. Therefore, since ultimately our identity with and relatively our relation to [the divine power] is incontestible, the perspective of the Kriyātantra is accompanied by the firm belief that through our perseverance in patterning ourselves after the god's form, speech, and mood, our temporal activities become significant, and that ultimately the god's essence is realized by us.

Kriyā is known to refer to six divine powers. This, in brief, means that one concentrates on such experiences as the visualization of the god's form, the hearing of his message, and the feeling of his mood, as well as the manifestation of the god's palace and the emanation and reabsorption of light rays. One then creates this mood again and again by repeating the god's specific mantra as if one's life were at stake and so causes the god's grace to descend upon one, just as if iron were touched by the philosophers' stone.

Inasmuch as the recitation of the mantra is effective in a ritual context, but otherwise remains barren like a seed without water and manure, one must exert oneself in performing such ritual acts as taking a bath and changing one's clothes thrice a day, worshipping, and making offerings, as detailed in the Tantras.

By such efforts, as temporal gifts, any of the ordinary attainments are won, such as the body of a Vidyādhara [8] who is equal in fortune to a god of the sensuous world, and, as a lasting result, the essence of a god of any of the three action patterns [9] is realized within a period of sixteen human lives.

In the Caryātantra, outwardly, ritual purity, as effected by ablutions and other observances and, inwardly, creative imagination are of equal importance. It is claimed that by viewing oneself and the god as being brothers or friends, realizations are won.

Here, too, there is the distinction between perspective, creative imagination, conduct, and their fruition.

Since [in this type] the conviction of the identity [of man and god] in the ultimate sense is still stronger than in the Kriyātantra, we and the god are of equal status like brothers or friends. Since temporal and lasting good is realized by reliance on the god envisaged as he really is, when appearance as a concatenation of interdependent entities has subsided, the perspective of the Caryātantra is accompanied by belief in the profoundness of the two truths.

Creative imagination means that when one has clearly visualized the god as the embodiment of primordial awareness he will come near, and that ultimately there is nothing left of logical fictions or propositions claiming truth.

This is to observe the various rites of ablution and ritual purity to the best of one's ability.

Temporarily one's activities become significant and finally the level of a Vajradhṛk of four action patterns is attained within a period of seven human lives.[10]

Further, one speaks of a 'twofold Tantric spiritual course' because [in this type], inwardly, creative imagination as in the Yogatantra and, outwardly, observances as in the Kriyātantra are equally distributed. Actually, however, the realization of one's goal is quicker because the perspective here is wider than in the previous Tantra.

The Yogatantra comprises two varieties: (i) an outward Yogatantra and (ii) an inner unsurpassable spiritual course. (The latter is discussed at the end of the following chapter.)

(i) While [in this Tantra] ritual purity and other observances are merely considered to be friends and helpers for the realization of the path, inwardly the contemplation of the working of the mind is stated to be of primary importance. It is claimed that realizations are attained through the contemplation of non-duality when by way of four 'seals' and five 'intuition-awakenings' there has come about a fusion of subjectivity and objectivity: subjectivity being the individual transfigured into a being committed to the service of the god, and objectivity being the god as the embodiment of primordial awareness, invited to come from his pure realms.

Here, too, there is the division into perspective, creative imagination, conduct, and their fruition.

Since this view of the absolute is superior to that of the two preceding Tantras, one knows for certain that one is actually identical with the god [one visualizes], that even in our relative world (man and god) become identical like water poured into water. In this state of heightened awareness, the perspective is accompanied by the special certainty of the realization of the essence of the god (of one's choice) by means of assiduously enacting as the four 'seals' [in one's being] the god's nature of existing, communicating, thinking, and acting. This deep concentration empowers one to feel that one *is* the god whom one has visualized, since all phenomena are manifestations of the working of a mind.

Creative imagination is to 'seal' one's three action levels [i.e. body, speech, and thought] and their operations as the expressions of the god's acts of existing, communicating, thinking, and acting with the four seals of Mahāmudrā, representing the act of existing, Dharmamudrā, being the act of communicating, Samayamudrā, being that of thinking, and Karmamudrā, being one's (perceptual) activity as it expresses itself through the emanation and reabsorption of light rays.[11] One performs this act of sealing after one has taken refuge [in the Three Jewels], developed an enlightened attitude, and effected, out of a sphere a nothingness, a transfiguration by means of five 'intuitions.' These are (i) the intuition of a lotus and a moon, forming a throne, being the cause factor of the existence of divine realms and habitats; (ii) that of letters as the elements of communication, being the cause factor of the most sublime message; (iii) that of a mood as the cause factor of a temporality which cannot be defined conceptually but is eternally present; (iv) that of perfected form-endowed existence in and with an entourage, being the cause factor of the sublime teacher and his followers; and (v) that of the god as embodied primordial awareness, being the cause factor of the very fact of absolute existence or of most exalted awareness. Even in this ritual activity one resorts to deep concentrations until the desired realization has been won through mastery and proficiency.

Although ritual purity and other observances are practised from time to time in the proper way, it is through attending to the experience of the inner processes of contemplation and imagination that one's activities become more harmonious and steady than they were in practising the previous forms of Tantra.

While temporarily the value-character of one's experience and understanding improves more and more, finally, within a period of three human lives, the five psycho-physical constituents, the five capacities and the five emotive reaction patterns become purified and are turned into the Buddha-nature of five Buddha-action patterns representing five forms of primordial awareness.[12]

These three Tantras in their totality conceive of the two truths [of appearance and nothingness] as alternations. They insist, however, on the importance of contemplating the ultimate as beyond judgments and propositions when all objective reference has been lost after the relative world of common appearance has been imagined as divine and when afterwards the appearance of it as a divine power has dissolved in itself.

CHAPTER EIGHT

THE UNSURPASSABLE REALIZATION

WHILE THE PRECEDING disciplines aimed at an ever more marked 'inwardness' and a growing enrichment of perception, the Anuttarayogatantra, which is listed as the next phase, is less their climactic fruition than a beginning from where they had left off. The 'inwardness' is now used to produce a 'profounder' awareness of the intrinsic qualities and values of the world of appearance and a 'vaster' range of potentialities. 'Profoundness' and 'vastness,' as a matter of fact, are the keynotes of this new and surpassing experience.[1] As far as words are able to convey its significance, the experience is described as complete; it needs nothing further and is sufficient unto itself. But inasmuch as every perception, however perfect and complete in itself it may be, translates itself into action, the manner in which a person conducts himself at this stage of his development and growth is one of 'choiceless' activity in which he no longer wastes his efforts. What at other times takes straining and struggling now 'comes of itself.' Conduct is free from blocks, more spontaneous, natural, unaffected and frank. This has been made possible through the individual's having become more able to fuse with the world, which has lost its 'thing'-character and is envisaged as an inspiring, aesthetically satisfying apparition. In gaining a new perspective through intrinsic perception and thereby 'creating' a more meaningful world, the individual can become one with it, as when the appreciator *becomes* the music and the music becomes *him*. This is ordinarily a very momentary and occasional achievement. As a rule, we compare, judge, approve, condemn, relate, and use. When this happens we perceive man and his world as part of the universe and in relation to the rest of it in many complex and devious ways.

But when the rift between an experiencing-self and an observing-self has been remedied by finding a more integrated point, the individual is 'all there' in the experience and need not drag in expectations based on past situations, and hopes or apprehensions based on planning for the future. Desire and fear, acceptance and rejection, those two formidable obsessive powers harassing a fictional self, have nothing to rest on or to haunt, because the individual has become most truly *himself*. His being, which is also his awareness, is an act and not a passive state, as it involves the whole living person and the world he lives in.

The new state is referred to in symbols, since only symbols can convey a glimpse of the richness that constitutes this unity of being and awareness. Examples of such symbols are 'citadel of Vajradhara' and 'Mahāmudrā.' 'Citadel' aptly illustrates the powerfulness of the locality which here is the centre of the personality which in itself acts as an integrator, and 'Vajradhara,' the Sceptre-bearer, is the Lord of the 'Indestructible' which is the very mystery of Being. This mystery is fundamentally the human situation itself as a quest: man is a being who, in his Being, is in search of his Being, of who (not what) he is. The other symbol, Mahāmudrā, literally translated means 'great seal' where 'great' (*mahā*) is used in an elative sense, 'there being nothing greater than this.' The second component, 'seal,' is not so much an imprint left on something as a vitalizing fulfilment, comparable with the vivid aesthetic perception of the artist as contrasted with the 'thing'-perception of ordinary persons. This symbol–term has been translated into Tibetan as either a masculine (*phyag-rgya chen-po*) or a feminine noun (*phyag-rgya chen-mo*), and this translation must be considered as an advance on the Sanskrit term which is exclusively feminine. The distinctive Tibetan translation reflects the polarity inherent in every living developmental process. Some contemplatives have a greater affinity with the feminine element in life, others with the masculine one. The way in which the symbol is verbalized merely indicates the individual's preference, but does not say anything about the symbol as such, which is a 'neutral' power and as such allows itself to be interpreted in either male or female images. The vitalizing power of the symbol is clearly attested to by Klong-chen rab-'byams-pa who gives the following explanation of *mudrā* (*phyag-rgya-ma*):

> "*phyag is* 'to hold to,' that is, to grasp the level of Buddhahood (which is going) beyond Saṃsāra; *rgya* is 'to seal,' that is, to seal Saṃsāra with enlightenment; *ma* is like invigorating food. Without food we die. Since enlightened understanding does not come without resorting to a *mudrā* (*phyag-rgya-ma*), we are fettered to the triple world without such understanding." [2]

However, to speak of a symbol must not make us overlook the eminently practical concern of the higher Tantras. Contemplation is not an end in itself but a means to make life more meaningful. It is here that much of what the Tantras have to say has been a source of perpetual misunderstanding with its attendant condemnation. The symbol-term *mudrā* also signifies 'woman' who must be understood as a 'way of doing,' a 'mode of activity,' a typical manner of conduct rather than as a typical kind of thing. That is to say, whereas a house is not itself 'in' the sign but only indicated by it, in this case the 'sign' (i.e., *mudrā*) indicates its 'signification' (i.e., the woman). The *mudrā*-woman thus actualizes Being and is its actuality, just as my body expresses my existence and as the concrete actualization of Being is both the 'expression' and the 'expressed.' When further it is said that no understanding is possible without the *mudrā*-(woman), the dialectic of lived experience is indicated. This lived experience is the tension of one existence towards another existence. It is essentially equivocal; everything which we live or think always has several meanings. Since existence, indeterminate in itself, manifests and expresses itself in the individual's body as sexuality and is manifested and expressed by the sexuality of the body, Mahāmudrā as absolute Being is equally indeterminate but manifests itself as masculinity or femininity which becomes *embodied* in a man and a woman. Masculinity and femininity belong to a plane of reality where male and female have little meaning. Male and female are only the adaptation to organic life of a basic polarity pertaining to the very process of becoming. As the higher Tantras deal with an individual's lived existence they quite naturally include sex, not because they advocate what other disciplines bashfully try to conceal but because they realize that sexuality is coextensive with the life of man. They are aware of the fact that sexuality cannot be reduced to existence nor can existence be reduced to sexuality. Man as embodied Being is sexual because he is the concrete expression of a basic polarity.

It is on the basis of the dialectic of lived experience that a distinction is made between 'Father'-, 'Mother'-, and 'Nondual' Tantras. What exactly is meant by this differentiation in opinions were held by the followers of the 'old' tradition (rNying-ma-pa) and by those of the 'new' one (dGe-lugs-pa). The latter, throughout their history, have been extreme traditionalists, paying attention to the words of the texts rather than to their meaning and therefore stressing the 'external' features. The 'old' tradition, on the other hand, claims that it brings out the spirit of Buddhism and does not cling to dead letters. To judge from textual evidence, their claim is not only well founded, it also reveals the tremendous difference in viewpoint between these two major trends. Accepting the Indian tradition almost to the letter, with its emphasis on epistemology and its restriction of its investigation to the analysis of concepts, the follower of the 'new' tradition must not put anything of himself into the investigation, and of necessity is forced to sidestep the human condition and what is of utmost concern to a living individual. Being metaphysically minded and concerned with an overall interpretation of experience or view of the world, the follower of the 'old' tradition continuously sees the world in new ways and acts on his vision too. Thus, whereas the 'new' tradition, which believes that the whole truth about the world is already known and that all that is necessary is to repeat the texts proclaiming this truth, is not in a position to produce original thought and offer moral advice, the 'old' tradition constantly tells us that things are not at all what they seem to be and, therefore, instead of leaving everything as it is, it engages in an on-going quest. As a consequence the Anuttarayogatantra, with its division into 'Father'-, 'Mother'- and 'Non-dual' Tantras, becomes a gradation rather than a uniformity. This gradation is technically known as Mahāyoga, Anuyoga, and Atiyoga, and since the Anuttarayoga turns out to be essentially a quest, even the last phase is again subdivided into three phases of an ever-increasing 'inwardness' and referred to as *sems-sde, klong-sde* and *man-ngag-gi sde*.

The starting point for the Mahāyoga is the metaphysical idea of the 'Two Truths,' which from the very moment it was first formulated in early Buddhist philosophy distinguished between what is ultimately real and what is empirically real. But here it is related to man's lived experience as an existing, communicating, and responding being. It does not take away anything from the phenomenal world, and certainly does not declare it to be 'unreal'; it rather frees the play of appearance from its fragmentation into things. In its transparency it is as nothing, but even so it *is,* and, regardless of its later qualifications as either this or that by a judgment which, as a matter of fact, presupposes Being as its possibility, its truth of being implies knowledge about Being. Knowledge is not added to Being but is implied by it. Therefore, ultimate Being is cognitive being and, in its being, knows about itself as Being, and implicitly also about what there is as object. In other words, Being-as-such is 'responsive,' and its response is the awareness of Being by Being-as-such. In this response subject and object are inseparable in a specific way. In the act of knowing, the subject *qua* subject knows itself as subject and counterpart to its object, and also knows it (the object) as counterpart to itself. In thus taking the object as its 'partner' it actually recognizes it as a subject in its own right which, in turn, *has* an object, namely the original subject, because *being* subject is tantamount to *having* object, and *having* object means to assume a certain attitude towards and to express a certain opinion on it, or simply, to function, to intend. There thus exists a 'response' relation of subject to object which may be unilateral or reciprocal. In the latter case there occurs what may be called 'a coming to terms' in which the object responds to the attitude of the subject and the subject aims at a certain response by the object. In case the subject's intention should aim at an attitude by the object suitable for setting up a state anticipated by the subject, the object's attitude would tally with that of the subject without, however, being identical with it. Applied to the 'Two Truths' this would mean that the 'superior conventional truth,' though not being the 'superior ultimate truth,' nevertheless is the latter's mode of Being, inasmuch as it exhibits the latter's functional intention in its own way. This is known as the indivisibility of the two truths. From a purely philosophical point of view the implication is tremendous, because the shallow subjectivism of all idealistic systems with their postulate of an absolute subject to which the object is dependently subordinated has been overcome. And as far as the human subject in his quest for Being is concerned, he is not swallowed up by an insensate absolute, euphemistically called Mind (with capital letter) or Brahman, and his world has lost nothing of its reality. Its dignity of being is not only recognized but even emphasized and never turned into a second-rate 'illusion.' This liberation of the individual from any kind of subjectivism widens his mental horizon and creates a new perspective involving a vast visual symbolism which not only adequately sums up the way in which the universe is comprehended, but also aids in the evocation of this comprehension. In this visual symbolism the so-called spell-letters (*yi-ge*) play an important role.[3]

While the Mahāyoga may be said to be essentially concerned with a visionary experience, the Anuyoga emphasizes the feeling tone of this vision. The emotional quality of what is best termed a peak experience is one of exaltation and pure happiness, and its symbolic characterization as 'son' marks the fusion as well as resolution of the ordinarily dichotomous and polar forces of reality, which are seen more clearly and felt more profoundly as harmonious and as essentially good and beautiful. Here again the terms Samantabhadra and Samantabhadrī are significant, since they concretely describe the 'all-round good' character of the polarities of masculinity and femininity which, to re-emphasize a former statement, are *facets* of being and not parts of it. The experience is infinitely rich, and the continued gaze and feeling can go from one aspect of the perfection of reality to another, now concentrating on one aspect (Samantabhadra), now on another (Samantabhadrī) in a continuous though fluctuating delight which itself is the unity and unification of the polarities. The richness to which the gaze may turn is technically termed a *maṇḍala,* which Klong-chen rab-'byams-pa, following an old tradition, explains as

> "The Indian term *maṇḍala* is in Tibetan *dkyil-'khor.* It means to surround any prominent facet of reality with beauty." [4]

His explanation reflects the spirit of the experience which other writers tried to reconcile with their traditionalism and slavish dependence on words. This may be gleaned from Blo-gsal rgya-mtsho's interpretation:

> "The previous learned men of Tibet explained the term *dkyil* as meaning 'the foremost' and *'khor* as 'the surrounding,' or *dkyil* as the god and *'khor* as his mansion, or *dkyil* as 'transworldly' and *'khor* as 'the worldly,' and so on. Here I follow the [etymology of the] Sanskrit word *maṇḍala. Maṇḍa* is the same as *sāra* and means 'essence' and *la* means 'to play,' 'to take,' 'to hold to.' Therefore *dkyil-'khor* means to 'take the awareness of great bliss' which is the essence [of the experience]." [5]

The beauty of the world to which reference is made is not its quality or value as separable from it. The world is beautiful because it *represents* beauty or absolute Being, and because it *is grounded* in it. Its beauty is an 'image' and 'appearance' pointing to its eternal perfection and completeness. In this experience of beauty and goodness the individual is entirely content; wherever he gazes he encounters beauty, and correspondingly expresses beauty and goodness in his very Being.

While the Mahāyoga aimed at presenting a new vision and the Anuyoga centered on the feeling tone of this vision, the

Atiyoga is concerned with bringing into existence the very foundation of cognitive life. About this foundation all we can say is that it *is,* but we cannot say what it is precisely because it is nothing at all in particular. Since it is *no* thing, it is not relative to anything else and thus is 'absolute.' Absoluteness, however, means that what *is* remains as it is. However it may appear, this does not mean that it loses its is-ness. This the texts indicate by saying that the whole of reality, that is, whatever there is, remains in self-same absoluteness (*mnyam-nyid*). In other words, if Being-as-such is absolute and therefore eternally remains the same, then whatever there is, is in view of its very being, which is Being-as-such, equally absolute and eternally the same; and, whatever there is, is relative to something else, and this relativity is the absoluteness of whatever there is. Since furthermore Being-as-such is absolute by virtue of the fact that it just *is,* it follows that it is not grounded in whatever there may be, that is, whatever appears before a person's mind. 'Appearance' in the Atiyoga is not a correlate to an unknowable thing-in-itself, nor is it to be identified with semblance. It is the distortions of an identical, self-same thing by the observer. The statement that appearance is delusive only means that it is futile to seek any sort of being in it other than the Being-as-such, which alone can claim the status of absoluteness or true Being. Since Being-as-such is coterminous with cognitive absoluteness (*sems-nyid*), it is essentially intentional. That is to say, inasmuch as Being-as-such or cognitive absoluteness is not a thing, not a content in cognition, it is an utter openness or rather an opening to, a shedding light by and on the intentional structure of a person's awareness. All our conscious acts are stretched out into a world that is relative to us and to our meanings. Consciousness knows itself, not objectively, but in its act of being and being-conscious. It is irradiative in revealing a horizon of meaning which encompasses all that can be known by feeling, thought, imagination and other forms of cognition. But while every cognitive act is the cognition *of* something, in order to comprehend one pole of its intentional structure that makes up the cognitive act, it is necessary to comprehend the other pole as well. It is impossible to understand a desirable object without also understanding the intentional act of the desire desiring it. We may speak of a primordial *thinking with* in view of the co-presence of absolute Being and cognitive absoluteness. This co-presence in itself is Dharmakāya, while the together-with is Sambhogakāya which by its irradiativeness indicates the manner in which Being-as-such spontaneously refers itself to its horizon of possible meanings. This horizon is constituted by Nirmāṇakāya, the responsibility embodiment of ultimate being. An individual's body is not something external to his existence, rather it is the concrete actualization of it. In this way it functions as a sort of implicit knowledge of the world whose structure is delineated by the body and its movements, acting as an orientation point to the individual's world. Thus, in the Atiyoga, the well-known triad of Dharmakāya, Sambhogakāya, and Nirmāṇakāya is dealt with existentially rather than postulationally-theoretically.

The Atiyoga is also known as 'Absolute Perfection and Completion' (*rdzogs-pa chen-po*). Its 'completeness' is summed up in a couplet often quoted:

Complete in one, complete in two, complete in mind:
Complete in one is complete in created by mind;
Complete in two is complete in perfect harmony;
Complete in everything is complete in becoming enlightened.[6]

This rather cryptic statement is elucidated by Klong-chen rab-'byams-pa as follows:

> 'Created by mind' means that the impure or the constituents of Saṃsāra, that is, whatever presents itself as appearance and possibility, the world as container and the beings as its content, summarized by the psycho-physical constituents, their elements and the interactional fields, as well as perspective, creative imagination and conduct based on them, considered as the foundation, way and goal by the various spiritual courses, are but the tendencies of a mind in its going astray [from its original integrity], because [all this] has been ephemerally created

by the water mill called mind. Although in their manifestation as errant appearance and in the mistaken belief in their reality they seem to be veridical for all practical purposes, actually they have no essence (of their own) and have never moved from the range of original awareness. Therefore [the words] complete in one [are used].

'Complete in perfect harmony' means that the very nature of original awareness, which is a radiant light, is an utter openness or Dharmakāya; that its actuality is irradiativeness Sambhogakāya, and that its sensitive responsiveness is intrinsic perception or Nirmāṇakāya. Inasmuch as the three Kāyas have been complete in their own right ever since they have been, there is no need to look for them elsewhere and to prove them somewhere. Therefore [the words] complete in perfect harmony [are used].

'Complete in becoming enlightened' means that whatever appears as possibility [for the judgment of being] pure and impure and the way in which it appears, is grounded in original awareness, starts from it and remains with it, just as a person's sleep and his various dream experiences are grounded in his psyche, arise from it, and stay with it. Therefore cognitive absoluteness [is referred to by the words] complete in becoming enlightened.[7]

The repeated reference to 'mind' (*sems*) must not induce us to understand this word literally, as when in us the sight of a dog ordinarily evokes the utterance of the word 'dog,' where the word refers to the thing. The word 'mind' is merely a *symbol* of the experience of those who have had the experience which the Atiyoga attempts to bring about in those who follow its lead. A person who then wants to communicate the experience which he and others who have had it consider to be the most worth-while of all experiences available to human beings, must resort to language, and if he attempts to convey it intellectually, he will most likely use terms ordinarily used in mentalistic disciplines; if he wants to communicate his experience of bliss, he will use terms related to the world of feeling. This accounts for the further subdivision of the Atiyoga into *sems-sde* 'mentalistic section' and *klong-sde* 'feeling-tone section.' However, these subdivisions still imply conceptualizations which are illegitimate because Being-as-such cannot be conceptualized. To do so is to negate its Being and to reduce it to a mere fiction. In order to be consistent, a follower of the Atiyoga must be silent. To bring this out is the task of the *man-ngag-gi sde* 'guidance section.' Here the individual does not try to set up extraneous rules, but allows himself to be 'guided' by the totality of Being. He can do this because he himself is this Being in embodied form. Inasmuch as Being is dynamic, man as an embodied being is guided from and in the light of the future of what he is going to be. This is the process of becoming enlightened which goes on forever.

FROM

THE SUMMARY OF PHILOSOPHICAL SYSTEMS

YID-BZIN MDZOD-KYI GRUB-MTHA' BSDUS-PA

foll. 30a. ff.

THE INNER UNSURPASSABLE SPIRITUAL COURSE OF THE YOGATANTRA *

Concerning the unsurpassable spiritual course one must first of all know the difference between the outer and inner aspects relating to the triple division into Starting Point, Path, and Goal.

THE STARTING POINT

The outer aspect is present when at the time of the maturing initiations the 'jar-consecration' is of primary importance; the inner one is given when the three higher consecrations figure more prominently.[8]

THE PATH

When contemplation proceeds in such a way that the Developing and Fulfilment Stages form a unity and not an alternation because the symbol-character and the absolute self-sameness [of reality] are envisaged as not implying any acceptance or rejection, the inner aspect is given. If this is not possible the outer aspect prevails. As a consequence, when conduct is based on acceptance or rejection of the ritual purity in place, food, dress and so on, the outer aspect obtains; when there is impartiality, the inner one.

THE GOAL

This is freedom. As to the particular time [of its realization] the inner aspect obtains when Buddhahood is realized in this life, the outer one when in a future life.

The general idea underlying the inner aspect of these great

* See *The Yogatantra*, p. 189.

Yoga disciplines of the special Tantra is as follows: the totality of reality subsumed under Saṃsāra and Nirvāṇa, or appearance and possibility, resides in utter self-sameness. Here, 'profoundness' is the purity [of all reality] in having the same value as the absoluteness of the Great Middle,[9] devoid of all judgments and propositions moving within four confines;[10] 'vastness' is its contemplation in the knowledge that the psychophysical constituents, the biotic forces, the sense fields, the five action patterns of Buddhahood and so on, constituting the specific appearance from the 'profound,' are one great *maṇḍala* rich in symbolism. And so whatever appears need not be rejected, but, as a most excellent means that is free in itself, is turned into a helper for traversing and scaling the paths and levels of spirituality. When then in all one's actions 'vastness' as the Developing Stage and 'profoundness' as the Fulfilment Stage, forming a unity in which from their very beginning they have never been joined or separated, are contemplated as [the working of] the absolute and original awareness in which the two truths [of appearance and nothingness] are indivisible, Mahāmudrā, the highest realization, integration, the citadel of rDo-rje-'chang, is reached.

In particular a division is made into 'Father'-, 'Mother'-, and 'Non-dual' Tantras with respect to the nature of counteracting the three poisons of emotivity and the intellectual acumen [of the followers of the Tantric disciplines] as well as other features.

One speaks of 'Father'-Tantras within the framework of the Anuttarayoga-Tantras when the primary concern is with the Developing Stage and its corollary, the methods of enacting the various attendant rites, as well as with the feeling of having an apparitional nature which is the manifestation of original awareness serving as the means of realization, the Fulfilment Stage as [the awareness] of inner sensations (*rlung*), and exorcism.[11] It is declared to be a means of training those who are swayed by antipathy and who cling to outward forms.[12]

One speaks of 'Mother'-Tantras when in the same framework emphasis is put on the Fulfilment Stage, on the discriminative-appreciative awareness of nothingness (*stong-nyid*) rather than on ritualism, and on the progressive experience through the Yoga of irradiative light, the feeling of bliss which is due to the free movement of creative life constituting the 'path of action,' and the ritual of subjugation. It is stated to be a means of training those who are in the clutches of passion, who are capable of identifying themselves with their body as lived in by a mind, and who are of mediocre intellectual acumen.

One speaks of the unsurpassed 'Non-dual' Tantras when emphasis is laid on the ultimate nature of the existence of all that is, which is the awareness of the symbol-character (*dag-pa*) [of all this is] and its absolute self-sameness, the self-aware enlightenment-mind as the sole creative power. No importance is attached to the Developing or Fulfilment Stages or action and contemplation in isolation. It is shown to be a means of training those who are [simply] not-knowing-better [but otherwise are not in a worse condition by additional hatred and love], and (who) as superior beings can proceed without stress and strain.

Some followers of the 'new tradition' of the Tantras claim that all Anuttarayoga-Tantras are alike in establishing the importance of unity, but are classified as either 'Father'- or 'Mother'-Tantras when they emphasize action or intuition respectively. It is also said that the division into 'Father'- and 'Mother'-Tantras is determined by the predominance of either gods or goddesses in a *maṇḍala,* the position of the principal gods or goddesses, the ornaments and dresses, the circumambulation from either the right or the left, the beginning of the ritual acts at night or during the day, the symbol-awareness and so on.

Also, there is according to the 'new tradition' a further triple division of the inner Tantras. The 'Father'-Tantras consist of the Guhyasamājatantra and others, the 'Mother'-Tantras of the Cakrasaṃvaratantra and others, and the 'Non-dual' Tantras of the Kālacakratantra. Since the latter clearly explains the a priori awareness which shines forth in the moment of the fourth initiation, while the other Tantras only obscurely hint at it, it is in all authoritative works extolled as the climax of the Tantras by such attributes as 'the neutral citadel of Vajradhara' because it does not side either with action or intuition, or as 'the opening of the casket of precious Buddhahood' because it teaches a non-dual self-same absolute.

According to the 'old tradition' the inner Tantras are classified as follows. The 'Father'-Tantras correspond to the *Mahāyoga,* the 'Mother'-Tantras to the *Anuyoga,* and the 'Non-dual' Tantras to the *Atiyoga.* It is stated that the Mahāyoga which deals with the Developing State is like the ground for everything else; the Anuyoga, which deals with the implementation [of what is the ground of human existence], is like the path; and the Atiyoga, which is the Fulfilment, is the goal. Accordingly the Mahāyoga, which is like the foundation, serves as the continuing factor for the two subsequent ones. The Anuyoga is like the progression on the path because it clearly explains and points out the profound path of action dealing with the empathetic identification with one's body as lived in by a mind and the inner structure and processes in it and, in view of the continuity [of Being], it is the elucidation of the meaningfulness of Being.[13] The goal to which ultimately all paths lead is the absolute original awareness. This has been revealed here in all its perfection and immediateness. It is therefore the climax of the Tantric path and in relation to the two preceding phases it is classified as the 'guidance'-Tantras.

MAHĀYOGA

The Mahāyoga will be discussed under the three headings of laying the Foundation, practising and experiencing the Path, and reaching the Goal.

THE FOUNDATION

The superior conventional truth is that the whole phenomenal world, present since beginningless time as the triple *maṇḍala* of embodied Being, communication, and responsiveness, is as if nothing, and the superior ultimate truth is the fact that this nothingness, which cannot be established as an object, is both Being and awareness, though not in an additive or disjunctive sense. The indivisibility of these two superior truths is ever present as ultimate cognitive Being. Through the axioms of the four kinds of understanding,[14] the scriptural authorities, and logical investigations, it is ascertained as not being an object, but irradiative and beyond the reach of conceptualizing mind.

THE PATH

The experience starts from a feeling of utter openness, the apparitionalness of compassionate action, [the adoption of a] single attitude, of elaborate postures and gestures, arrangements of flowers in a ritual ceremony and so on. Gradually it leads to spiritual maturation, control over one's span of life, the realization of Mahāmudrā and entering the citadel of Him who has spontaneous knowledge.

THE GOAL

When through the power of this profound path the infinite variety of impurities involved in 'deviation' [15] has been removed, the citadel of Vajradhara being of the nature of twenty-five aspects is reached on the Yi-ge 'khor-lo tshogs-chen level.[16]

ANUYOGA

The Anuyoga follows the same division as the Mahāyoga.

THE FOUNDATION

The things of the phenomenal world constitute the spontaneous *maṇḍala* [surrounding] Samantrabhadra, and nothingness, freed from all limitations, as its actuality is the primordial *maṇḍala* [surrounding] Samantabhadrī. Their self-same absoluteness in the sense that their essences are not additive or disjunctive, i.e., their son, is the *maṇḍala* of the enlightened mind in great bliss.

THE PATH

Although these *maṇḍalas* have been forever inseparable from one's mind and although all entities of reality gather in it, one has to apply the appropriate means to bring into immediate reality this original bliss-awareness by an empathetic identification with the structures, motility, and creativity (of embodying Being). This is in order to remove the obscurations that come with the involvement into the world of appearance representing a variety of opposites such as good and evil, acceptance and rejection, due to the movement of dichotomizing thought in its polarities of subject and object of which the latent possibilities of the three 'light'-manifestations have become the cause-factor.[18] By [the application of the appropriate means] one gradually traverses the stages of the preparatory path or 'aspiration,' the connecting path or 'clear insight,' the path of seeing or 'the great respite,' [19] the path of attending to the seen or 'the great revelation,' and the path of no-more-learning or 'perfect creativity.'

THE GOAL

This is the realization of Buddhahood, existence as great bliss on the *rdzogs-spyir-chib* level,[20] where understanding and abandon have come to an end.

ATIYOGA

The Atiyoga follows the triple division.

THE FOUNDATION

This is the certainty that the whole of reality is the sole creativity of a self-same absolute original awareness. That is to say, all the entities of reality are but an appearance before one's mind. But since no essence in this appearance can be found, it is a delusive presence. Cognitive absoluteness, which is nothing in itself, is noetic Being, its irradiativeness as actuality is communicative Being, and its sensitive responsiveness, which constitutes the horizon of meaning, is authentic Being.[21] It thus has been ever present as the three existential norms, and in its presential value of the indivisibility of purity and spontaneousness it is the absolute and spontaneous self-same *maṇḍala* in which the whole of Saṃsāra and Nirvāṇa need not be accepted nor rejected.

THE PATH

By such 'felt' knowledge the significance of reality gradually dawns upon us when we leave it as what it is in original awareness which is effortlessly present, and which is not in need of being affirmed or negated, refuted or posited. Although this process looks like making the effortlessly operating original awareness one's path of development, it really means that error subsides where it has started from, and the four light-experiences reach their final stage,[22] by the four types of concentrations through which the absolute having no determinate observable qualities is experienced, and by the three visions of the *thod-rgal,*[23] through which spontaneity with its determinate observable qualities is experienced.

THE GOAL

Here the openess of self-aware enlightenment, devoid of all incidental obscurations, abandon and attainment having reached their end,[24] is unchangingly present, inseparable from the all-encompassing primordial Lord Samantabhadra, on the level of absolute awareness.[25]

In this doctrine of Absolute Completion both the *Sems-sde* and *Klong-sde* are concerned with the immediate experience of the Absolute, the former by emphasizing the perspective through which the self-certain awareness or the very fact of enlightenment is envisaged, and the latter by focussing on the meditation on the self-same Absolute by overcoming Saṃsāra and Nirvāṇa through the five forms of original awareness.[26] The *Man-ngag-sde* lets [us] hold firmly to the real without becoming mistaken about it when the inner-light awareness is sensorily experienced. Hence it emphasizes the experience of spontaneity.

The many details about setting out on the path [of spiritual development] in each of these sections may be learned from the Tantras and from Klong-chen rab-'byams-pa's other writings.

Although there are many aspects, actually there is only one way of arriving without effort at this original awareness in which absolute purity and spontaneity form a unity, once this cognition absoluteness has been realized as what it really is, free from the obscurations of mentation.[27] Here all spiritual courses and philosophical tenets have reached their end.

Selected Bibliography

A. Tibetan Sources

(mf: microfilms, ms: manuscript copies in the author's possession)

Bi-ma snying-tig mf Collection of rNying-ma-pa works in 15 vols.

Bla-ma yang-tig Collection of smaller works by Klong-chen rab-'byams-pa, n. pl., n.d.

Chos-dbyings rin-po-che'i mdzod-kyi 'grel-pa lung-gi gter-mdzod autocommentary on the *Chos dbyings rin-po-che'i mdzod* by Klong-chen rab-'byams-pa. publ. by Dodrup Chen Rinpoch, Gangtok

Grub-mtha' chen-mo by 'Jam-dbyangs bzhad-pa'i rdo-rje. publ. by Bhikshu Guru Deva Lama, Sarnath 1964

Grub-pa'i mtha'i rnam-par bzhag-pa rin-po-che'i phreng-ba by dKon-mchog 'Jigs-med dbang-po, publ. by the (late) Mongolian Dalama rNam-rgyal rdo-rje

rGyal-tshab, *Collected Works,* Tashilhunpo edition, n.d.

rGyud-rgyal gsang-ba snying-po'i 'grel-pa by Rong-zom Chos-kyi dpal bzang-po mf

Lam-zab-kyi rnam-par bshad-pa zab-lam-gyi snye-ma by Padma dkar-po ms

dPal gsang-ba snying-po'i rgyud-don gsal-byed me-long by g'Yung-ston rdo-rje dpal-bzang mf

dPal Kye-rdo-rje'i phyi bskyed-rim-gyi rnam-par bshad-pa legs-bshad nyi-ma'i 'od-zer by Blo-gsal rgya-mtsho (publ. by the Mongolian Dalama)

Sa-lam-gyi rnam-bzhag go-bde-ba'i ngang-gis bshad-pa by bsTan-pa dar-bzang ms

Sa-lam-gyi rnam-bzhag theg-gsum mdzes-rgyan by dKon-mchog 'Jigs-med dbang-po ms

Theg-pa chen-po'i man-ngag-gi bstan-chos Yid-bzhin rin-po-che'i mdzod-kyi 'grel-pa padma dkar-po autocommentary on the

Yid-bzhin rin-po-che'i mdzod by Klong-chen rab-'byams-pa mf

Theg-pa'i mchog rin-po-che'i mdzod by Klong-chen rab-'byams-pa mf

Theg-pa mtha'-dag-gi don gsal-bar byed-pa Grub-pa'i mtha' rin-po-che'i mdzod by Klong-chen rab-'byams-pa mf

Tibetan Buddhist Studies of Kloṅ-rdol bla-ma Ṅag-dbaṅ-blo-bzaṅ publ. by Dalama, Laxmanpuri, Mussoorie 1963

Tsong-kha-pa, *Collected Works,* Tashilhunpo edition, n.d.

Yid-bzhin-mdzod-kyi grub-mtha' bsdus-pa by Mi-pham 'Jam-dbyangs rnam-rgyal rgya-mtso, publ. by Tarthang Tulku n.pl., n.d.

B. OTHER WORKS

Abhidharmakośa L'Abhidharmakośa de Vasubandhu. Traduit et annoté par Louis de la Vallée Poussin. Paris. Paul Geuthner, Louvain, J.-B. Istas 1923–1931.

Abhisamayālankāra *Abhisamayālankāra nāma prajñāpārami topadeśaśāstra.* Ed. by Th. Stcherbatsky and E. Obermiller: Bibliotheca Buddhica 23, Leningrad 1927.

Guhyasamājatantra Guhyasamāja Tantra or Tathāgataguhyaka. Critically edited with introduction and index by Benoytosh Bhattacharyya, Oriental Institute, Baroda, 1931.

Mahāyānasūtrālankāra Asanga, Mahāyāna-Sutrālaṃkāra. Exposé de la doctrine du grand véhicule selon le système Yogācāra. Édité et traduit d'après un manuscript rapporté du Nepal par Sylvain Lévi. 2 vols. Paris, Librairie Honoré Champion, 1907–1911.

Sandhinirmocaṇasūtra Saṃdhinirmocanasūtra. L'explication des mystères. Texte Tibétain édité et traduit par Étienne Lamotte. Bureaux du recueil, bibliothèque de l'université,

Louvain; Librairie d'Amérique et d'Orient Adrien Maisonneuve, Paris, 1935.

Vijñaptimātratāsiddhi Vijñaptimātratāsiddhi. La Siddhi de Hiuan-tsang. Traduite et annotée par Louis de la Vallée Poussin, Librairie Orientaliste Paul Geuthner, Paris 1928–1948.

Guenther, Herbert V., *sGam.po.pa—Jewel Ornament of Liberation* Rider & Company, London 1959.

———, *The Life and Teaching of Nāropa,* Clarendon Press, Oxford 1963.

———, *The Spiritual Teacher in Tibet* (= Hermès. Recherches sur l'Expérience Spirituelle, Paris 1967).

———, *Tibetan Buddhism without Mystification* E. J. Brill, Leiden 1966.

Lamotte, Étienne, *Histoire du Bouddhisme Indien. Dès origines à l'ère Saka.* Publications Universitaires, Louvain 1958.

Takakusu, Junjiro, *The Essentials of Buddhist Philosophy* 3rd ed. Office Appliance Co., Ltd. Honolulu 1956.

NOTES

Notes to Chapter I

[1] The four qualities stand for the ways in which a person behaves. He may be one who is victorious by the path, who points out the path, who lives by the path, and who makes a mockery of the path. See *Abhidharmakośa* IV 39.

[2] These are mentioned in the *Vinaya,* the *Milindapañha,* the *Visuddhimagga.* There is, however, no evidence that they were ever widely adopted. The Pāli texts usually enumerate thirteen practices.

[3] See *Mahāyānasūtrālankāra* xx–xxi 16, for the thirty-seven topics. The five paths are: the path of preparation, the path of linking one's preparations with the path of seeing, the path of seeing itself, the path of attending to what has been seen, and the path of no-more-learning. The three poisons are: passion-lust, hatred-aversion, and infatuation-bewilderment.

[4] The three types are the misery of conditioned existence, the misery of change, and the misery of misery in itself. See H. V. Guenther, *sGam.po.pa—The Jewel Ornament of Liberation,* pp. 55 ff.

[5] See above note 3.

[6] This is the Sautrāntikas' conception of Nirvāṇa. They have often been equated with the Pratyekabuddhas.

[7] This refers to the famous story that Māra appeared before Upagupta in the guise of the Buddha.

[8] The four axioms are: everything is transitory; everything transitory is frustrating; nothing has or constitutes a principle through which something is what it is; and Nirvāṇa is bliss.

[9] The word 'countless' indicates a certain number in the number mysticism that was current in ancient India.

[10] The two prerequisites are merits and knowledge.

Notes to Chapter II

[1] This name covers a number of 'schools' and their subdivisions. However, tradition is not unanimous. According to Étienne Lamotte, *Histoire du Bouddhisme Indien. Dès origines à l'ère Śaka,* (Louvain 1958) pp. 578, the *Sarvāstivādins* comprised:

1. The Vātsīputrīyas and their subdivisions: Dharmottariya, Bhadrayānikas, Sāṃmitīyas, Saṇṇagarikas;
2. The Mahīśāsakas and their subgroup: Dharmaguptakas;
3. The Kāśyapīyas (or Suvarṣakas); and
4. The Sautrāntikas.

This last group may not have been identical with the later Sautrāntikas.

[2] Hence their name Sarvāstivadins (*sarvam asti*).

[3] See Chapter IV.

[4] The Mahīśāsakas listed as the fourth particular existent the state of mental immobility (*āniñjya*); and the forerunners of the Yogācāras also included the state in which sensation and feeling have ceased to be operative (*saṃjñāveditanirodha*). See Louis de la Vallée Poussin, *Vijñaptimātratāsiddhi. La Siddhi de Hiuan-tsang*, p. 678.

[5] The analysis here follows the exposition of Klong-chen rab-'byams-pa in his *Theg-pa mtha'-dag-gi don gsal-bar byed-pa grub-pa'i mtha' rin-po-che'i mdzod*, fol. 37a. (In the following this work will be referred to in the abbreviated form *Grub-mtha'-mdzod*).

[6] *Grub-mtha'-mdzod*, fol. 37b.

[7] The qualification 'of what there is' is to distinguish the use of 'ontology' in the Buddhist context from the customary Western use of the word.

[8] This does not mean that the one borrowed from the other. Rather, this concretistic type of thinking was 'in the air.'

[9] It is on this 'path' (*mthong-lam*) or at this moment that the Four Noble Truths are 'seen,' and this vision initiates the actual process of spiritual growth.

[10] The later count is given on page 56 f. The earlier count is found on the table facing p. 72 in Junjiro Takakusu, *The Essentials of Buddhist Philosophy*, Honolulu 1956.

[11] The term *shes-pa*, translated here by 'the noetic,' is not an exact equivalent of the Sanskrit word for mind, *citta*, which in Tibetan is *sems* and which is more adequately rendered by 'responsiveness' than by the traditional translation of 'mind.' What we understand by 'mind' is a total state of responsiveness and those mental events and processes which give it a determinate and specific character. The subtle difference between *sems* (*citta*), *sems-byung* (*caitta*), and *shes-pa* (*jña*) can be stated as follows: responsiveness (*sems*) and mental events (*sems-byung*) entail the noetic (*shes-pa*), but the noetic does not entail responsiveness, because a mental event is the noetic but not responsiveness.

For the Vaibhāṣikas the noetic is a particular existent. Similarly, mental events are not derivatives or states of a mind, but separate particular existents.

[12] For the importance of being a human being see H. V. Guenther,

Tibetan Buddhism without Mystification, pp. 4 ff. Man can work out his way of growth only as man, but this does not entail the fallacious argument that man is the measure of all things. This psychology of excessive dominance is absent in Buddhism.

[13] See *Abhidharmakośa* VII 31 ff.

[14] dKon-mchog 'Jigs-med dbang-po in his *Grub-pa'i mtha'i rnam-par bzhag-pa rin-po-che'i phreng-ba,* fol. 4b states: "If someone declares that the Vātsīputrīyas should not be counted as Buddhists because they recognize a self, the objection is unfounded. The non-absolute character of the entities of reality, which is mentioned as one of the four axioms [lit.: seals], is recognized by the five schools of the Sāṃmitīyas [that is, the Gokulikas, Dharmaguptikas, Bhadrayānikas, Vātsīputrīyas and Dharmottarikas], for whom this non-absolute character is merely the non-existence of an eternal, single, and sovereign Pure Ego, while the self which they recognize is of the nature of a self-sufficient substance."

[15] Colour-form (*gzugs*), feeling, sensation-ideation, motivation, and perceptual processes.

[16] Accumulation of merits and perfection of knowledge are the beginning of the 'Path' (*lam*) which is a name for man's spiritual growth. The central phase of this growth is the 'Path of Seeing' reality as it is, which means not to expect more of it than it can offer. Viewed from this central phase the accumulation of merits and perfection of knowledge are peripheral and must be 'linked' to the centre if the aim of the individual's growth, integrity, is to be fulfilled. This 'linking' is the second phase of the 'Path.' However, these stages, preparation, and linking, are marked by endeavour, and every kind of endeavour is bound to arouse affective states due to the feeling of success or failure. Every affective state disrupts the integrity of man's being and prevents him from seeing himself and his world properly, because it makes him biased.

[17] The qualifying adjectives 'coarser' and 'subtler' refer to the evaluative division of the universe into a world of sensuality, (aesthetic) forms, and formlessness. Each subsequent 'world'-experience in this schema is more subtle than the preceding one. Meditative concentration and attention is considered as a fluctuation between these three worlds.

[18] Names (*ming*), words (*tshig,* inflected nouns and verbs), and letters (*yi-ge*) are the material out of which significant patterns are built. This material itself is not a significant form or pattern (*gzugs*). Insofar as the Buddha-word conveys meaning it is significant form; insofar as it consists of letters and elements of speech it is a disjunct entity.

[19] See above note (14).

[20] They are: passion-lust (*'dod-chags*), aversion-hatred (*zhe-sdang*),

and bewilderment-error (*'kkrul-pa*). They derive their names from their overt manifestations but are not merely these. 'Error' does not imply culpability but describes man's straying away from his authentic nature into a world of 'things.' See n. 3, chap. I.

[21] The four patterns are: (a) one does not understand the profoundness and subtleness of the Buddha's teaching, (b) one does not know what is going on at a distance, (c) one does not know the past nor the future, and (d) one does not understand the manifoldness of reality.

[22] They are those of (a) Śrāvakas, (b) Pratyekabuddhas, and (c) Bodhisattvas.

[23] The Truth of the Path is what is otherwise known as the Noble Eightfold Path. While for all other schools this path was knowledge, the Vaibhāṣikas recognized only five of its eight members as being of the nature of knowledge. Right speech, right action, and right livelihood were for them 'significant form' (*gzugs*). 'Form' (*gzugs*) was a particular existent different from the 'noetic' or 'knowledge' (*shes-pa*).

[24] The Path of Preparation, consisting of the accumulation of merits and the perfection of knowledge, is of an inferior, mediocre, and superior quality. The practises which belong to each grade have been pointed out in H. V. Guenther, *sGam.po.pa—The Jewel Ornament of Liberation,* London 1959, p. 233.

[25] Six types of saints were recognized. Only the highest one would not fall from his height. However, although the five lower saints might fall, they would not fall so low as to find themselves on the level of an ordinary being. See *Abhidharmakośa* VI 56 ff. 'Rejection' is the relinquishing of all affective states, and 'attainment' is the state of happiness operating in the present, because the disturbing affective states have been eliminated.

[26] The twenty varieties of Śrāvakas are enumerated in *Abhisamayālankāra* I 23–24. There are eighty-one affective states or potentialities that can be overcome by the truth one has seen. They distribute as follows: nine belong to the world of sensuality and sensuousness, thirty-six to the world of aesthetic forms (nine to each of its four levels), and thirty-six to the world of formlessness with also nine to each of its four levels. According to the Vaibhāṣikas each of the eighty-one affective states is overcome in succession, starting with the first belonging to the world of sensuality, then its second, and so on, until one arrives at the last one which belongs to the world of formlessness. A person who overcomes nine at a time is one who abandons the first of each of the nine affective patterns belonging to the nine levels of the three world-spheres. Then he overcomes the second nonary and so on up to the ninth nonary.

[27] The Buddha-marks are enumerated in *Abhisamayālankāra* VIII

13–17. This is the well-known episode in the life of the Buddha before enlightenment. The conquest of Māra (*Devaputramāra*) is essentially a spiritual phenomenon. Māra is a shorthand term for the feeling of pleasure through meditative exercises which are so easily misunderstood as a means of producing this feeling rather than as the vehicle by which one passes beyond affective states. Meditation, in whatever sense of the word we may understand it, is a step into another world which we cannot but designate divine (having both benign and fearful features). Hence, in personalistic terms one speaks of gods (*deva, devaputra*) or, when there is a strict dualism, of heaven and hell. The divine, however, has meaning only in relation to the humane; it is not superior in an absolute sense, although its superior power is often too much for human beings. Whether man is involved in 'blunt facts' or lives in a world of 'gods' does not alter his being at the mercy of dark powers. The preoccupation with the things of this world is in no way different from the preoccupation with the world of gods. To be so involved in either aspect of reality is technically known as Saṃsāra, and Saṃsāra is synonymous with Māra. Thus, in the conquest of Māra man casts off his shackles and finds freedom as a mode of being.

[28] There are twelve episodes of particular significance in the life of a Buddha; however, the count varies. They are: (i) the resolve to be born in the world of man (since this happens in another realm this incident is sometimes not counted as a Buddha-act); (ii) the descent from the Tuṣita heaven; (iii) entering the mother's womb; (iv) physical birth (however, if no. i is counted, nos. iii and iv are taken together as one incident); (v) accomplishment in worldly arts; (vi) a life of pleasure with women; (vii) withdrawal from it; (viii) ascetic exercises; (ix) sitting under the Bodhi-tree; (x) conquest of Māra; (xi) becoming a Buddha; (xii) promulgating the teaching; (xiii) passing into Nirvāṇa.

[29] The *Grub-mtha'-mdzod*, fol. 37a offers the clearest presentation. Discussing the nature and number of relatively stable patterns (*gzugs*) its author says: "Relatively stable patterns that can be shown and present [certain] limitations are as follows: The atoms of earth-solidity, water-cohesion, fire-temperature, and wind-movement, being indivisible, are ultimately real particular existents. Out of their collocation which retains intervals between them, the 'coarse' physical-material [universe] is set up. "Relatively stable patterns that cannot be shown while presenting [certain] limitations are the following: the five senses of sight, hearing, smelling, tasting and the tactile organ (the body) as well as [their referents], colour, sound, taste, fragrance and touch.

"Relatively stable patterns that can neither be shown nor have

[any] limitations are discipline, absence of discipline, and that which is neither the one nor the other, all three pervading the whole body like a raging fire."

80 The *Grub-mtha'-mdzod,* fol. 37b states: "Mind is the six sensory perceptions: visual, auditory, olfactory, gustatory, tactile, and intellectual. When the five sense organ functions (*dbang-po*) sense their respective objects and the five sensory perceptions (*rnam-shes*) perceive their respective objects, it is the intellect (*yid-kyi rnam-par shes-pa*) that interprets [the perceptions] as to past, future, particular existent and so on. Otherwise intellectual perception would have to be claimed to *sense* objects which are concealed, because of its nature of not being limited." This passage shows that perceiving and conceiving begin when we select and attend to connections which have already been 'thought' in sensory awareness, although they have not yet been 'thought about.'

81 This difficult passage is clarified in the *Grub-mtha'-mdzod,* fol. 38: "(1) Each perception (*rnam-par shes-pa*) as the primary factor has its own objective reference by relating itself to one object; (2) it has its own observable quality as it investigates qualities similar to it [i.e., in the case of colours it will observe their nuances, but not timbre which belongs to sound]; (3) it operates simultaneously because perception occurs at one time; (4) it operates from its specific basis because it starts from its specific sense-organ [which give perception its sensory name]; and (5) it has its substantial foundation because in a certain person (*gang-zag*) it does not start from visual perception alone nor from one of the attendant functions."

82 In the Sāṃkhya system time is the mode of constituting things in their different stages of becoming manifest in the course of their evolution (*adhvan*). For the Nyāya-Vaiśeṣikas it was a substance (*dravya*) existing by itself which in accordance with the changes of things reveals itself as past, present, and future.

83 The four points are: being, non-being, both being and non-being and neither being nor non-being.

Notes to Chapter III

1 Thus Klong-chen rab-'byams-pa in his *Theg-pa chen-po'i man-ngag-gi bstan-chos Yid-bzhin rin-po-che'i mdzod-kyi 'grel-pa padma dkar-po,* vol. VAM, foll. 36a f. (In the following abbreviated as *Yid-bzhin-mdzod*).

2 *Grub-mtha'-mdzod,* foll. 40b.

3 In this school the essential works on Buddhist logic originated. They are: *Pramāṇavārttikā; Pramāṇaviniścaya; Nyāyabinduprakaraṇa; Hetubinduprakaraṇa; Sambandhaparīkṣaprakaraṇa; Codanānāmaprakaraṇa;* and *Santānāntarasiddhi.*

[4] For the Vaibhāṣikas only the first fifteen moments were the 'Path of Seeing'; the sixteenth moment, because it could only repeat itself, was already the path of attending to what had been seen.

[5] The 'Path of Seeing' consists of three phases; the first is an obstacle-removing one, the second a free progress, and the third cannot be predicated as either of the two former.

[6] *lKog-gyur, lKog-na yod-pa,* lit.: 'existing in hiding.' The Sautrāntikas were, comparatively speaking, closer to the phenomenalists in European philosophy than to the critical realists. Phenomenalism declares that a physical object can exist even if it is not actually perceived. It is enough that it is capable of being perceived. To speak of a physical object that could not be seen, heard, smelt, tasted and touched, even under any specifiable conditions, would be a contradiction. It remains unintelligible how Western interpreters could impute Kant's unknowable thing-in-itself to the Sautrāntikas. This is against all evidence. As a matter of fact, the Sautrāntikas clearly state that that which is not apprehended in direct sensing, can be inferred as 'knowable.' Certainly 'to be invisible' or 'to be hidden' and 'to be unknowable' do not mean the same. 'To be invisible' may well mean 'available.'

[7] *Yid-bzhin-mdzod,* VAM, foll. 36a f. quotes *Abhidharmakośa* II 61–62 is support of this explanation. It then explains a perceptual situation as follows: "The cause situation of visual perception is what was a germinal state of the noetic in the antecedent noetic moment. The similar immediate cause-factor is the cessation of the antecedent noetic moment. The referential cause-factor is a colour-form; and the dominant cause-factor is the eye.

[8] Those who held this view are discussed in Chapter IV.

[9] See also *Yid-bzhin-mdzod,* VAM, foll. 37a.

[10] This account is presented from a later viewpoint which effectively pointed out the fallacies in assuming 'atoms.' The difference between the Vaibhāṣikas and Sautrāntikas was that the former accepted spaces between the punctiform atoms, while the latter did not.

[11] 'Impermanence' is distinguished here from the 'momentariness' of the particular existents. Strictly speaking, 'impermanence' and 'momentariness' are identical. If 'impermanence' is considered merely as an interpretative schema, then it would contradict the very instantaneousness or momentariness of the other particular existents, and the eternalistic Vedāntic theory about mind (*cit*) would follow.

[12] The theory of interdependent origination.

[13] The four 'names' are feeling, sensation-ideation, motivation, and conscious perception.

Notes to Chapter IV

[1] *Tibetan Buddhist Studies of Kloṅ-rdol bla-ma Ṅag-dbaṅ-blo-bzaṅ,* ed. from the Lhasa xylograph by Ven. Dalama. Laxmanpuri, Mussoorie 1963, Vol. I p. 244.

[2] *ibid.,* p. 243.

[3] *ibid.,* p. 244.

[4] Indian texts do not always distinguish clearly between Dharmakāya and Dharmajñānakāya. This has created considerable misunderstanding on the side of those who came to Buddhism from without. Many Western translations will have to be retranslated in view of the ambiguous use of 'Dharmakāya,' and reinterpreted according to the functional and ontological implications of this term.

[5] He was a famous Lama of Sera monastery, who lived from 1350–1425 A.D.

[6] This account does not necessarily imply an atomistic view: we do not see several disjunct colours and then infer from them that it must be a butterfly's wing; we directly see the butterfly's wing in all its coloured splendour. Another point to note is that the use of the word 'sensation' is a very loose one. Usually we tend to use 'sensation' to stand for certain mental contents or experiences. In so doing, we uncritically take over the legacy of idealism, which confuses an experience with the object of that experience. True, we have visual and auditory sensations, but we see a butterfly's wing and hear a Bach sonata. The Tibetan term, *rnam-pa* (*ākāra*), is used to stand for what we directly see or hear: colours and sounds. They are what we experience, and this is what phenomenalism calls 'sense-datum' (usually in the plural 'sense-data') or 'the given,' which includes the data of dreams and imagination. Naturally the question remains, what is actually given and what is added to it by interpretation. Nevertheless, something is given on which we base our interpretation. This shows that the translation of this term by 'representation' is wrong. To begin with, we say that in our 'perceptual' world the 'physical' world is 'represented,' 'symbolized.' But the mentalists say that there is no 'physical' world *apart* from the 'perceptual' world. So what is it of which we are supposed to have a 'representation'? It seems that many Western interpreters and their Eastern imitators in their eagerness to *force* Western ideas upon Eastern doctrines confused something which could not so easily be equated with idealism or mentalism (although it was quickly labelled 'idealism'), with representative realism with which it unfortunately has nothing to do.

[7] This seems to be an attempt to describe what happens when a person intuits an object without his being in any way sensorily

affected. All that would be needed would be his capacity and capability of simple detection and inspection.

[8] This seems to be a critique of the seemingly atomistic views of the previous theories.

[9] IV 53a ff. Of particular importance is the qualifying attribute 'suitable' (*rigs-mthun*). This is to say, the colours of a butterfly's wing are, to be sure, a function of the observer, of the rods and cones in his eyes, just as they are equally surely a function of the character of the butterfly's wing.

[10] *Grub-mtha' chen-mo* IV 52b. This is essentially the attempt to solve the age-old problem of reconciling the 'perceptual' world with the 'physical world,' the 'analytic' processes with the 'integrative' ones. On this problem see W. Russel Brain, *Mind, Perception and Science* (Oxford, 1951), pp. 60 ff.; Judson C. Herrick, *The Evolution of Human Nature* (Austin, 1956), p. 273 with reference to further literature on this subject.

[11] *Grub-mtha' chen-mo* IV 54b. This seems to refer to a purely aesthetic and intuitive experience.

[12] The eight are the 'substratum-awareness' (*kun-gzhi rnam-par shes-pa ālaya, vijñāna*), the 'human constant' (*yid, manas*), and the six perceptive functions, five of which are sensory and the last one abstractive-intellectual. As so often, the terminology has given rise to different interpretations. The dGe-lugs-pas defined the 'substratum-awareness' as an indeterminate cognition, and insisted on the unitary character of the eight awarenesses. Other schools, such as the rNying-ma-pas, distinguished between a 'substratum-awareness' and a 'substratum.' They also conceived of the eight awarenesses in a genetic way. All these problems have been discussed from the dGe-lugs-pa point of view by Tsong-kha-pa in his *Yid dang Kun-gzhi'i dka'-gnas rgya-cher 'grel-pa legs-bshad rgya-mtsho* (Collected Works, Tashilhunpo, ed., vol XVIII, no. 3). The six are the perceptive and abstractive-intellectual processes with the exception of the 'substratum-awareness' and the 'constant' or 'seventh' awareness.

[13] *sems-kyi ngo-bo*. The term *ngo-bo*, often translated by 'essence,' does not mean what is understood by 'essence' in classical and traditional philosophy, as that which marks one finite thing off from another. This would be *rang-gi mtshan-nyid* but not *ngo-bo* nor even *ngo-bo-nyid*. *Ngo-bo* corresponds to our notion of 'facticity.'

[14] 'Deviant' is to be understood as a movement away from real Being. *'khrul-pa* (*bhrānti*) emphasizes the going astray. The translation 'deviant' is preferred to 'erring' because it does not convey the implication of culpability.

[15] The Five Divisions are: *Yogacaryābhūmi, Śrāvakabhūmi* and *Bodhisattvabhūmi* as the First Division; *Yogacaryābhūmiviniś-*

cayasaṃgraha as the Second; *Yogacaryābhūmau vastusaṃgraha* and *Yogacaryābhūmau vinayasaṃgraha* as the Third; *Yogacaryābhūmau parāyasaṃgraha* as the Fourth; and *Yogacaryābhūmau vivaraṇasaṃgraha* as the Fifth. The Seven Treatises on Logic are: *Pramāṇavārttikā; Pramāṇaviniścaya; Nyāyabinduprakaraṇa; Hetubinduprakaraṇa; Sambandhaparīkṣāprakaraṇa; Codanānāmaprakaraṇa;* and *Santānāntarasiddhi.*

16 'Awareness,' *rjes-thob, pṛṣṭhalabdha-jñāna.* Its nature varies according to the spiritual pursuits of Śrāvakas, Pratyekabuddhas, and Bodhisattvas. This varying character is discussed in the extensive, but hitherto neglected, literature on the 'spiritual levels and paths' (*sa-lam*). See *Abhisamayālankāra* viii 13 ff. for Buddha-marks.

17 That is, the metaphysical absolute in and as itself.

18 *stong-(pa)-nyid, śūnyatā.* See note 4 to chapter V.

19 That is, feeling, sensation-ideation, motivation, conscious perception.

20 Acts are both individual and collective. The former lead to a life as a particular individual being, the latter condition the environment in which each individual being will find himself.

21 The five function patterns are the complexity of any momentary situation (*sparśa*) (the rapport that exists between the various components of a situation), directiveness of the process (*manaskāra*), feeling-tone or mood of the situation (*vedanā*), sensation-ideation (*saṃjñā*), and qualitative conditioning (*cetanā*). The 'seventh' awareness, which is constantly disturbing the substratum-awareness, and in so doing originates the subject-object dichotomy, deserves the name 'constant' for two reasons: it is constantly disturbing the substratum-awareness, and it is constantly present in all our conscious acts which are but a segment of the total psyche.

22 Reality is not mere facts, it especially comprises value. Seen as value it is triple: wholesome (positive), unwholesome (negative), and neither (indeterminate). The latter is of two kinds: uncontaminated-indeterminate and contaminated-indeterminate. The latter, psychologically speaking, is contaminated because it is about to develop into emotively toned actions and reactions, but indeterminate insofar as the determinate emotively toned response or the affect content is not yet at hand.

23 See note 13 to Chapter II.

24 For the six primary affective patterns and the twenty secondary patterns, see page 64.

25 See *Abhisamayālankāra* I 23–24.

26 One 'countless aeon' consists of as many human years as would be expressed by a 1 followed by 140 zeros.

27 That is, Sambhogakāya and Nirmāṇakāya.

[28] This is the *Ārya-saṃdhi-nirmocanasūtrasya vyākhyāna,* the most exhaustive commentary on the *Saṃdhinirmocanasūtra.*

[29] 'Incidental' has the meaning of a free possibility. It does not imply that something from some other source can affect the purity. It is not to say that the 'incidental stains' can be wiped off and dumped somewhere, leaving something blank behind.
The Svābhāvikakāya, which is here conceived of as cognitive absoluteness (*sems-nyid*), may be viewed from two angles, either as what it is in itself, or what it is when realized. The former is 'pure in being-itself,' the latter is 'pure as regards incidental stains.' From the Prāsangikas' point of view the Svābhāvikakāya is 'nothingness' (*stong-pa-nyid, śūnyatā*) in the sense of explicit negation (*med-dgag*): Nothing whatsoever exists ontologically.

[30] See above note (21).

[31] See above note (12).

[32] See chapter II.

[33] See H. V. Guenther, *Tibetan Buddhism without Mystification,* pp. 19 ff.

[34] This collective term comprises the individualized Sambhogakāya and Nirmānakāya.

[35] 'Error,' *'khrul-pa.* That is, the process of straying into a world of 'things' which are but fictions of the mind, comprising a subject and an object believed to exist in their own rights.

Notes to Chapter V

[1] *ngo-bo-nyid med-par smra-ba.* This is short for *bden-grub-kyi ngo-bo-nyid med-par smra-ba.* The current rendering is to use the Sanskrit term: *niḥsvabhāvavādin.* This term is usually left untranslated or, if a translation is attempted, it is based on the mistaken assumption that words are understood by their etymology instead of by their use due to stipulation. Moreover, lexical translations have singularly failed to adduce any reason why the Sanskrit term *svabhāva* should be translated into Tibetan as *rang-bzhin* in one case, and as *ngo-bo-(nyid)* in another. The fact that the Tibetan translators of Sanskrit texts thought about what might be intended by the texts which they translated—which lexical translators painstakingly avoid doing—forced them to use different words for one term. The term *rang-bzhin* is similar to our concept of 'essence,' 'being-itself.' In distinction to *rang-bzhin* we have *rang-gi mtshan-nyid* 'being-what-something-is' indicating the constitutive principle through which something is what it is. Quite different is *ngo-bo-(nyid)* which corresponds to our 'fact' and 'facticity.' The Mādhyamikas did not deny the 'fact' of things, but they denied that this fact was itself something existing as such (*bden-grub*). In other

words, they most vigorously eschewed any substantival kind of ontology.

[2] *rtags, linga.* In a general way this term is used in the same way as we use the 'middle' in logic. However, the wide range of application of the term *rtags* has been obscured by the fact that in dealing with Buddhist logic one has thought too much in Aristotelian terms, rather than considering it in its own right.

The first principle that has to be satisfied is the triple relation of identity, that is to say, *S* can be *P* only because of something else that *S* is, namely *M*. Moreover, "if S is P because it is M, this can only be because of what M is and not because of what it is not. More specifically, what M must be is P, if one is ever to demonstrate that S is P through the fact that it is M" (Henry Babock Veatch, *Intentional Logic,* p. 310). The second principle can best be expressed symbolically:

$$(x). \Phi x \supset \Psi x.$$

The third principle is what is known as the obverted contrapositive.

[3] Duality is of three kinds. The first is the subject-object division against the background of nothingness; the second is the dialectic of negation; and the third is the conventionally true as against the absolutely true.

[4] The sixteen types of nothingness are frequently mentioned in the Prajñāpāramitā literature. The four types bear the following names: *'dus-byas stong-pa-nyid, 'dus-ma-byas stong-pa-nyid, rang-gi ngo-bo stong-pa-nid,* and *gzhan-gyi ngo-bo stong-pa-nyid.* These descriptive terms mean that there is nothing concrete that exists in truth, nor anything abstract, nor any fact by itself, nor any fact other than itself. The rejection of the translation of *stong-pa-nyid* (*śūnyatā*) by 'emptiness' or 'void' is based on the following consideration: *śūnyatā* is not a container that can be emptied nor is there anything that could be taken out of *śūnyatā.* The choice of the term 'emptiness' dates back to the time when under the influence of idealism mind was conceived as a container of ideas, and when the ideal seemed to be to leave an empty blankness. Something like this must have inspired the doctrine of Jo-nang-pa Dol-po Shes-rab rgyal-mtshan (1292–1361 A.D.) who spoke of what is technically known as *gzhan-stong* 'empty of something else.' This doctrine has been generally rejected, particularly so by the dGe-lugs-pas. While for this doctrine the term 'emptiness' would have been appropriate, it should have been avoided where it did not apply.

Of course, 'nothingness' is also not a very helpful term, but it may assist in abolishing the attendant notion of 'thingness' in talking about the things of the world and of our experiences. For the Dge-lugs-pas *stong-nyid* (*śūnyatā*) is explicit negation (*med-dgag*): things do not exist as such apart from our labelling them to be this or that.

[5] Śrāvakayāna, Pratyekabuddhayāna, and Bodhisattvayāna.

[6] 'Continuity concentration' is a state in which everything that is heard is of the nature of the Buddhist teaching being proclaimed. 'Most sublime reality,' *mchog-gi sprul-sku,* lit.: 'most sublime Nirmāṇakāya.' Nirmāṇakāya is essentially a name for the manifestation of Buddhahood in its active aspect through sentient beings; it signifies living a life of authenticity in the world of man. Three types are distinguished: *skyes-pa sprul-sku* or the various forms through which the later Buddha passed previous to his enlightenment (described in the collection of *Jātakas* or 'birth stories'); the *bzo-pa sprul-sku* or gifted artist; and lastly the *mchog-gi sprul-sku* 'He who performed the twelve Buddha-acts.'

[7] The four patterns are known by their Indian names: Svābhāvikakāya, Dharmakāya, Sambhogakāya, and Nirmāṇakāya.

[8] Dharmakāya and Rūpakāya, the latter consisting of both Sambhogakāya and Nirmāṇakāya.

[9] The four are: being, non-being, both being and non-being, neither being nor non-being.

[10] rGyal-tshab, *dbU-ma rtsa-ba'i dka'-gnas chen-po brgyad-kyi brjed-byang* (*Collected Works,* Vol. I, No. 6).

[11] The three factors are: the cognizing agent, the object of cognition, and the act of cognition.

[12] For the Sautrāntikas, Yogacāras and Mādhyamika-Svātantrikas only the present was a 'particular existent' and a 'thing,' while for the Vaibhāṣikas and Prāsangikas the past and the future were both a 'particular existent' in the sense of a not-now.

[13] There are two types of impermanence: (a) coarse, or the impermanence of the living and (b) subtle, the impermanence of the material world.

[14] With the exception of comparative judgment the other three types are recognized by the Svātantrikas and others. What I have translated as 'existential judgment' means that here we pass to a new symbolic formulation of the same existent fact; for instance, in recognizing impermanence we also recognize the concrete nature of that which is impermanent. 'Metaphorical judgment' is to understand that 'Phoebus' means the sun, and 'doctrinal judgment' is to understand the proposition that generosity brings satisfaction. See also Tsong-kha-pa, *Collected Works,* Vol. xviii, No. 5, fol. 6b.

[15] That is to say, concepts, propositions, arguments, fictitious beings have absolutely no existence apart from or independent of the psychological operations that produce and give rise to them. This emphasis on the psychological processes distinguishes the

Prāsangikas from the Svātantrikas who made the distinction, known also in scholasticism, between the logical and the real. For the Svātantrikas a concept of a jug is necessarily such as to intend a jug, but the real jug which is thus intended does not intend anything else; it is, and it is what it is.

16 Passion-lust, aversion-hatred, bewilderment-error.

17 The Prāsangikas follow here the *Sha-ri'i bu-la rjes-su zlos-pa'i mdo* which declares that, when a Śrāvaka or Pratyekabuddha saint in utter composure concentrates on nothingness (*stong-pa-nyid*), there is no residue of the misery of the world to be found, and the experience of Nirvāṇa is that of the non-residual one. But when he comes out of this state of composure, the misery of the world reasserts itself and the experience of Nirvāṇa that lingers on is that of the residual one.

18 See above note 8.

19 Sambhogakāya and Nirmāṇakāya.

NOTES TO CHAPTER VI

1 *Guhyasamājatantra,* p. 153.

2 *rGyud rgyal gsang-ba snying-po'i 'grel-pa,* foll. 14a ff.

3 *lta-ba.* This is essentially an unbiased perspective from which things are seen as they are, rather than being dealt with by a distorted view of them which demands more from them than they can possibly offer.

4 For a detailed analysis of these technical terms see H. V. Guenther, *The Life and Teaching of Nāropa,* Clarendon Press, Oxford 1963, pp. 268 ff.

5 *Theg-pa'i mchog rin-po-che'i mdzod,* foll. 60a ff.

6 *Theg-pa'i mchog rin-po-che'i mdzod,* fol. 60a.

7 *ibid.* fol. 60a.

8 The 'four lamps' are symbolic terms for certain mystical experiences.

9 *Theg-pa'i mchog rin po-che'i mdzod,* fol. 61b.

10 This situation has been summed up by Aristotle in his *Nichomachean Ethics,* ed. H. Racsham, Loeb Classical Library, No. 73, II, VI, 14: "Evil is a form of the unlimited, and good of the limited." In his dialogue *The Timaeus,* Plato tells us that the aesthetic factor, in his later books called *eros,* is the female principle in the nature of things, while the *logos* is the male one. When he brands the female principle as evil and the male one as good, he does not proceed 'quite arbitrarily,' as F. S. C. Northrop, *The Meeting of East and West. An Inquiry concerning World Understand* (The Macmillan Company, New York 1949) states (p. 59), but follows the pre-Socratic conception of the *peras* 'the limited and formed' as good and the *apeiron* 'the unlimited' as evil.

[11] In particular see H. V. Guenther, *The Spiritual Teacher of Tibet,* Hermès, Recherches sur l'expérience spirituelle 4, Paris 1966–67, pp. 226 ff.

[12] These are the 'substratum awareness' (*kun-gzhi rnam-par shes-pa*), the 'human constant' (*yid*), and the six perceptive functions. See also above, Chapter IV.

[13] While the traditional and purely Indian classification recognizes four classes of Tantras, the rNying-ma-pas accept six classes.

A. Kriyā-	Caryā-	Yoga-	Anuttarayoga-tantra		
B. Kriyā-	Caryā-(or Uba)	Yoga-	Mahā-	Anu-	Ati-.

[14] *sku gsum: dharmakāya, sambhogakāya, nirmāṇakāya.* See also above, Chapter IV.

Notes to Chapter VII

[1] *Grub-mtha'-mdzod,* fol. 159b.

[2] *ibid.*

[3] *sbyor-ba,* the transitive form of the intransitive *'byor-ba* in *rnal-'byor,* is explained as *shes-rab-kyi spyod-pa* by Rong-zom Chos-kyi dpal bzang-po in his *rGyud-rgyal gsang-ba snying-po'i 'grel-pa,* fol. 99a. The functional character of *shes-rab* as converting 'thing'-orientated perception into aesthetic perception and appreciation is clearly elaborated in *Bi-ma snying-tig,* vol. Nga, foll. 97b sqq. In this respect it is justifiable to speak of *shes-rab* as 'intelligence,' because a person using his intelligence is analytical and appreciative and is unlikely to use it for 'non-intelligent' or 'metaperceptual' ends.

[4] *Grub-mtha'-mdzod,* foll. 159b sqq.

[5] *mdzad* is 'existential' (*sku*), 'communicative' (*gsung*), and 'responsive' (*thugs*); each of these 'enactments' operates externally (*phyi*), internally (*nang*), and mystically (*gsang*); and each of these levels has four activities. See Klong-chen rab-'byams-pa, *Theg-pa'i mchog rin-po-che'i mdzod,* foll. 6b sqq.

[6] Past, present, future, and that which is none of them.

[7] *rGyud-rgyal gsang-ba snying-po'i 'grel-pa,* foll. 20a sqq.

[8] *rig-'dzin* 'he who holds to (*'dzin*) intuitive, aesthetically moving awareness (*rig-*(*pa*)).'

[9] They are *De-bzhin-gshegs-pa'i rigs, Padma'i rigs,* and *rDo-rje'i rigs* (in Sanskrit *Tathāgatakula, Padmakula,* and *Vajrakula* respectively).

[10] This is *rdo-rje-'dzin* Vajradhara as distinguished from *rdo-rje-'chang;* the former still implies separateness from the Absolute, the latter self-same absoluteness. The four action patterns are the same as those mentioned in note 9, to which *las-kyi rigs* (*Karmakula*) or *rin-chen-rigs* (*Ratnakula*) is added.

[11] i.e., the progression and regression of aesthetic perception.

[12] The five constituents are: colour-form as corporeality, feeling, concept-formation, motivation, and perception. The five capacities are: faith, zeal, inspection, integrative concentration, appreciative discrimination. The five patterns are: passion-lust, aversion-hatred, infatuation-dullness, conceit-arrogance, and envy-jealousy. According to the *Lam-zab-kyi rnam-par bshad-pa zab-lam-gyi snye-ma,* foll. 24b sq., the relation between the psycho-physical constituents, emotions, and awarenesses, together with their Buddha-nature which expresses the polarity of masculinity and femininity, can be tabulated as on the next page.

Notes to Chapter VIII

[1] The term 'profoundness' (*zab*) and 'vastness' (*rgyas*) were also used in the Sūtras where they indicated *shes-rab* (*prajñā*) 'appreciative discrimination' and *thabs* (*upāya*) 'ethically positive action.' Here, in the Tantras, they have been reinterpreted in terms of immediate experience.

[2] *Theg-pa'i mchog rin-po-che'i mdzod,* foll. 108b–109a.

[3] The level reached by a follower of the Mahāyoga is termed *yi-ge 'khor-lo tshogs chen sa* 'level where the universe is present as a rotating procession of spell-letters.' Each 'letter' evokes a vision which links up with other letters in an endless progression.

[4] *Theg-pa'i mchog rin-po-che'i mdzod,* fol. 101a.

[5] *dPal Kye-rdo-rje'i phyi bskyed-rim-gyi rnam-par bashad-pa legs-bshad nyi-ma'i 'od-zer,* fol. 131a–b.

[6] See for instance *Grub-mtha'-mdzod,* fol. 168b; *Chos-dbyings rin-po-che'i mdzod-kyi 'grel-pa lung-gi gter-mdzod,* fol. 63b.

[7] *Grub-mtha'-mdzod,* foll. 168b ff.

[8] On the initiatory confirmations and consecrations see H. V. Guenther, *The Life and Teaching of Nāropa,* pp. 143 ff.

[9] *dbu-ma chen-po.* This is a specifically Buddhist technical term for what in philosophy is called 'the Absolute.' *dbu-ma* 'middle' is so termed because it steers clear of the extremes of judgment (positive or negative); *chen-po* because there is nothing 'greater' than this.

[10] i.e., being, non-being, both being and non-being, and neither being nor non-being.

[11] *rlung.* For a detailed analysis of this technical term and its meaning in Tantrism see H. V. Guenther, *The Life and Teachings of Nāropa,* pp. 270 ff. (Note F).

[12] So also *Grub-mtha' mdzod,* fol. 163a.

[13] *dgongs-(pa).* This term corresponds to the concept of 'intentionality' in modern philosophy. The 'meaning' or 'significance' of an action is of primary importance.

[14] They are specified by g-Yung-ston rdo-rje dpal-bzang in a lengthy discussion in his commentary on the *gSang-ba*

A Pycho-physical constituents	:	B Elementary forces	=	C Buddha (male aspect)	:	D Buddha (female aspect)	=	E Emotions	:	F Awarenesses
Perception		Cohesion (water)		Akṣobhya		Māmakī		Aversion-hatred		Mirror-like awareness
Feeling		Spatiality (space)		Ratnasambhava		Dhātvīśvarī		Conceit-arrogance		Identity awareness
Concept-formation		Warmth (fire)		Amitābha		Pāṇḍarāvasinī		Passion-lust		Distinctness awareness
Motivation		Movement (wind)		Amoghasiddhi		Tārā		Envy-jealousy		Finality awareness
Colour-form-corporeality		Solidity (earth)		Vairocana		Locanā		Infatuation-dullness		Absoluteness awareness

Columns A,B,E refer to that which is the object to be "purified," that is, to be spiritually transformed;
Columns C,D,F refer to the outcome of spiritual transformation. The spiritual transformation process itself is the understanding of the polarity symbolism manifesting itself in the imagery of C and D.

snying-po, the *dPal gsang-ba snying-po'i rgyud-don gsal-byed me-long,* fol. 133b.

[15] *'khrul-pa.* Unlike our 'error' this term does not imply culpability. It indicates the straying away from the significant and meaningful.

[16] See note 3.

[17] *rtsa rlung thig-le.* For a detailed analysis see H. V. Guenther, *The Life and Teachings of Nāropa,* pp. 270 ff. (Note F) and 273 ff (Note I).

[18] See H. V. Guenther, *The Life and Teachings of Nāropa,* p. 275 for the meaning of these terms.

[19] This is a highly conscious moment, relatively free of the particular objects around us; a moment in which we can breathe and, if we observe ourselves, actually do breathe more deeply. It is a very relaxed moment.

[20] 'Riding on completion in a general sense.'

[21] 'Cognitive absoluteness,' *sems-nyid.* This term is carefully distinguished from *sems.* The latter refers to the working of the mind, mentation with its creation of concepts and the belief in the reality of its fictions. *sems-nyid* is an index-word without standing for anything concrete. 'Noetic Being,' *chos-sku, dharmakāya.* 'Communicative Being,' *longs-sku, sambhogakāya.* 'Authentic Being,' *sprul-sku, nirmāṇakāya.*

[22] The four light-experiences are:

chos-nyid mngon-sum 'the immediate awareness of the aesthetic object apart from the beliefs about it,'

nyams gong 'phel-ba 'the intensification of the aesthetic experience,'

rig-pa tshad-phebs 'the aesthetic awareness having reached its highest peak,' and

chos-nyid zad-pa 'the aesthetic experience as such.'

For a detailed discussion see *Bla-ma yang-tig* IV 8b ff; 58a ff.; V 18a ff.

[23] *thod-rgal.* This term refers to a person who takes up an intermediate position between the one who proceeds step by step (*rim-gyis-pa*) and the one who achieves his enlightenment in a sudden breakthrough (*'khregs-chod*).

[24] *spang-rtogs,* the abandoning of all that makes a person emotionally unstable and the understanding of the significance of what is.

[25] *Ye-shes bla-ma.*

[26] They are the 'mirror-like' awareness revealing the nature of reality rather than merely 'reflecting' something appearing before it; the awareness of the self-same nature of what is real; the awareness by being aesthetically alert; the awareness of significant action; and the awareness of absoluteness as absolute.

[27] *sems.* See above note 21.

INDEX OF SUBJECTS

perspective, 158, 200, 228 n.3
phenomenal, 19
phenomenalism, 15, 221 n.6
physical, 16; material, 33, 54, 56, 63, 66, 81, 86, 116
pluralism, 81
pluralist; differentiating-attribute, 15, 34; specific property, 14
plurality, 99
point-instant, 38, 66
poison, three, 26, 58, 204, 215 n.3
polarity, 193, 198
positivism, 169
possibility, 45, 47, 165, 167, 224 n.29
potentialities, 58
power, 176ff., 180f., 187, 191
Pratyekabuddha, 20, 22, 50, 59, 61, 77, 87ff., 111, 133f., 136, 142, 147, 215 n.6, 218 n.22, 224, n.16, 228 n.17
prerequisites, two, 29, 215 n.10
present, 80f., 227 n.12
presentation, 125
principle; absolute, 82, 110ff., 133, 147; constitutive, 97f., 107, 113, 115f., 130, 132, 143; formative, 161, 163; ontological, 115; self-evident, 131; ultimate, 136, 146
process; analytic, 223 n.10; cognitive, 76; perceptual, 217 n.15; psychological, 76, 91, 227 n.15
profoundness, 192, 204, 230 n.1
project, 127, 145
Pure Ego, 40, 46f., 57, 82, 83, 144, 217 n.14
purification, 128
purity, 181, 208, 210, 224, n.29; ritual, 188f., 203
pursuits, three spiritual, 20, 58, 86, 133

Quality, 184; observable, 82, 93; positional, 37

Rapport, 34f., 64, 88, 114, 116, 224 n.21
rationalism, 169
reaction; favourable, 33; unfavourable, 33
real, 15, 17, 36, 107; absolutely, 54; conventionally, 19, 132; empirically, 36, 54, 196; relatively, 19, 108; ultimately, 19, 36ff., 79, 116, 132, 196
realism, 15, 31
Reality/reality, 15f., 19, 31, 33, 36, 58, 60, 87, 108, 113, 123, 125, 130, 134, 159, 169, 185, 197f., 204, 208, 224 n.22; absolute, 86; awareness of, 160; concrete, 114; ultimate, 42, 139; vision of, 43
reason, 159
rebirth, 43
recognition, 82, 145
reflection, 85
rejection, 170, 172, 203, 208, 218 n.25
relation, 73, 99, 108, 119, 150; cognitive, 70f.; subject-object, 99
relative, 100f., 107, 113, 115ff.
representation, 177
response, 20; affective, 44; motive, 27; emotional, 39; compassionate, 44
responsibility, 200
responsiveness, 21, 91, 178, 180ff., 201, 206, 208, 216 n.11
returner; no, 49; once, 49
rite, 189, 204
ritualism, 205
Rūpakāya, 121, 227 n.8

Saint, 44, 49, 59, 66, 83, 108, 111, 133, 146, 218 n.25
Sambhōgakāya, 60, 103, 112, 200f., 227 n.7
Saṃsāra, 28f., 32, 114ff., 162, 164, 171f., 185, 200, 204, 209, 219 n.27; cause of, 153
sceptre, 180, 182
seal, 181, 184, 189f., 193
self, 20, 22, 46f., 58, 96, 109ff., 115f., 132f., 136, 145f., 217 n.14; individual, 28, 58, 81ff., 87ff., 146; ineffable, 63, 65, 67; functional character of, 47
self-cognition, 78
self-development, 127, 129, 158
self-evident, 17, 110, 132
self-identification, 88
selfishness, 20
self-knowledge, 53, 70
self-realization, 22
self-sameness, 204f.
semblance, 74
sensation, 16, 86, 90, 94, 105, 159f., 204, 217 n.15, 222 n.13, 222 n.6; pure, 92, 121
sense-organ, 41, 57, 220 n.31

INDEX OF TECHNICAL TERMS

A. Sanskrit

B. Tibetan